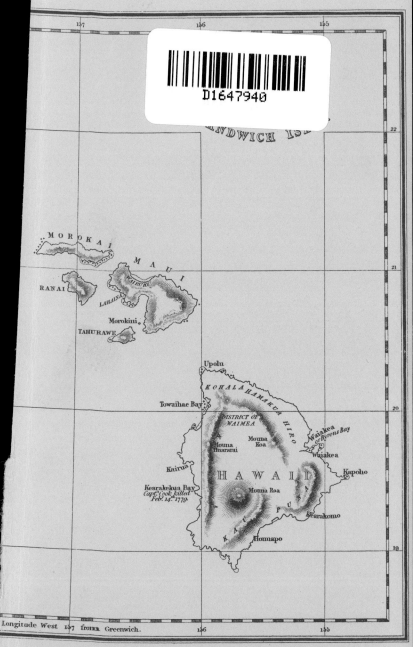

SANDWICH IS

22

MOROKAI

MAUI
21

RANAI
WUKU
LAHAINA

Morokini
TAHURAWE

Upolu

KOHALA HAMAKUA HIRO

Towaihae Bay
DISTRICT OF
WAIMEA
20
Waiakea
or Byrons Bay
Mouna
Koa
Mouna
Huararai
Wanakea
Kairua
HAWAII
Kapoho
Kearakekua Bay
Capt. Cook killed
Feb. 14. 1779.
Mouna Roa
KAU
PUNA

Kearakomo

Homapo
19

...er. Son & P. Jackson, 1828.

J.R.Murry. del.

J.Bürichett. sculp.

View in the Valley of Ua, Island of Oahu.

Published by Fisher. Son & C⁰. Caxton. London. April. 1828.

JOURNAL

OF A RESIDENCE IN THE

SANDWICH ISLANDS,

DURING THE

YEARS 1823, 1824, AND 1825:

INCLUDING

REMARKS ON THE MANNERS AND CUSTOMS OF THE INHABITANTS;
AN ACCOUNT OF LORD BYRON'S VISIT IN H. M. S. BLONDE; AND A
DESCRIPTION OF THE CEREMONIES OBSERVED AT THE INTER-
MENT OF THE LATE KING AND QUEEN IN THE ISLAND OF OAHU.

———

BY C. S. STEWART,

LATE AMERICAN MISSIONARY AT THE SANDWICH ISLANDS:

With an Introduction, and occasional Notes,

BY WILLIAM ELLIS.

————

A MAP, AND PLATES.

————

Facsimile Reproduction of the Third Edition of 1830
Index by Margaret Apple

UNIVERSITY OF HAWAII PRESS
for
FRIENDS OF THE LIBRARY OF HAWAII

HONOLULU, HAWAII
1970

DU
623
S85
1970

This edition is a facsimile reproduction of that originally
printed by H. Fisher, Son, & P. Jackson of London
Library of Congress Catalog Card Number 71-135064
ISBN 0-87022-772-6
Manufactured in the United States of America

ADVERTISEMENT.

———

When I left the United States for the Sandwich Islands, I thought I bade farewell to my country for ever, and felt it a duty to transmit to those most deeply interested in my destiny, a minute account of the scenes and events of a voluntary exile. With this view, the following Journal was addressed to Mrs. John M. Bowers, of Bowerstown, Otsego, New York, one of the nearest of my relatives, in the expectation of its being read by other family connections and personal friends. In the number of the last was the Rev. Dr. Green, during whose Presidency of the College of New Jersey, I had the privilege of being a student at Nassau Hall; and to whose ministry of the Gospel, in the grace of God, I trace the origin of the principles and affections which resulted in my becoming a Missionary to the heathen. By him, extracts from the manuscript were introduced into the pages of the Christian Advocate of Philadelphia; others appeared in the Herald of the

American Board of Commissioners for Foreign Missions, at Boston; and both gave rise to various and repeated applications, on my arrival in America, for the publication of the whole in a connected form.

It was believed, that a record of facts and circumstances, made, at the time of their occurrence, for the gratification of private friends only; and necessarily unfolding the motives, feelings, pursuits, and success of those engaged in the Missionary enterprise,—would have a salutary influence. To prepare a document of the kind for the public eye, so as to guard, on the one hand, against an obtrusion of points too private and personal for general perusal; and, on the other, against an obliteration so fastidious, as to take from the work its original and appropriate character, I foresaw must prove a delicate task. But the prospect of an advantage, however slight, to a cause to which I have devoted my life, has been sufficient to induce the experiment.

The original manuscript was written under every disadvantage of place and circumstances; and its highest pretension was that of a true delineation of scenes and characters, as they passed before me: in assuming a printed form, it can prefer no other claim. The only alteration I have made, in a hasty and interrupted revisal of the original, is that of collecting, in some cases, under a single date, remarks and facts upon the same subject found under several; and, in one or two instances only, that of adding, from other memoranda, matter never transmitted to America, the introduction of which became necessary for the elucidation of points which otherwise could be but imperfectly understood.

The Chart of the Sandwich Islands is a copy, from one in the third edition of a "Tour through Hawaii," by the Rev. Mr. Ellis, recently published.

Trusting to the kindness of my readers, on the point which has given me most anxiety, the extent of erasure desirable,—without other apology than the explanation given, I cheerfully place the volume in their hands.

New York, January 1, 1828.

CONTENTS.

———

CHAPTER IV.

CHAPTER V.

CHAPTER VI.

CHAPTER VII.

CHAPTER VIII.

CHAPTER IX.

CHAPTER X.

CHAPTER XI.

CHAPTER XII.

CHAPTER XIII.

CHAPTER XIV.

CHAPTER XV.

INDEX

INTRODUCTION.

In the course of the last eight or nine years, public attention, in Europe and America, has been frequently directed to the SANDWICH ISLANDS. The demolition of the ancient temples—the destruction of the idols—the renunciation of the national religion in 1819, and the establishment of a Christian Mission among them early in the following year, were events remarkable and important, in the estimation of all who take an interest in the propagation of Christianity throughout the world. The discovery of vast numbers of sperm whales, first in the Northern Pacific, and afterwards on the coast of Japan, has occasioned an increase of the shipping accustomed to resort for repairs and refreshments to the Sandwich Islands, to so great a degree, that instead of a few uncertain calls, not less than one hundred vessels touch at the Islands in the course of a year. The visits they have received from Capts. De Freycinet, Vasselieu, and Kotzebue, in the French and Russian ships of discovery, which have recently traversed the Pacific, together with the more subsequent ones of Lord Byron and Capt. Jones in British and American vessels of war—the peculiar facilities afforded by their local situa-

b

tion, to the important and growing commerce which the establishment of the South American states has now opened between the
western shores of the new continent and the eastern parts of
India, and China—have naturally attracted the attention of
Europe and America, and probably rendered a settlement
among these interesting Islands an object of desire with more
than one maritime power of the present day.

In addition to these circumstances, a project so bold and
patriotic as that of the Rulers of a people, with whom we
had been accustomed only to associate ideas of all that was
degrading in ignorance, and ferocious in savage life, traversing a distance greater than half the circumference of our
globe, in order to visit and behold for themselves a country
whose fame had long reached their distant and isolated
shores,—with the sincere desire to improve the condition of a
nation, which Providence had committed to their government
and care,—justly attracted no ordinary attention. The dignified
propriety of their manners, and the mild benevolence of their
dispositions, were not less agreeable, than their complexion,
language, native costume, and the varied productions of their
country, which they brought, were curious and strange. The
interest produced by their visit was evinced in the general
sympathy awakened by their illness and death, and by the
apprehension, almost universally entertained, that suspicion
would arise in the minds of the affectionate people whom they
had left behind, that they had fallen victims to some unfair
treatment in England, and, perhaps, had suffered in revenge
for the death of Capt. Cook, who had been murdered, half a
century before, on their own shores. The costly and delicate
respect shown by the British government to the bereaved nation,
in despatching the Blonde frigate, commanded by a nobleman, to
convey the bodies of the King and Queen, that they might be
deposited in the sepulchres of their ancestors, and that the nation

might have the melancholy satisfaction of paying the last tribute of affection to the remains of their departed rulers, tended in no small degree to give a salutary direction to the sensations to which their sudden decease had given birth. These combined circumstances have secured to the Sandwich Islands a greater degree of attention, than had been manifested since the announcement of their discovery, or the publication of those fascinating accounts of their natural beauty, and the interesting circumstances of their inhabitants, which were at that period given to the public.

The pleasing, and in many instances decisive change that has taken place in the moral and religious state of the people, is by no means the least important circumstance connected with the Sandwich Islands. It has furnished occasion for grateful acknowledgments to Almighty God, from all who duly appreciate the benefits conferred by our holy religion on any nation by which it is received, whether barbarous or civilized. It has afforded fresh encouragement to all interested or engaged in its propagation throughout the world, and has augmented the evidence already possessed, of the adaptation of Christianity to improve the condition of mankind, and its tendency to elevate their intellectual and moral character, and to ameliorate their present condition, whilst it inspires them with the hopes of immortality.

The recent publication of the narrative of the Blonde's voyage, and some other works relating to the Sandwich Islands, together with the various letters and journals which have, at intervals, appeared in several literary and religious periodicals, have sustained in a great degree the interest in those Islands, which the preceding events inspired.

The writer of the following sheets is one of a small body of Missionaries from America, whom the most disinterested benevolence led to those Islands, for the purpose of attempting to communicate to the unenlightened minds of the inhabitants the principles of human knowledge and inspired truth. Although connected with families of the first respectability in America, and favoured with the fairest prospects of realizing all he could desire in his profession at home, he relinquished them, and devoted himself to the service of his Saviour among the heathen :

> —— Denied to self, to earthly fame
> Denied, and earthly wealth— he kindred left,
> And home, and ease, and all the cultivated joys,
> Convenient and delicate delights,
> Of ripe society.——

Between three and four years he had resided in the Islands, principally in Maui, had acquired the language, become familiar with the habits and character of the people, and having surmounted the difficulties inseparable from the first period of a Missionary's residence among uncivilized heathens, was looking forward with confidence to years of delightful occupation and extensive usefulness, wnen the distressing illness of Mrs. Stewart became so alarming, as to leave no doubt, that the only hope of life was in her immediate removal to a colder and more congenial climate   No means of conveyance to the United States were at that time at hand ; and the symptoms of her disorder became so urgent, that the least delay threatened to be fatal even to the faint hope they were allowed to indulge.

At this critical period, a British ship, the Fawn, bound for London, providentially put into Oahu for refreshments ; and the master, Capt. Dale, generously offered Mr. Stewart and his family a gratuitous passage to England, where they would meet with every facility for proceeding to America. In April, 1826, they arrived in London ; and although Mrs. Stewart's health was materially improved by the voyage, it was deemed expedient that she should endeavour, in some degree, to recruit her strength before embarking for her native country. This circumstance, while it detained them from their friends in America, afforded the directors and officers of the Missionary Society, with many other friends to the Missionary cause, an opportunity of becoming acquainted with Mr. and Mrs. Stewart. I shall only add, that the result of this intercourse was an impression most favourable to the character of the visitors, which is still vivid and delightful in the recollection of many.

Their arrival excited mingled emotions in my own mind. I could not but sympathize with them under an afflictive dispensation, the bitterness of which, I had myself so fully tasted; yet the feeling of regret on this account was somewhat counterbalanced by the satisfaction I enjoyed in their society, during the interesting period of our public anniversaries in the month of May. Mr. Stewart and myself attended most of the public meetings together, and in the proceedings of several we both took a share—a fact that brought powerfully to my recollection the services, similar in kind, yet very different in their accompanying circumstances, in which we had so often unitedly engaged in the Sandwich Islands.

After about three months' residence in England, Mr. Stewart, with his family, embarked for America. He has since been employed in visiting, on behalf of the American Missionary Society, different sections of the United States, and advocating the cause of Christian Missions. A residence in her native land has somewhat improved Mrs. Stewart's health; but while both are anxious to resume their labours in the Sandwich Islands, it is by no means so far established as to afford any immediate prospect of embarkation.

After the ample details already noticed respecting the Sandwich Islands, any further accounts might appear superfluous; but

during the period of Mr. Stewart's residence there, events trans-
pired, of deeper interest and higher importance, than those that
had happened in any former period of their history. Of these, so
far as they came under his own observation, Mr. Stewart has given
a faithful account; and though many of the details necessarily
resemble those on the same subjects, contained in the Voyage of
the Blonde, and the Tour of Hawaii, yet it will not, perhaps, be
uninteresting to combine the narratives given on the other side
of the Atlantic, with those which have already appeared in our
own country. Much, however, of the matter contained in
Mr. Stewart's volume is entirely new; and his letters respecting
the Sandwich Island Mission, which have appeared in the
Appendix to Mr. Orme's Defence of the Missions in the
Pacific, are so clear and satisfactory, that they must have pre-
disposed all by whom they have been read, to feel interested in
the perusal of whatever, in connexion with these Islands, may
proceed from his pen.

In reference to the resemblance between his Journal, and the
Tour of Hawaii, Mr. Stewart, in a letter which I received with the
sheets of his volume, after speaking of two or three points, for descriptions of which he was indebted to the "Tour," remarks, "I
believe that in all other cases, however closely our descriptions or
statements may approximate, that I had the originals of my own, *ver-
batim et literatim*, before I ever saw the 'Tour.' My description
of the volcano was written with a pencil in a blank book, just
after the excursion, and was printed as it is, excepting one or two
words, before I reached the United States. My picture of the
people presents them at a time, and under circumstances, not
touched in yours."

I have read his Journal with real pleasure, and doubt not
it will be very favourably received, even should my warm attachment to the writer have led me to form a partial opinion of its

merits. Of this, however, the public will decide. For myself,
I must confess that I esteem the friendship I formed with Mr.
Stewart and his family in the Sandwich Islands, among the happiest
of the many pleasing events connected with my transient labours
there. The striking resemblance between our circumstances has
also united our hearts. We have both, from the same painful
cause, been obliged to leave interesting and important fields of
labour. Mr. Stewart, on his way home, spent some time in
Britain, while I could only reach England by way of America.
We have both been engaged, since our return, in promoting the
interest of the Missionary enterprise—are at length both favoured
with some faint hopes of resuming our labours—are cheered by
the anticipation of meeting again in our former stations, and
combining our efforts in promoting the best interests of the
inhabitants of Hawaii, with those of our colleagues, who have
been honoured to remain on the field.

Respecting the establishment of the first permanent mission
in Hawaii and Maui; the conversion, baptism, and death of
Keopuolani, the first Hawaiian convert; the first admission of
natives to the Christian church; the remarkable and general
attention paid to instruction; the character of the present young
prince and princess of the Sandwich Islands; the determination
of the late King to visit Great Britain; the flagrant outrages of
several Europeans, who have visited the Islands; the first intelligence received by the natives, of the death of the King and
Queen; the arrival of the bodies of the deceased sovereign and
his consort; the honourable conduct of Lord Byron; the circumstances connected with the visit of the Blonde; and the eruption of
the great volcano, which took place during an excursion, which, in
company with Lord Byron and a party of officers and gentlemen
from the Blonde, he made to this grand and stupendous natural
phenomenon;—Mr. Stewart has furnished a mass of information
that cannot fail to be deeply interesting.

The progress of Christianity among the people, and their gradual improvement in morality, intelligence, and civilization, have not been less decisive and encouraging since the departure of Mr. Stewart, than they were during his residence in the Islands. A series of events, of great importance to the natives, has taken place, among which might be mentioned the hopeful piety of Nahienaena the young princess, who, according to a journal kept by Toteta, a native teacher from the Southern Islands, and published in the American Missionary Herald, embraced Christianity in the beginning of the year 1825. Notwithstanding the dying admonition, and affectionate prayer, of Keopualani, her departed mother, she remained until that time indifferent to religious instruction, and at times openly sanctioned the practice of idolatry; she now appears to have experienced an entire change of sentiment and feeling, which has been attended with a corresponding change of conversation and deportment. In a conversation with *Taamotu*, a female native teacher from Huahine, published also in the Missionary Herald, she said, "I am exceedingly alarmed on account of my former sins: I have despised the Lord Jesus Christ, and spoken evil of his good word; I have been unwilling and afraid to have the people of God pray with me. I am sorry in my inmost heart for all my former sins. I will by no means return to my former evil ways." In reference to her humility, Taamotu observes, "She does not wish to be exalted by men. This is wnat she desires and longs to have rehearsed—Jesus Christ alone; let him be lifted up; let him be exalted; let all rejoice in him."

Kaahumanu, the queen-dowager, and regent of the Islands, has also taken a most decided stand in favour of religion and morality; and under her sanction, together with that of Karaimoku and other leading chiefs, the principles and the precepts inculcated in the Decalogue, have been presented to the nation as the basis of the laws by which they are for the future to be governed. Efforts have also been made by the chiefs to suppress the immorality connected with the increasing number of ships annually visiting the Islands.

When in England, Boki was strongly recommended to attend to the cultivation of such articles as would increase the resources of the Islands; and since his return to Oahu, he has enclosed several plantations, and it is hoped that the cultivation of coffee and cotton, with the view of promoting habits of industry among the people, and increasing the commerce of the Islands, will be successful.

During the latter part of Mr. Stewart's residence in the Islands, and since his return, the instruction of the inhabitants has produced so rapid an advancement in the acquisition of useful knowledge, as to awaken feelings of astonishment and delight. On the island of Maui, in the year 1826, not less than eight thousand scholars received instruction in the schools; and it was presumed, that, with a larger supply of books, the number might be increased Forty schools existed in Hawaii; and the Missionaries, in writing to America, express their conviction, that had they the means of extending their schools, 10,000 might, in the course of the year, be taught to read with facility and correctness the word of God, in their own language. Early in the same year, sixty-nine schools, containing between two and three thousand scholars, attended a public examination at Honoruru. And during the preceding year, 1825, 78,400 spelling books and tracts had issued from the press. In January, 1827, the schools in the same island contained 8303 scholars. The translation of the Gospel by Matthew was finished about the same time, and, having been revised by the Missionaries, was sent to America, where it will probably be printed by the American Bible Society, and forwarded to the Islands; 20,000 copies of which, it is estimated, may be advantageously distributed among the people of Hawaii alone.

The progress of a work so decisive in its nature, and so extensive in its influence, affecting not only the religious, civil, and political institutions of the people, but changing entirely the principles and habits which had heretofore marked their intercourse with those by whom they were occasionally or periodically visited, would, it was natural to expect, be branded with opprobrium, and resisted with virulence, by those whose interests it would oppose, and whose inclinations it would restrain. This has been the case; and, indeed, had it not been so, the moral change that has taken place in these Islands, would have wanted one of the strongest demonstrations of that unequivocal origin and character under which it now appears before the world. Some account of the nature and causes of the opposition to that process, which is now rapidly transforming the face of Hawaiian society, will be met with in the following sheets. Numerous additional instances might be cited, were it necessary, to shew the influence of Missionary efforts in restraining the vices, and proportionably diminishing the miseries, of the people. But I am convinced, that those recorded in Mr. Stewart's volume, with others already before the public, will be sufficient to remove whatever erroneous impressions may have thereby been made, from any minds open to conviction, and influenced in reference to Missionary efforts, only by the simple declarations of honest truth. I was recently informed by an officer, who, in his Majesty's ship Cornwallis, visited Hawaii some few years ago, that not less than 400 females came on board the vessel, on the night of her anchoring in one of the harbours; but such is the change since that time, that when the Blonde arrived, not one female ascended her sides. Yet so violent has the opposition been in the Islands, that the persons and the lives of the Missionaries have only been safe under the protection of bodies of armed natives, by whom their dwellings have been surrounded and defended.

The most injurious misrepresentations have also been cir-

culated both in England and America, by those from whom
better things might have been expected; and it is greatly to be
regretted, that a leading literary journal, in our own metropolis,
should have so far indulged its prejudices, as even to hazard
its claim to public confidence in the correctness of its communications, by giving its authority as the verification of a document,
bearing the marks of improbability and self-refutation on the
very front of its assertions. It will be evident that I refer to
the fabricated Letter from Boki, the chief, and which appeared
in the beginning of 1827. Convinced, as soon as I saw the
Letter, that it had not been written by the individual whose name
was appended to it, I communicated to the Editor my reasons for
believing he had been *mistaken*, at least, in supposing it genuine.
In the following number I received a public reply, asserting,
"that the Letter certainly did come from the Sandwich Islands,"
(which I had never questioned,) and stating at the same time,
"that its genuineness neither has been, nor is, doubted either
by the officer of the *Blonde* who received it, or by his *Captain*.'
This statement being at entire variance with a communication
I had received from Lord Byron personally, I wrote to ask
his Lordship's opinion, and received shortly afterwards, in
reference to that part of my letter, the following reply:—

" You ask my opinion respecting the Letter said to be written
" by our friend Boki, and signed with his name. I have no
" hesitation in saying, that I do not believe Boki either wrote or
" dictated that Letter. It is not his manner of expressing him-
" self, and you are aware that he can scarcely form his letters.
" I do not mean to say, that the Letter *did not come from the
" Islands,* but it certainly was manufactured by some other per-
" son."

This answer, which his Lordship has so obligingly returned,
is decisive, and shews most distinctly the snare into which the

Editor of the Quarterly Review has fallen on this point, as well as on other matters in relation to the Sandwich Islands. I should not have alluded to these facts, but from the connexion in which they stand with this volume; and from the republication of the supposititious Letter from the Islands in other periodicals, and the daily papers, and the extensive circulation thus given to it through the country. It is, therefore, an act of justice to give the public the means of correcting any erroneous opinion which may have been formed; although, to every unprejudiced mind, the Letter itself would convey an antidote to the poison it was designed to instil.

W. ELLIS.

Hoxton College, April 2, 1828.

CHAPTER I.

THE Sandwich Islands are situated in the North Pacific Ocean, between 18 deg. 50 min. and 22 deg. 20 min. north latitude, and between 154 deg. 53 min. and 160 deg. 15 min. west longitude, from Greenwich. They are about 2800 miles distant from the coast of Mexico on the East—about 5000 from the shores of China on the West—and 2700 from the Society Islands on the South.

The Islands are ten in number, stretching, as may be seen from the chart, in a flattened curve, E. S. E. and W. N. W. in the following order: HA-WAI-I, MAU-I, MO-RO-KINI, TA-HU-RA-WE, RA-NAI, MO-RO-KAI, O-A-HU, TAU-AI, NI-HAU, and TAU-RA.

HA-WAI-I, the most southern and eastern Island, is the largest of the group. It is about ninety-seven miles long,—seventy-eight broad—covering a surface of 4000 square miles—and containing 85,000 inhabitants.

MAU-I lies N. W. from Ha-wai-i, and is separated from it by a channel twenty-four miles wide. This island formed by two mountainous peninsulas, connected by a narrow neck of low land, is forty-eight

B

miles long, and, at its greatest width, twenty-nine miles wide. It covers about 600 square miles, and is supposed to have a population of 20,000 people.

MO-RO-KINI is a barren rock, rising only fifteen or twenty feet above the level of the ocean, at a distance of four or five miles from the western shore of the southern peninsula of Mau-i. TA-HU-RA-WE lies in the same direction from Mau-i, six or eight miles beyond Moro-kini. It is only eleven miles long and eight broad, and has but few inhabitants.

RA-NAI is situated twenty miles N. W. from Ta-hu-ra-we, and ten or twelve miles directly west from the northern peninsula of Mau-i. It is seventeen miles long and nine broad, covering about 110 square miles, with a population of two or three thousand.

MO-RO-KAI lies W. N. W. from Mau-i, and is separated from it by a channel ten miles wide. A passage of about the same width, divides it, on the south, from Ra-nai. Mo-ro-kai is forty miles long, and seven broad—covering 170 square miles—and containing three or four thousand inhabitants.

O-A-HU lies twenty-seven miles N. W. from Moro-kai—is forty-six miles in length, and twenty-three in breadth—with a surface of 520 square miles, and a population of 20,000. It affords the best harbour in the group, and is the most fertile and beautiful of the islands.

TAU-AI is seventy-five miles N. W. from O-a-hu. It is thirty-three miles long, and twenty-eight broad —covering 520 square miles—and has about 10,000 inhabitants.

Ni-hau lies s. w. from Tau-ai fifteen miles, and is twenty miles long, and seven broad. The number of its inhabitants is small. Tau-ra, situated seventeen miles s. w. of Ni-hau,—like Mo-ro-kini—is an uninhabited rock, visited only for the eggs of seafowl, which frequent it in great numbers, and there hatch their young.

These islands were discovered, in the year 1778, by Captain James Cook, of the British navy; and from him, in honour of Earl Sandwich, then First Lord of the Admiralty, received the name by which they are at present designated. The tragical and lamented death of this celebrated navigator at Ha-wai-i, in the succeeding year, caused their existence to be made known to the civilized world, with an excitement of feeling that deeply stamped the event on the public mind.

No foreign ship visited the group again, till the year 1786, when the ill-fated La Perouse touched at Mau-i; and about the same time two vessels, engaged in the trade of the North-west Coast, procured refreshments at the island of O-a-hu. These were early succeeded by several others; and, in 1792 and 1794, by the expedition under the command of Vancouver.

At the time of their discovery, the four principal islands—Ha-wai-i, Mau-i, O-a-hu, and Tau-ai—were governed by separate and independent kings; but within the ten years preceding Vancouver's visit, Ta-meha-meha, originally a chief of inferior rank, possessing only one or two districts in Ha-wai-i,—a man of ambitious spirit, and great powers both of body and mind, had by his talent and prowess not only secured to himself the sovereignty of his native Island, but was then pushing his conquests to the islands of Mau-i and O-a-hu. During the sanguinary conflicts attending this usurpation, some of the chiefs, apprised, by their intercourse with the few ships that had then been at the island, of the importance of guns and fire-arms, in a time of warfare; and sensible of the superiority that would be given to the party who could gain the possession of a foreign vessel; had made treacherous and violent attacks upon several traders—and, in one instance, were unhappily successful in seizing an American schooner, and in putting her crew to death.

Ta-meha-meha, too wise not to perceive the bad policy of attempting, in this manner, to avail himself of the advantages of his visitors, adopted a course directly opposite; and, by his unwearied kindness, and every pledge of friendship, endeavoured to secure their confidence and good will. This policy in an especial manner characterised his treatment of Vancouver; and, in 1794 he formally ceded to this commander, as the representative of the British nation, the island of Hawai-i, in expression of his respect for that government, and a desire to have the protection of its power. In return, Vancouver aided this chieftain in building a small vessel, which was of essential service in his future expeditions: and in the course of the succeeding year, by the death in battle of the king of O-a-hu, he became the uncontrolled master of the Windward Islands. The king of Tau-ai and Ni-hau, intimidated by the success and invincible power of Ta-meha-meha, despatched an embassy to him, on this event, with a surrender of himself as a tributary prince ; and the supreme government of the whole group became thus established in the hands of the conqueror.

This great political change, with the known kindness of the king to foreigners, opened the way to a safe and increasing intercourse with the American and European nations. The number of vessels, especially of American merchantmen, touching at the Sandwich Islands, soon became very considerable : and the discovery of the protected and excellent harbour of Honoruru, in the island of O-a-hu, which had escaped the vigilant search of Vancouver in his survey of the coast, caused them to become to ships in general, traversing the North Pacific, a place of resort for undergoing repairs—obtaining water and other refreshments.

Sandal wood—an article of value in the Chinese market—was discovered in the mountains of the different islands, and soon became the means on the part of Ta-meha-meha of extensive commerce with foreigners. The articles of barter first given in exchange by traders were of the rudest kind—such as pieces of iron hoop, nails, coarse cloth, &c. &c. Then knives, hatchets and axes—guns, muskets, and ammunition— and eventually whole cargoes of rich American Chinese goods—and vessels of various sizes, from small schooners to brigs of upwards of a hundred tons burden.

By this intercourse with the inhabitants of other nations,—by the partial introduction among the chiefs, of European and Asiatic manufactures—by the erection of fortifications—and by the purchase, equipment, and management of ships—promise was given of, at least, a degree of future civilization.

Early in the present century, the natives began, occasionally, to enter into the service of foreign vessels as seamen, and in this manner several made their way to the United States.   In this number was Obookiah— an individual whose name and character is now extensively known, and whose wanderings were made, in the wise providence of God, to result in consequences of unspeakable importance, not only to himself, but to his whole nation.

This lad arrived at the city of New-York in the year 1809; and, shortly afterwards, became an inmate of the family of the commander of the ship in which he made this voyage, at New-Haven, Connecticut.   He was naturally of an observing and inquisitive mind; and the wide contrast, presented by a civilized and christian people, with the ignorant and degraded idolaters of his own nation, made a deep impression upon him.   Having learned the design of the extended edifices of Yale College, he frequently visited the grounds of that institution, and was at length discovered weeping at the entrance of one of the buildings.   The cause of his tears was ascertained to be a sense of his own ignorance, and an anxious desire for instruction. A gentleman of intelligence and piety immediately received him as a private pupil.   He made rapid advances in knowledge—became a sincere convert to Christianity, and, fired with zeal for the salvation of his countrymen, began to qualify himself to return to his native islands, for the purpose of making known the existence of the only true God, and the redemption that is in Jesus Christ.

The character of Obookiah was early reported to the American Board of Commissioners for Foreign Missions —a society formed in the year 1810, for the propagation of the Gospel among the Heathen. This information led to the establishment of an institution at Cornwall, Connecticut—called the " Foreign Mission School"—for the education of pagan youth found on our shores, preparatory to their being returned, as teachers, to their respective countries. Here Obookiah was placed. Other Sandwich Islanders were found, and entered on the same foundation.

Among them was a young chief, George Tamoree, son of Taumuarii, the tributary king of Tau-ai. Eight or ten years previously, his father had sent him, when only nine years old, to America to be educated. The sea-captain who had charge of him had been provided by the king with the means of meeting the necessary expenditures, but dying suddenly, within the year of his arrival, without designating these funds, they were lost in the wreck of his own fortune. George, permitted to wander from a school at which he had been placed, enlisted in the naval service of the United States. On his discharge, at the close of the late war, he was discovered at the navy-yard at Charlestown, Massachusetts; identified as the son of Taumuarii; and removed to Cornwall for education.

Obookiah, unhappily, as was thought, for the proposed introduction of Christianity at the Sandwich Islands, died before completing his course of instruction,

in February, 1818. But the event excited so great and
so general an interest in the American churches, that
by it the way became more speedily prepared for sending
a christian mission to his native shores, than might otherwise have been the case ; and in the autumn of 1819,
a company of Missionaries, under the patronage of the
American Board of Commissioners for Foreign Missions,
embarked from the city of Boston for that destination.

It consisted of the Rev. Mr. Bingham, and Rev. Mr.
Thurston, ordained ministers of the Gospel ; Mr.
Ruggles and Mr. Whitney, catechists and teachers ;
Dr. Holman a physician, Mr. Loomis a printer, and
Mr. Chamberlain an agriculturist, all married men.
And of the Sandwich Islanders, John Honorii, Thomas
Hopu, William Tenui, and George Tamoree. George
was returned to his father, by the Missionary Society,
as a passenger only, without any official connection
with the mission family.

The affecting death of Capt. Cook, and the massacre
of several other foreigners at a later period, had deeply
impressed the public mind with a belief that the Sandwich Islanders were more barbarous and sanguinary than
most other Islands of the Pacific. The unvarying testimony of voyagers who had visited them, when consulted
in reference to the contemplated mission, had been —
" The natives are too much addicted to their pagan
customs ever to give them up. They will never abandon
their sacrifices and tabus. The Missionaries may attempt to convert them, but they can never succeed ;
they will be robbed and driven away, even if they
escape violence and death."

It was with just reason, therefore, that the Society under whose auspices this enterprise had been projected, waited with deep solicitude for the period when they might hear of the arrival of this devoted company at their destination, and of the character of their reception by the people. Seventeen months elapsed before this anxiously desired moment came. But, though the suspense had been long, it was broken by sounds of gladness, which yet vibrate joyfully on the ears of many, who look for the coming of the kingdom of God.

The Missionaries had not only made the islands in safety, but the first word of intelligence that reached their vessel was in the astonishing, and, to them, overwhelming exclamation, " THE GODS OF HA-WAI I ARE NO MORE !—TA-MEHA-MEHA IS DEAD—RIHO-RIHO IS KING—THE TABU IS ABOLISHED—AND THE TEMPLES AND IDOLS ARE DESTROYED !"

The eldest son of the Conqueror of Ha-wai-i had ascended the throne, and the very opening of his reign had been marked by a measure which is without a parallel in the history of the world. A pagan king, unbidden and uninstructed, had in a day cast off all the gods of his people; and, by a single stroke of boldness, overthrown a superstition, which, for ages, had held a degraded race in the bondage of fear.

The idolatry of the Sandwich Islanders was of a form peculiar to the Polynesians, called TABU, from an appendage to the ordinary worship of images, expressed by that term, so singular in its nature as justly to give name to the whole system. The tabu, though intimately connected with the services of religion, did not consist of any fixed and unchanging observances—but was uncertain and arbitrary in its requisitions. It was an instrument of power, in the possession of the priests and king, which might be made to assume any shape, which interest, passion, or even caprice, might dictate, and to extend to all things civil as well as religious. And, every breach of tabu being punishable with death, it was a system under which the people were governed as with a rod of iron.

The word, itself, has generally been considered by foreigners as synonymous with the English word *prohibition*. But its literal and peculiar meaning implies a *consecration*. Thus the priests, the king, the chiefs, who claimed descent from the gods, and the temples,. were *tabu*. So also an animal, or cluster of fruit, or other article, set apart for sacrifice—and a day, week, or month appropriated to the worship of the gods.

The tabus varied greatly both in extent and duration. Sometimes a single tree, or a single animal only, would be made tabu, and at others, a whole grove or herd ;— sometimes a single house, or piece of land, or fishing ground, at others a whole district, or even island. Sometimes the tabu would be limited to a day, at others, would continue for weeks and months. Tabus of *time* varied in the degree of rigour with which they were to be observed ; sometimes requiring only a cessation from ordinary work and amusement; at others, an entire seclusion ; when, to be seen abroad, was death. Every fire, too, must then be extinguished—every sound, even to the crowing of a cock or barking of a dog, prevented—and the silence and desolation of death, be made to reign throughout the whole extent of the tabu, whether of district or island.

But though thus various in its features, and changeable in its forms, there were points, in the tabu, which were general and unalterable. One of these, was the tabu of all the best kinds of food for sacrifice to the gods, and for the use of the men: the women were thus excluded from the use of hogs, fowls, cocoa-nut, bananas, several kinds of fish, &c. &c. Another was, a tabu excluding the females from the houses of the men. A woman was not permitted to enter the habitation, even of her father or husband, nor to eat in company with any man. These were the points, a breach of which, the king determined to make the signal for the abolition of the whole, and for the downfall of idolatry.

Having secretly consulted the high priest and principal chiefs upon the subject, and gained their consent and co-operation, he made a great entertainment, in the month of November 1819, to which all the foreign traders, mercantile agents, and residents, then at the islands, were invited, together with the whole company of chiefs. Two long tables, one for males and another for females, in conformity to the tabu, were spread in an open bower, around which a great concourse of common people assembled. After the food was served up, and all the company had taken their seats, the king evidently much agitated, arose with a dish of the food denied to females, in his hand, and walking first round the table of the men, as if to see that all were properly provided, hastily turned to that of the women, and seating himself between two of his queens, began to eat with them, from the dish he had carried. At this, the whole astonished multitude burst into the exclamation, AI NOA! AI NOA!—(*ai* food—*noa* common, or general, in contradistinction to *ai tabu*—food sacred.) The high priest himself rushed to fire an adjoining temple; and messengers were instantly despatched, in all directions, to perpetrate a similar conflagration. In a very few days, every heathen temple, in the group, was mouldering in ashes, and the idols, which had not shared the same fate, were cast useless on the beach, or reserved merely as objects of curiosity.

That it was the pleasure of the king, thus to cast off the tabu, and to abolish idolatry, seemed sufficient to satisfy the minds of the people. One ambitious young chief of rank, however, attempted, by it, to excite the natives to a rebellion; but, in this, he was unsuccessful —his party were defeated, and himself and wife slain in battle, in the winter of 1820.

The causes which led Riho-Riho to a determination so bold and so important, are not fully known; but probably were, a conviction of the falsity of idolatry, derived from an intercourse with foreigners and from the indifference, if not contempt, they may have manifested for the gods and sacrifices of his nation; a knowledge of the destruction of the idols at the Society Islands, a people known to him to be altogether like his own; and strong attachment for his queens, who were restricted in their privileges and enjoyments by the tabu. Whatever may have been the immediate cause or causes of this singular event, the pious heart will recognize in it the hand of Him, who doeth all things according to his good pleasure, and who, only can " IN THE WILDERNESS, PREPARE THE WAY OF THE LORD, AND MAKE STRAIGHT, IN THE DESERT, A HIGHWAY FOR OUR GOD!"

The intelligence thus communicated from the shore, prepared the Missionaries for a favourable reception by the king and government. They were early and happily established on the islands of Ha-wai-i, O-a-hu, and Tau-ai; and with such prospects of immediate and wide-spreading usefulness, that the first communications from them to their patrons were accompanied by an earnest application for more Missionaries. This application was repeated again and again, and in the year 1822 was complied with, by the American Board of Commissioners for Foreign Missions, in the selection of a reinforcement, consisting of three ordained ministers: the Rev. Mr. Bishop, Rev. Mr. Richards, and myself; two licensed preachers, Mr. Ely and Mr. Goodrich; Dr. Blatchely a physician, all married men; Mr. L. Chamberlain, agent for secular affairs; Betsy Stockton, a coloured female; a domestic and assistant Missionary in my own family; and three Sandwich Islanders, from the Foreign Mission School at Cornwall,—Stephen Pupuhi, Richard Karaioula, and William Kamahoula.

The embarkation took place, on board the ship Thames, in the harbour of New-Haven, on Tuesday the 19th of November, 1822; immediately after which, the following Journal was commenced.

CHAPTER II.

COMMENCEMENT OF THE VOYAGE.

Ship Thames, at Sea, Nov. 22, 1822. The letters of the 20th instant, sent on shore by the pilot, will inform you, my dear M——, of the manner in which the first day of our embarkation was spent. Our ship, from the gentleness of her motion, seemed less willing than ourselves to exchange the smooth waters of the sound, and the rich and cheerful landscapes along the shores of Connecticut and Long Island, for the troubled bosom and unbroken horizon of the ocean; and it was not till yesterday morning, at day-break, that we passed Montauk Point, and gained the open sea.

A few hours afterwards we lost sight of Block Island, the last part of our country in view—without scarce noticing it, however, from the excessive sickness which had already seized most of our number. H—— is extremely ill, so much so, as to be almost entirely insensible. I have, myself, escaped altogether, and am happily enabled to devote my whole attention to her. The wind yesterday was fresh, and the sea rough—but to-day the weather is much more boisterous. Since even-

iug we have had heavy squalls, with occasional dashes
of rain, and there is now every appearance of an approaching gale.

Saturday, 23.   After taking reef on reef, and furling sail after sail, during the night, it became necessary
this morning, from the violence of the storm, to heave
the ship to, and let her drift with the wind. The scene
is new and terrific. The dead-lights are in ; and
besides the gloom thus thrown over all below, the cabin
has been made still more comfortless by a heavy sea
which broke over the ship, and poured a torrent of
water down the companion-way. Every thing not
strongly lashed is driving from one side to the other,
while we ourselves, some seated on the floor, some
on trunks and boxes, and others braced in our births,
are obliged to cling to whatever is within reach, to prevent being dashed about in the same manner. The
wind howls dismally through the spars and rigging, and
every wave that rushes along the sides of the vessel, or
breaks above the bulwarks and thunders over our heads,
seems to threaten destruction.

At 9 o'clock I went on deck : I had anticipated a
scene of grandeur, but its sublimity and fearfulness far
surpassed my expectation. No description can convey
a just impression of it to your mind. Imagine for a
moment, the mountains of Otsego to be rolling in
every direction, with high and broken swells over the
lake and valley. Just so monstrous are the billows
that rage around us. We are in the gulf stream, and
the current and storm being in opposite directions, the
waves are not only high and heavy, but irregular in

their course, and so rapid in their succession, that, before the ship, in her descent, is half way down the abyss between them, the next sea often collects to a tremendous height above her bowsprit, over which it appears impossible for her to rise. Still she as often mounts its threatening waters, and rides in triumph on its summit. But the labour is excessive, and, as she plunges from the top of one wave to the gulf below, and, after a momentary pause, rushes again to the height of another, every timber groans in the effort, and at times she trembles to her keel as if foundering in the struggle.

was above, when she made the most fearful plunge we have yet felt. Several of the crew were, at the time, securing the flying-jib-boom, and, with the bowsprit and whole head of the ship, were instantly buried in a mountain of water. An involuntary shriek, as their hats were seen sweeping topmast-high on the passing wave, expressed the fear that they too were swept to destruction. But happily they maintained their hold, and, though bruised and breathless, escaped a watery grave.

Never before was I so deeply impressed, as in this conflict of the elements, with my insignificance as a creature, in the sight of Him who " commandeth the winds and the waves, and they obey him." A momentary unbelief would persuade me to think myself too unimportant an object to share in the protecting power of such a Being. How happy for us is the assurance that every hair of our heads is numbered, and that without Him not even a sparrow falleth to the ground.

All the fortitude of the Christian is requisite, to pre-
serve an ordinary degree of composure, amidst the
terrors of the Lord, as thus displayed, in the wonders of
the deep; how is it, that the careless and ungodly sinner can behold them, and not tremble!

Evening. The storm has rapidly abated, and we are
again under sail; but the sea is still dreadfully high,
and almost every wave washes our decks.

Sabbath, 24. The weather continues too tempestuous
to allow of any religious service; and our Sabbath and
sanctuary must be those only of the heart. But though
denied the peculiar privileges of the day, we are cheered
by the persuasion, that we are not forgotten by our
already distant friends, who have gone up to the courts
of God, renewedly " to be satisfied with the fatness of
his house," and " to drink of the river f his pleasures."

The remembrance of Sabbaths in a christian land,
now past to us for ever, has been accompanied by
recollections of home of the deepest tenderness. For
the first time since we sailed, I have felt the reality of
my separation from all I have held dearest on earth;
and, as the conviction has pressed itself upon my soul,
friend after friend has crowded on my imagination, till
I have escaped agony of heart, only by hurrying my
thoughts to that world of gladness, where there will be
no more separation, and from whence " sorrow and
sighing shall for ever flee away." O how happy, how
glorious the hope of an interminable meeting there!—
Would to God that all the objects of love, on whom
the warm remembrance of this day has rested, had secured this hope to their souls " as an anchor sure and

steadfast;" then, though widely dispersed, we should pass safely through all the tempests of life, and ride securely together, at last, in the haven of eternal rest.

Tuesday, 26. We have to-day been gratified by an incident, always cheering to those at sea, that of speaking a ship homeward bound. Animation beamed from every eye, as the cry of " Sail ho !" echoed from voice to voice. A fine ship under full sail, is a noble object, and we watched our mutual and rapid approach with delight. It proved to be the William Penn of Philadelphia; and as we rushed past each other, we requested to be reported, " *All's well—a week at sea.*" and followed her with our best wishes and prayers.

Saturday 30. Another severe gale of wind compelled us to lay-to the whole of Thursday night, and part of yesterday, Confinement to the cabin, and the tossing of the ship, has greatly increased H——'s sickness. She has indeed been very, very ill; so much so, as even to excite, at times, serious apprehensions of the result. She has scarce opened her eyes, or spoken a word, since we gained the open sea ; and has suffered more, in that period, than in all her life before.

This circumstance has given me an opportunity of judging what my thoughts and feelings will be, when I see her enduring all the privations of the Missionary life—should she be spared to meet them. When I look back a fortnight, and view her as she then was, healthful and animated, with happiness beaming on every feature, and see her now pale, emaciated, and spiritless, from a sickness which might have been avoided, I am ready to ask myself, " Could it have been my duty thus to expose one so delicate, and so unused to fatigue and hardship?" Something within me would answer, " No, it could not." But it is not the spirit of the Christian, nor of the Minister, nor of the Missionary ; all these, more promptly and more decisively exclaim, "It could, and it is." Yes, whatever I myself, whatever H—— may suffer, I am fully persuaded, that I have done right, and that she has done right, in forming the determination, and in pursuing the measures, we have. We are not on a warfare at our own charge ; nor do we undertake to build, not having counted the cost. We have engaged in this enterprise, not from a sudden impulse of unenlightened enthusiasm, but from a long process of reasoning, which, we trust, will bear the scrutiny, equally, of philosophy and of religion.

Did self-enjoyment constitute the highest object and blessing of our present existence, in " the elegant sufficiency" of an American home, we could have been so well satisfied as scarce to have wished for a change, even to that " better country" whose fulness, only, can meet the desires of an immortal spirit. But while such is not the case, and, next to the salvation of our own souls, the glory of God and the good of man ought to be our chief concern, we most willingly bid farewell to all the charms of civilized life, and welcome the simplicity and rudeness of a Missionary hut, if thereby we can most fully achieve these great ends of existence.

If the Bible be true—and where my soul can confidently repose, every minor good may be securely trusted—I fear no evil in this measure, except that which may arise from the deceitfulness of the human heart. To me, the duty involved in Christian Missions to the heathen, is clear as the sun at noon-day; and to deny it, is, in my opinion, at once to oppose the whole spirit and genius of our faith—as well as expressly to reject the authority of the scriptures. Unto the Gentiles the gospel of Jesus must be preached. On whom, then, does the obligation of this necessity fall? I answer, on those ministers of the cross, at least, who can devote themselves to the work, without neglecting or forsaking a prior and superior duty, incompatible with the undertaking; and who are not disqualified by physical or other causes, from entering upon it. Of this number, after a careful, and, I may add, at the time unwelcome examination, I proved myself, to my own conscience, to be one. And what reason could I plead, why an exemption should be granted to me? Could I say—" My attachment to my family and friends, to my home and country, are too strong—I cannot tear myself from them ?" The same argument might be equally urged by all others; and he who trusted in it, might justly apprehend the righteous judgment of Heaven on the heart, that loved the objects of its earthly affection more than it feared its God. Could I plead the too great sacrifice of the indulgences and elegancies of life? In so doing, by what data could I discriminate between a supreme attachment to these, and that " friendship of the world which is enmity with God ;" and how well might I dread the sentence—" Thou fool! -this night thy soul shall be required of thee." No plea could stand the test,—and it was only left for me to say—" Lord, here am I, send me."

This surrender was not made, I admit, without a struggle—not the struggle of a day—nor of an hour —but of months : and a struggle of agony too; but— thanks be to God—it was that also of triumph, and from the moment of victory, all within my own bosom, on this point, has been peace.

Both myself and H—— have acted in this matter only in conformity to the precepts of the Gospel— to the dictates of reason and conscience—and to the leadings of the Providence of God.   We may find that the hand that guides, bears the rod to afflict; still we will fear no evil : blessings rich and satisfying will arise in the path of duty—if not in one form—in others, perhaps less expected, but not less full.

With these views of the subject, and they are those of our inmost hearts, we cheerfully turn for ever from the comfort, the social happiness, and refined enjoyments we might so fully have secured in our native land, and welcome, with contentment, the self-denial and privation—the toil and care, we have in prospect. Whatever else we lose, we gain

" A peaceful Conscience, and approving Heaven"—

a treasure, too rich to be exchanged or forfeited for all the fleeting and unsubstantial pleasures of the world.   When, then, we recount our sufferings,— when we give a candid statement of our situation, however afflictive it may be—do not think that we consider it strange that such things have befallen us, but that deeming the service we perform as done unto the Lord, we even "count for joy" the trials that may await us in its accomplishment.

Our humble friend B—— daily proves more and more kind, affectionate, and faithful. She has been most thoughtful and assiduous in her attentions to H ——, and we consider her an invaluable acquisition to our family

Monday, Dec. 2, *N. lat.* 36 *deg., W. long.* 49 *deg*
The weather now is delightful—the air as mild and balmy as that of a morning in May. The sea too is less disturbed than at any time since we came out. Indeed, until Saturday we were in a constant gale. You can scarce imagine the difference made in every thing by the change. Before, we could not see two hundred yards for the green billows heaping in mountains around us; now, we can look, in any direction, to a distance of many miles over a beautiful surface of deep blue, variegated here and there by the snowy curvings of a breaking wave.

Contrary to my expectation, I find no difficulty in profitably employing my time on board ship. In this I am happily disappointed;—from what I had heard of sea life, I was fearful the voyage would prove almost a blank. We are quite systematic in our regulations as a family. The rousing bell is rung in the cabin at sunrise, and that for morning prayers at half past seven o'clock. We breakfast at eight, dine at one, take tea at six, and have evening worship immediately after the setting of the first night-watch, that all the crew may attend.

The establishment of regular worship has been a source of much satisfaction, and the respectful attendance of the captain, officers, and crew, gives us sincere pleasure. When the weather admits, the evening service is held on the quarter-deck ; and it is sweet, indeed, to hear our hymns of praise floating on the breeze, and to listen to the voice of prayer addressed, from the midst of these mighty waters, to Him who protects, and who only can defend, and bless us.

Our other religious services are, a prayer-meeting in the forenoon of the Sabbath, and a sermon in the afternoon. Bible classes have also been established among the sailors. We cannot but hope, and do most fervently pray, that these means of grace may not be lost on the souls of those, by whole skill we are enabled to bear the glad tidings of salvation to the distant islands of the ocean.

Dec. 4. We are at present nightly enjoying a lovely exhibition—that of moonlight at sea. At this season of the year, even in these mild latitudes, the queen of night ascends her throne through dark and wintry clouds floating on the horizon ; and, for the last few evenings, I have stood hour after hour, gazing at her, as she has burst, in all her glory, from behind one and another of these dark masses, or, from her concealment, has fringed their edges with a splendour equal to her own.

> " Nor undelighted, in the solemn noon
> Of night,"—

have I watched ner progress through the sky, while the mild radiance above, and the playful reflection below, have presented a scene of tranquillity and peace, un-rivalled but in a vision of fancy. Then, too, our ship, as she hastens on her course, looks more majestic than in the day; her lofty masts seem, from the deck, to tower among the stars, and her full, swelling sails, tapering to their very tops, add no small degree of the beautiful to the sublime.

Dec. 9. Five days ago, we fell in company with the ship Winslow, of New-Bedford, bound, like ourselves, to the Pacific. We are still sailing within a short dis-tance of each other. Arrangements were made for a religious service on board of her on the Sabbath; and the novelty of an excursion, in a small boat, in the midst of the Atlantic, was assigned to me. I was ac-companied by Captain Clasby, and Mr. Chamberlain, and preached from the text, " My son, if sinners entice thee, consent thou not." The whole ship's company, neatly dressed, attended on the quarter-deck, and ap-peared interested in the exercises. The crews of Ame-rican whale-ships are, generally, composed of respect-able young men, of a class altogether superior to ordi-nary seamen. Intelligent, active, and enterprising, they cannot be regarded with indifference; and I re-joiced in the opportunity of preaching to these, the unsearchable riches of Christ. May it not be in vain! but may they hear, obey, and live! At the close of the sermon, Mr. Chamberlain furnished them with a quan-tity of tracts, and we returned to the Thames in time for the afternoon worship.

For the last few days we have been perfectly be-calmed. A very heavy swell is, at the same time, roll-

ing from the westward, giving to our ship a long, slug-
gish motion, almost as fatiguing as that in a gale.

Dec. 19. *N. lat.* 24° *W. long.* 20°. During the
last week, my taste for sea life; has greatly increased;
principally, perhaps, because of the rapid and almost
entire recovery of H——. She is quite herself again.
The weather, too, has been delightful; the sky clear
and mild, the wind fresh and fair, and our progress
rapid and exhilarating.

Dec. 23. Just after breakfast yesterday, a shoal of
large fish, a species of whale, (*Physeter Catodon,*) called
blackfish by the crew, were descried close to our ship.
H—— and myself were walking the quarter-deck at
the time, and had a full view of them as they tumbled
and spouted on their way, directly under the stern.
Not less than fifty were in sight. Three of our boats
were lowered and manned in a moment, and a chase
after them commenced. At the distance of half a mile
we saw the darting of a harpoon; immediately after,
the water dashing high into the air; and then the boat,
oars "apeak," rushing with astonishing velocity after
the animal to which it was fastened. From a defect in
the iron, however, this one was not secured. Shortly
after, the first officer struck another, which instantly
spouted a column of blood ten or fifteen feet high, and
began plunging in the agonies of death. He threw his
immense body almost entirely out of the water, and,
while dying, thrashed the waves, till he was covered in
a bed of foam.

All hands were engaged in towing the prey to the
ship, when another shoal appeared just under our bows:

D

a boat was quickly in the midst of them, as they sported along unconscious of danger ; and one of the largest became alarmed only in time to receive a harpoon fully in his side, as he plunged round to escape it. He sprang once nearly his whole length into the air, and then diving into the deep was soon out of sight ; but the swiftness with which the boat cut the waves after him, and the purple stream that marked its wake, told that the blow had been true. The boat continued to be hurried, with the speed of a race-horse, first in one direction, and then in another, for more than half an hour before the creature died.

With some exertion, both were brought alongside the ship, and hoisted upon deck. They were of one size, about twenty-one feet long, fifteen-feet in circumference, and each weighing nearly three tons. The blubber was immediately cut off; and, after reserving the livers, and a few *steaks*, for the crew, the huge carcases were launched again into the deep.

Unaccustomed to such feats, the whole scene was to us an exhibition of singular intrepidity. The process in taking a whale is precisely the same. The boats for this purpose are of the most light, and apparently fragile construction, formed to move with the utmost rapidity, and to ride even on the crest of a wave. The harpooner stands erect on the bow, with a firmness and gracefulness which practice only could secure, while the boat bounds from height to depth and from depth to height of the swelling sea. At a proper distance. his eye fixed on his victim, he darts the instrument with a force, which would seem, inevitably, to throw him from his narrow foot-hold into the water while the floundering animal, writhing in the desperation of death, puts the boat in constant jeopardy.

The danger is by no means imaginary; many boats are destroyed, and many lives lost, in whaling voyages. The line, many hundred yards in length, to which the harpoon is attached, is coiled in a tub in the forepart of the boat, and permitted to run off according to the power and speed of the whale to which it has been fastened; while one of the boatmen stands with a hatchet to cut it off, at a single blow, in case it should become entangled; the delay of an instant, might prove fatal, and the boat be irresistibly taken down by the animal. It not unfrequently happens, that an arm or leg of some of the men is caught in the line, as it glides with the quickness of lightning from the tub, and, should not the limb be at once severed from the body by it, the wretch is, in a moment, hurried to an irrecoverable depth.

Our crew are engaged to-day in *trying* the blubber, for which purpose all whaling ships have a fixture of two or more large boilers and a furnace, on the foredeck. The oil of the blackfish is principally used by curriers in dressing leather;—that now preparing is for our lamps, there having been a mistake in the quantity of spermaceti put on board the Thames for the voyage.

Dec. 24. For the last fortnight we have been anticipating the pleasure of touching, for a day, at one of the Cape de Verd Islands; and, for the time, had almost lost sight of our more distant destination. Last night we supposed ourselves so much in the neighbourhood of

them, that we fully expected to hear the cry, "land
ho !" early this morning.   But instead of land, we have
a heavy breeze, high sea, and thick and gloomy atmosphere.   The uncertainty of our real distance from the
group,—the impossibility of getting an observation,—
and the threatening aspect of the weather, made the
captain so doubtful of the prudence of running towards
land, as to consult the passengers on the subject.   We,
of course, begged him to follow his own judgment;
when, with one more inquisitive look to the windward,
and an expressive shake of the head, he gave the command—" *Up with the helm, and square the yards;*"
and, in five minutes from the first suggestion of sailing
by without our promised visit, we were running before
the wind towards the equator, at the rate of ten miles
an hour.   A principal desire for stopping, had been, to
send letters to America : and when I saw the ship
actually about, and, in imagination, the land for which
we had been so eagerly looking, fading in the distance,
I felt a momentary regret and disappointment.

   Saturday, 28.   After a most rapid run of several days,
we, this morning, reached " *the swamp*"—as the captain calls the calm and rainy latitudes between   the
north-east and south-east trade-winds—a few degrees
north of the equator.   Clouds and tempests seem gathered
before us, having indeed, in point of gloom, the appearance of some of the dismal swamps of our own continent; and we begin to apprehend the proof of a
geographical description I have seen, stating that " the
regions of the equator are given up to calms and rain—
thunder, lightning, and water-spouts."

Evening. A violent squall has just swept over us; and, before our sails could be secured, the lee-bulwarks of the ship were nearly under water. Every thing had an aspect more like that of the gale in the gulf stream, than at any time since. The wind rushed so loudly through the rigging, as to require a full exertion of lungs in the captain and mates to cause their orders to be heard, and the rain poured in torrents. Both wind and rain continue, in an abated degree, and the ship is still reefed down so as, in sea-phraseology, to be " *all snug.*"

There is something in this state of things, that produces a peculiar effect on my mind, and one which, you may be surprised to hear me say, is that of enjoyment. The low and scudding clouds—the driving rain—the sullen heavings of the ocean, and the roaring of the water at the prow—the rapidity with which we dash from wave to wave, while our lee-gunnels are almost buried in the deep—though they give, to all without, the aspect of suffering and of danger, induce a musing mood which I have found delightful. Every thing on deck, too, has a like tendency—nothing generally is heard, but the creaking of the masts and yards, and the rattling of the cordage, while the officers, in their watchcoats and tarpawling caps, stand at their respective posts, and the sailors shelter themselves, from the worst of the storm, under the lee of the boats or weather-bulwarks of the ship.

A situation of personal comfort, however, as well as a sense of safety, is essential to this kind of enjoyment: it is the contrast, indeed, thus afforded, that yields the principal pleasure. Feeling ourselves free from inconvenience and harm, we triumph over the ragings of the tempest, and forget the case of those who, unlike us, have no refuge from its fury.

Armstrong describes the same feeling, in reference to sleep, under circumstances familiar to every one—

> " O when the growling winds contend, and all
> The sounding forest fluctuates in the storm,
> To sink in warm repose, and hear the din
> Howl o'er the steady battlements, delights
> Above the luxury of common sleep."

Monday, Dec. 30. Within the last two days, we have, for the first time, had a sight of a dolphin—one of the most beautiful of the inhabitants of the sea. The general length of this fish appears to be about two feet. In its shape it bears little resemblance to the representation of it seen on vases, &c. and in marine emblems and armorial bearings, but is very similar to the white salmon-trout of the Otsego. When swimming in the water, its colours appear exceedingly delicate and beautiful. The head, back, and upper part of the sides, vary from the hues of burnished steel to that of deep azure and mazarine blue, shading off towards the under parts in pea-green and light yellow. The head fins are sky blue, and those of the tail pale green, terminating in yellow.

The dolphin is seldom taken with a hook and line, but only a short time ago, one was struck with a harpoon, and brought on deck.—we all hastened to witness the reported splendour of its colours when dying. We found them to be as truly beautiful as they have been described; consisting of rapid transitions from the deepest purple, approaching to black, through blue, green, gold of different hues, and several shades of silver, to an almost snow-white, and then to purple again. The sight, however, was painful, from a kind of sympathy with the beautiful sufferer;—we could but feel, that the gratification of our curiosity was at the expense of its life. The colours soon became less and less brilliant, and in five minutes entirely disappeared. A large shoal of the boneto were sporting round the ship in company with the dolphin;—they are a very active fish,—and frequently threw themselves several feet into the air.

In a Waterspout, we have also had one of the phenomena characteristic of the region in which we now are. It was at too great a distance to be seen very minutely. The end nearest the ocean was scarce perceptible, though the agitation of the water under it was very evident: the upper extremity terminated by a tubular expansion—similar in form to the large end of a trumpet—in a heavy black cloud. The part clearly visible was about 300 feet in length, and the cloud not less than 1500 feet in height. There was a shower of rain, almost immediately afterwards, of the largest drops I ever saw. It is perfectly calm, and the ocean glassy as a mirror, which made the appearance of the rain, as it struck the surface of the water, singularly beautiful—as far as the eye could reach, the whole sea seemed a plain of glass, studded with diamonds of the first magnitude.

Ten o'clock at night. The exhibitions of the day, have been followed to-night by a *phosphoretic scene* of unrivalled splendour and sublimity. We had often before observed luminous points, like sparks of fire, floating here and there in the furrow of our vessel; but now the whole ocean was literally bespangled with them. Notwithstanding the smoothness of the surface, there is a considerable swell of the sea; and, sparkling as it did on every part as with fire, the mighty heavings of its bosom were indescribably magnificent. It seemed as if the sky had fallen to a level with the ship, and all its stars, in tenfold numbers and brilliancy, were rolling about with the undulation of the billows.

The horizon, in every direction, presented a line of uninterrupted light, while the wide space intervening was one extent of apparent fire. The sides of our vessel appeared kindling to a blaze, and, as her bows occasionally dashed against a wave, the flash of the concussion gleamed half way up the rigging, and illumined every object along the whole length of the ship. By throwing any article overboard, a display of light and colours took place, surpassing, in brilliancy and beauty, the finest exhibition of fireworks. A charming effect was produced, by a line, coiled to some length, and then cast in the water at a distance; and also, by a bucket of water dashed from the side of the vessel. The rudder, too, by its motions, created splendid coruscations at the stern, and a flood of light, by which our track was marked far behind us. The smaller fish were distinctly traceable, by running lines shewing their rapid course; while, now and then, broad gleamings, extending many yards in every direction, made known the movement of some monster of the deep. But minuteness will only weary, without conveying any adequate impression of the scene;—it would have been wise, perhaps, only to have said, that it was among the most sublime, Nature herself ever presents.

The cause of this phenomenon was long a subject of speculation among men of science, but is now satisfactorily ascertained to be sea-animalcula of the luminous tribe, particularly the species *Medusa*. The *Medusa pellucens* of Sir Joseph Banks, and the *Medusa scintillans* of Mr. Macartney, emit the most splendid light. The degree and brilliancy of the exhibition are supposed to depend on the state of the atmosphere and sea. A more grand display than that which we have witnessed, probably seldom, if ever, takes place.

CHAP. III.

Monday, Jan. 6. Several days ago, we took a fine breeze from the south, which has proved to be the regular trade-wind. The "*swamp*" was much less formidable than we expected : we have had but little rain, only a short calm, and no thunder-storm, though "the artillery of the heavens" has been heard, almost constantly, at a distance. We crossed the Line, yesterday morning, in longitude 24 deg. west. The heat, though great, has not yet been very oppressive : the mercury in Fahrenheit, in the shade, has ranged from 79 to 83 deg., and in the sun stands at 116 deg.

Thursday, 9. *S. lat.* 8 *deg.* 34′, *W. long.* 27 *deg.* Early to-day, a sail was discovered with signals for speaking; and we bore down to her. It was a Portuguese vessel of very indifferent appearance. Our captain put the Thames so close alongside of her, that an apple could have been thrown on her deck. The commander could not speak English, and hailed through one of his crew : he merely wished to know our longitude ; and informed us he was bound to the Western Coast of Africa. With the knowledge of her destination, the horrors of a slave-ship at once rose on the mind; and the probability of her errand to that land of wretchedness, took entire possession of the imagination. The sighing of the captive, and the groaning of the oppressed, seemed already to be heard from her hatchways; and, as we dropped into her wake, gazing at her black hulk and bloody waist—colours well suited to her character—to the farewell wave of the hand, I could not add the customary ejaculation—" *God speed thee !*"

Never before was I so deeply impressed with the enormity of this trade. I involuntarily shrunk from the sight of men, who I believed to be engaged in its cruelties; and felt no inclination, as on similar occasions, to watch the lessening sail till it should sink beneath the horizon. Instead of impressions of beauty, before received, from the same object, every look brought with it associations of human misery. Oh ! what perversion of feeling, what destitution of principle, must there be in the heart, that can convert the ignorance and debasement of those, who, though sunk below the level of their race, are still " bone of our bone, and flesh of our flesh," into reasons for subjecting them to still greater degradation ! Surely, if any thing on earth calls loudly for the righteous judgment of God, it is the prosecution of the slave trade ; and, sooner or later, the retributions of a just avenger must fall on those who thus make the heavens to echo with the moanings of the bereaved, and the earth rich with the tears and blood of the enslaved.

Jan. 22, *S. lat.* 33°, *W. long.* 51°. For some time time past, the ocean around us has been enlivened by

immense numbers of flying fish, *(exocætus volitans.)*
This is a beautiful animal, six or eight inches in length,
and of slender and delicate form. Until now, I had an
impression that it received its name from springing in the
air, for a moment only, and then sinking into its native
element; but, within the last fortnight, flocks of forty
and fifty, and even of a greater number, have risen
about our ship, and flown yards before descending
again. When in this situation, a person ignorant of
their nature could not distinguish them from birds
of the same size. The large transparent fins, which
they use in flying, have every appearance of wings;
and when in a direction opposite to the sun, their
whole bodies are of a most dazzling silver white.

But in this case, as in that of the dying dolphin, we
have been led to commiserate as well as to admire.
At most times, when these little creatures thus take
flight, it is only to escape from some devouring enemy
in close pursuit. We have often caught a glimpse of a
boneto darting through the water under them, as they
have skimmed along its surface; and once, after watching with delight the lengthened course of an uncommonly beautiful fish, as time after time it dipped
for a moment, but scarcely touched the waves before it
rose again, and seemed to exert every power to pursue
its rapid way, we saw it fall directly into the jaws of
some ferocious monster, which, as if doubly ravenous
chase, leapt partly out of the water to receive it.

They seem peculiarly ill-fated; not unfrequently, a
flight from the enemies in their proper element, exposes
them to the rapacity of others equally destructive; and

they become the prey of gulls, cormorants, and other seafowl hovering over the water for food.   In their aerial course, they often also come in contact with vessels, and fall helpless on the deck.

Since taking the south-east trade-wind, we have had most charming weather.   The beauty, both of sea and sky, has been such, as to attract constant observation; and the perfect clearness of the atmosphere, except a rich bed of clouds floating on the most distant horizon, is peculiarly pleasant, after the gloomy heavens of the " *thunder-storm latitudes.*"   We are all in fine health and spirits, and truly happy.   Every thing, within and without, indicates prosperity and peace; and, occupied with a variety of useful employments, we have yet known nothing of the ennui so often complained of at sea.

We are not without evidence, of a more interesting and important kind, that the blessing of God is upon us.   A very visible change has taken place in the general deportment of our crew, and a great increase of seriousness is observable at the seasons of worship. Beneficial consequences are following our Bible classes. While they enlighten the mind on the subject important above all others, they give an access to the heart and conscience, which could not otherwise be readily secured; and the happy influence of which, is already manifest.   Another exercise, connected with evening prayers,—the repetition, by each of the Missionaries, of a single text of Scripture, indiscriminately chosen from the bible,—has been attended by a salutary effect.   The practice was adopted, from the incon-

E

venience of reading at night on the quarter-deck, and has been found more successful, in arresting the attention, than the ordinary manner of introducing the Scriptures at such services. There is something peculiarly impressive and solemn, in the sound of so many different voices, successively proclaiming, amid the darkness that covers the deep, the words of eternal truth.

Our Sabbaths also have, of late, increased in interest. There is now generally, during the sabbath an order and quietness in every part of the ship, becoming the character of the day.   The officers and crew, like ourselves, are occupied with their bibles, and other appropriate books ; and, in meeting the various duties of this happy institution, we often experience the truth of the assurance — " they that wait upon the Lord shall renew their strength."

Our evenings, too, are greatly conducive to a spirit of devotion : the vast expanse of water around us, almost insensibly leads the mind to the eternity, of which it is so often made an illustration.   The mild splendour of a tropic sky, here adorned by the CROSS— " the emblem of redeeming love"—and, the serenity of every thing within observation, seem better suited to emotions of seriousness, than the glare of day ; while the general silence of the ship, broken by

" No noise but water, ever friend to thought,"

leaves the mind to the free use of every contemplative power.   It is a time in which I delight ; and often, after most of our company are wrapt in sleep, I ascend the rigging, till, even the footsteps of " the patrolling watch," are lost in the dashing of the water, there to gaze on the heavens, " the work of the Almighty, and the moon and stars which He hath made ;" and, in view of their magnitude .and sublimity, with the psalmist, to exclaim—" What is man, that THOU art mindful of him ? or the son of man, that THOU visitest him ?"

Thursday, 23, *S. lat.* 34°, *W. long.* 51° 30'. Spoke the Hebe, of Philadelphia, from Buenos Ayres, bound to Rio Janeiro and Lisbon. The Thames was running under a press of sail before a strong breeze, against which the Hebe stemmed her way, *close hauled*, with double-reefed topsails only. She was but two days from port ; and having been newly painted, looked as fresh and fair as the fictitious being whose name she bears.

Evening. The most tremendous squall we have yet encountered has just swept by. It came raging so suddenly upon us, that the Captain had time only to exclaim—" *All hands on deck ! hand the royals— and the top-gallant-sails too !—clew up the mainsail ! mind your helm—quick ! quick !*"—while all became vociferation and confusion—before the wind struck us a full broadside, and instantly laid the ship almost on her beam ends. Every thing cracked, in her struggle against the blast, and she shot forward like a race-horse, with her gunnels in the water, and the waves on her lee towering yard-arm high.

All the furniture in the cabin was completely capsized, and those below, thinking the vessel going down, rushed on deck with looks and exclamations of horror.

For some time, I thought every successive moment would see us engulfed in the flood, which literally yawned to receive us. But all the halliards having been let go, and the helm seized by an experienced hand, the ship was got before the wind, and somewhat eased, till the violence of the gust gave place to torrents of rain, accompanied by lightning and thunder. A ship-wreck must, indeed, be horrible. I was not greatly agitated myself; the most unpleasant sensations I experienced, arose from the terror of others; for there was many a pale face and trembling lip, among both crew and passengers. Whatever the degree of danger may have been, the scene was of a character deeply to fix thoughts of that event, by which, sooner or later, we shall all be made to stand before the bar of God.

Jan. 25, *S. lat.* 37°, *W. long.* 52° 48'. At twelve o'clock last night, a gale commenced, and in an hour's time we were compelled to *lay-to*, under a storm-stay-sail only. The howling of the tempest—plunging of the vessel—and trampling and hallooing of the sailors, effectually prevented our taking any rest. The first person from the deck, this morning, reported the wind to be a hurricane, and the waves mountain high : the latter circumstance we were ready to believe, without ocular demonstration. One or two, only, of the passengers, attempted to take breakfast. While at the table, a sea struck the ship along her whole length, from the quarter deck to the bows, and threw her nearly on her beam-ends. She lay, trembling under the stroke, till I thought she would never rise again ; and, the water came pouring by the hogshead, down the companion-way, and through the steerage hatch. Every thing was swept from the table, though secured in the manner usual in such weather; and some of the family, mattresses and all, were thrown from their births, into the cabin. On deck, one of the boats was stove, and the ship, in its whole length, was washed by the wave.

The gale continuing to increase, and the sea to rise at a fearful rate, it became necessary for our safety, to have the upper yards and masts sent down. The seamen were obliged to mount to their very tops, a distance of seventy or eighty feet from the deck, to unloose the rigging; where,

> " Upon the high and giddy mast,
> In cradle of the rude, imperious surge,"

they were swung, every successive minute, with incredible velocity, through a space of little less than ninety feet; while, an inevitable grave yawned beneath them, should the slender yard, to which they clung, give way, or they once lose their footing. The unnatural sound of their voices, as their screams to make themselves heard below, were caught by the wind, and borne away on the tempest, came to the ear like the shrieks of the dying ; and, I dared scarce look up, for a moment, lest I should see some one, in despite of every effort, thrown into the raging sea, where no power of man could have secured him rescue. Anticipating the expression of hopeless horror, which the wretch thus perishing must give I often involuntarily closed my eyes, in the fear of beholding the agonizing reality.

The storm raged till evening with unabated violence and produced greater anxiety than any we have before

experienced. A tempest, such as this has been, is
indeed indescribably sublime ; but too dreadfully terrific, when at its height, to allow of much enjoyment.
When it begins evidently to abate, and hope tells you
that the worst is known, you are left to the indulgence
of unmingled and enthusiastic admiration ; and may
gaze with delight at the ever-varying scene, as wave
after wave rears its monstrous head, and " casts its
foaming honours to the clouds."   But, till this change
does take place—(while every successive blast blows
harder and harder, and each billow, threatens more
surely than its precursor, to bury you under its weight)—
it is impossible. Thoughts of fear must check, if they do
not take entire place, of the higher feelings of admiration.

But though the day has been one of gloom, it has
been marked by a circumstance, which has given me
more genuine satisfaction than any thing since we left
America.   In the dusk of the evening, while leaning,
alone, against the railing of the quarter-deck, feeling in
my own mind something of the desolation of the scene
around me, my arm was gently touched by some one,
on the spars behind : it was R——, one of the hardiest
of our crew.   As my eye fell upon him, I at once anticipated his errand ; and can scarce describe my
emotion, when I ascertained it, indeed, to be the jailor's
query—" What must I do to be saved ?"   Perceiving
me alone, he had stolen from his station forward, to say
that his spirit, like the troubled sea, could find no rest :
and to beg to be directed in the way everlasting.   His
words were few, but his look, while he trembled under

his guilt as a sinner, and earnestly supplicated an interest in my prayers, spoke volumes. So unexpected, though greatly desired and prayed for, was this event, that I almost doubted its reality. This state of feeling had been induced by a private conversation, on the subject of religion, immediately after the recitation of the Bible class, on the preceding sabbath; and he had scarcely eaten or slept during the whole week. Every thing, in his appearance, manifested sincerity and contrition. I would not be too sanguine, yet cannot but hope that the Spirit of God has begun in his heart that good work, which shall be performed " until the day of Jesus Christ."—" A little leaven leaveneth the whole lump;" and, should but one of this crew be truly converted to the faith and practice of pure religion, through the example, the persuasion, and the prayers, of that individual, all his companions, ere the voyage is completed, may be turned to the Shepherd and Bishop of souls.

Notwithstanding this incident, our spiritual state, as a little band far separated from all the world, may be best understood from the lines of a favourite hymn—

> " At anchor laid, remote from home,
> Toilling, we cry, " Sweet Spirit, come !"

Friday, 31. This morning, during a calm, we had the first full view of a whale. From daybreak till eight o'clock, many had been spouting at a distance; but this rose immediately at the bows of our vessel, The noise made by the suction of the water round the animal, and by its spouting, rendered the usual exclamation—" *There she blows !*"—unnecessary, in attracting our attention to the spot; and we all hastened forward to catch a sight of so welcome a visitor. We were fully gratified; for it continued to play round us on the surface of the water, within a stone's throw, for more than an hour; and at one time lay alongside of us for some minutes perfectly still and within a few yards of the ship. It was about eighty feet long, and proportionably large: its spout, appearing like pure and beautiful steam, was projected, by a single puff, nearly twenty feet into the air. The animal was of the species, called fin-back—*(Balæna Physalus)*—a kind too fleet and powerful often to be attacked by whalemen. It disappeared by diving headforemost, and casting its broad flukes perpendicularly out of water.

Monday, Feb. 3, S. lat. 45° 30′. We are now on the *Brazil Banks*—had soundings at 60 fathoms on Saturday afternoon. The difference of depth in the water is plainly visible to the eye; the colour having changed from deep blue to that of a beautiful light green. At four o'clock, yesterday morning, we fell in with the whaler Britannia, of London, cruising on the banks, and sent letters on board of her, to be transferred to the first ship she should meet, bound to America. Some of our number improved the opportunity to distribute tracts, which were gratefully received by her crew.

Thursday, Feb. 5, S. lat. 51s. All hands have been actively engaged to-day, in putting the vessel in trim for Cape Horn. The upper yards, masts, and rigging, have been sent down; and the ship drest in a complete suit of new sails, of the stoutest texture. These preparations look formidable, but seem justified by the

general aspect of the weather.   Just before night, there
was a very peculiar exhibition on sea and sky   For
half an hour before and after sunset, the whole heavens,
except a quarter of a circle in the west, which was
perfectly clear, were covered by dense, and unusually
lowering, clouds.   The elevation of the unshaded arch
was not more than five degrees; and under it, on the
farthest horizon, a mass or line of vapour extended, so
greatly resembling a distant coast, that, had we not
known it to be impossible, not all the power of vision,
aided by our sea-glasses, could have satisfied us that
it was not the American continent.

The rays of the sun, entirely shut out by the heavy
canopy above, came to us only in splendid reflections
from this fairy realm, and presented a succession of
mountains, and groves, and spires, and turrets, and
towers, and even *steamboats* and *lighthouses*, all in
the richest colouring, and glittering with silver.   For
some minutes, the splendour of the sight momentarily
increased, drawing from us enthusiastic admiration :
when the sun suddenly burst from behind its dark
drapery, and in an instant the whole mass of clouds,
over and around us, were changed, in all their ponderous
forms, from the blackness of night to the brightest
crimson; while the sea, before shrouded as in a funeral
pall, gleamed with the mingled reflections of purple and
gold.   The transition seemed one of enchantment; but
our admiration was not unaccompanied by emotions of
awe.   The lowness and thickness of the clouds made
the reflections of their colour so strong, that the sun,
though perfectly unobscured, glared with a fiery and

unnatural light; which, as it gradually faded into the
sickly shades of an eclipse, marked the sails and rigging,
and every countenance, with the hue of death. Minds,
that soar above the power of superstition, might have
felt a momentary uneasiness at such unusual omens;
and while sea-birds, which delight only in the drivings
of the storm, screamed round our masts above, or
silently gazed at us as they tossed on the waters below;
I could but exclaim—

> " Dark gath'ring clouds, involve the threat'ning skies; —
> The sea heaves, conscious of th' impending gloom—
> Loud hollow murmurs from the deep arise—
> They come—the spirits of the tempest come !"

Feb. 7. Our apprehensions of heavy weather have
not been realized; and we are making most rapid progress, with clear sky and fair wind. We have been
amused to-day by vast numbers of whale sporting near
us on every side, and often thrusting their broad backs
entirely above water, as they rushed past with the
velocity of lightning. These also were *fin-backs.*

Saturday, Feb. 8. We were roused, this morning,
at six o'clock, by the cry—" *Land ho !*" Staten Land,
seventy miles distant, being in sight. Points of Terra
del Fuego were also seen during the forenoon. At
mid-day we arrived directly opposite Staten Land; and
passed New Year Harbour, at a distance of ten miles.
The mountains are lofty, and broken, and fantastic in
their contour. Many of their summits were spotted
with white, but whether of snow or rock we could not
determine. The whole island appeared thickly covered
with wood, but of low growth; though one of our sea-

men, who has visited it for seal, says the trees, to the water's edge, are large, and afford good timber. The whole coast is iron-bound and precipitous, consisting of cliffs towering many hundred feet, against whose slippery bases, the surf constantly breaks fifteen and twenty feet high. Every thing wears an aspect of profound solitude, not a living creature being seen, but the sea-fowl wheeling round their inaccessible nests, or diving to the waters below.

Knowing the island to be uninhabited, we were surprised, on a nearer approach, to see a column of smoke, rising at the entrance of New Year Harbour. It was probably, from the fires of persons left by ships, for the purpose of catching seal. While accounting for it in this manner, I could but wonder at the inconsistency of those who condemn the Missionary to a heathen land as an enthusiast and a mad man, and yet look on such as these, who, for a little worldly gain, banish themselves for months and years to the most lonely and inhospitable climes, as praise-worthy examples of enterprise and hardihood.

After passing the most eastern point of the island, and directing our course along its southern shore, it assumed new and interesting forms; and its entire outline became more and more *outrè*. Were I to send you a sketch of it, you would almost believe me sporting with your credulity. The whole seemed but a range of obelisks, pyramids, domes, castles, and towers, which even a dull imagination might have transformed into the gigantic works of the fabled race, said to have inhabited the southern regions of the neighbouring continent. As the evening approached, the whole became empurpled, by the rich tints of the " sunset scene," so often the subject of the artist's skill, while many points of rocks, from the water's edge to the highest peaks, either from ice, or water, or metallic composition, glittered with the brilliancy of diamonds. It is pleasant, after having been seventy-nine days at sea, thus to have our horizon once more broken; especially as it is accompanied by the assurance, that we have very nearly reached the grand climacteric of our voyage—CAPE HORN.

CHAPTER IV.

VOYAGE.

Thursday, Feb. 20, *S. lat.* 57° 30′, *W. long.* 70° 30′. Immediately after finishing the preceding page, nearly a fortnight ago, we were assailed by the fierce winds of the Cape. We had just fallen asleep, after an uncommonly mild evening, when the rushing of an impetuous storm, followed by the alarming cry, " *All hands on deck !*"—(thundered with stentorian voice, down the maindeck, and forecastle hatchways) — effectually roused us from our slumbers. It was more than an hour, before the ship could be snugly hove to : and we have been in one uninterrupted gale ever since, making but little headway in our passage. Some apprehension existed, at one time, of our being too much in the neighbourhood of the Diego Ramerez, a cluster of rocks thirty miles south of Hermit's Island, on which Cape Horn is situated. But we shortly afterwards ascertained ourselves to be well to the westward of them ; and, on the morning of the 16th, at four o'clock, made Cape Noir, an island near Cape Gloucester, on Terra del Fuego, twenty miles distant. We wore ship immediately, and had only time to clear the coast before the wind, blowing " *dead on shore*," increased to a perfect hurricane, and for the last forty-eight hours has driven us with irresistible fury far eastward again. Here we still struggle with the elements.

H—— often says, " *With what terror would our friends witness our situation !*" At the very extremity of the globe, surrounded by an immense waste of angry waters, whose surface is unceasingly swept by wind, and hail, and rain, and snow, our only earthly hope, a few hundred feet of timber, which the ingenuity of man has formed to float upon the ocean ; liable to many accidents, and hourly exposed to a horrid death, it would not be surprising, if the bursting of the tempest above, and the roaring of the deep below, should sometimes make us " fearful and unbelieving." But they do not. We have an unshaken confidence that all will be well; and behold the terrors of our way without other emotions than those of gratitude and hope. We often view our good ship with a kind of sympathy : dismantled of much of her loftiness, and reefed and furled almost to bare poles, she looks, in her conflict, desolate as a solitary oak, writhing in the contentions of a winter's storm.

Saturday, March 1, *S. lat.* 52° *W. long.* 82°. After a tempestuous passage of twenty-one days, by the aid of a few hours of fair wind, we find ourselves completely round Cape Horn. The whole ship's company, passengers and crew, appear like captives on the eve of liberation from a gloomy and uncomfortable prison. You will not be surprised at this, when informed that we have scarce seen the sun for three weeks, and the moon but once, though she is now some days past her full. Not one of the officers or crew have had dry clothes during the whole of the time ; the deck has been constantly deluged, and the cabin dark and cold : for we have had no fire, though the mercury has stood as low as 34° and 36°. Our nights have been restless, from the violent motion of the vessel, and the groaning of her timbers ; and our days spent in stupidity and idleness, if an involuntary loss of time may be called by that name. We could do nothing, but wrap ourselves in our cloaks, hold on to any thing within reach, and, whether sitting up or lying down, roll and pitch with our labouring bark.

Notwithstanding these facts, this part of our voyage has by no means been uncommonly tedious or uncomfortable. The prevailing winds of this region are heavy gales from the west, the direct course to be steered in passing the Cape, and ships are often detained by them three times the period we have been, and meet with weather far more dangerous and severe ; so much so, that many vessels, after striving in vain for weeks here, to make a passage into the Pacific, have been obliged, at last, to bear away for the Cape of Good Hope, and make their voyage across the Indian ocean.

There is great cause for gratitude, that we have thus passed this dreaded goal, and are permitted to pursue our way without disaster or longer detention. Our crew have all been kept in life, where many a poor sailor has found a cold, unfathomed grave ; and our ship has rode in safety, where, not a few have met an untold fate.

March 4, *S. lat.* 48°; *W. long.* 84°. If the affections of my heart are ever roused to an enthusiasm of
joy, it is when I see a young man, in the fulness of his
health and strength, turning from folly and sin, to the
love of God. Such a sight I have lately had the happiness to witness in G——. I have had long and repeated
opportunities of conversing with him on the salvation
of the soul; and, for some time past, he has been
deeply serious.   More than once, I have seen him
stretched at full length in his state-room, apparently
under the influence of thoughts and feelings bordering
on agony.   The same emotions have been visible in his
countenance and manner, as he has walked his nightly
watch on deck; and he now stands, before the whole
ship's company, as one who is confessedly of a broken
and contrite spirit in the sight of his Maker and his
Judge.   I cannot but believe, that in him we have the
faithfulness of the promise, that the Spirit should be
sent " to convince of sin, of righteousness, and of judgment."

My interviews with R——, since the gale off the
Rio de la Plata, have been frequent.   He continues
greatly interested for his own salvation.   On two
nights, recently, I have spent a part of his watch on
deck with him, and at both times, by the sight of a
waning moon, have seen tears roll in torrents down his
hardy cheeks, while he has spoken of the things that
relate to his eternal peace.

To some of his shipmates he has become an object of
ridicule, while others seem to be like-minded with himself.   Shortly after passing Staten Land, he came to

me one morning, with a very animated look, saying, " O Mr. S——, I have much hope of C—— : he is greatly troubled, has *knocked off swearing*, and is constantly *overhauling his Bible.* He used, always to swear when reefing in a gale, but, on Saturday night, we were on the lee-yard-arm of the main-topsail together, for half an hour, and, though it blew a hurricane, and we could do nothing with the sail, he never swore a word : Let him only *cut cable, and swing from the fellows in his watch,* and I shall not fear for him !"

I do not wonder that the angels of heaven, who know all the bliss of true holiness, rejoice before the throne of God, at the repentance of a sinner on earth.   When I look on these rough sons of the ocean, and know that the breath, so lately spent only in profaneness and sin, is now addressed to God in prayer ; and that, from some secluded part of the ship, they daily and nightly offer the sacrifices of penitence—sinful as they have been, I at times feel ready to clasp them to my bosom, as those who shall yet be purified, even as Christ is pure. Oh ! that their number may here be increased, till every soul, by the renewing of the Holy Ghost, shall " be made meet for the inheritance of the saints in light."

March 6.   G—— is rejoicing in the possession of a Christian's hope.   He requested an interview with me last night, during his first watch ; and as I approached him in the dark, fell on my neck, with emotions that denied him utterance.   It was some time before he could tell me of the affections that had taken possession of his bosom.   So great and so entire a change had taken place in his views and feelings, as to constrain him to believe, that unto him " old things had passed away, and all things become new," and that he was "in Christ Jesus a new creature." After an interesting and exciting conversation, I left him as I found him, rejoicing in the fulness of hope; and praying in my own heart, that the affection throbbing within his manly breast, might prove to be the commencement of a joy, which, in the world to come would " rise immeasurably high."

A short time since, R—— was in great despondency, and said to me, " I know not what to do !" I have read my Bible, and have prayed; I have tried for weeks, and for months, to be religious, but I cannot; I have no true repentance, no real faith, and God will not hear my prayers; what can I do? I feel that my soul will live for ever; and without the grace of God, I know it must eternally perish." But to-night I met him, with his Bible in his hand, and his very heart in his face, and his first words were, " O Mr. S——, I have found the right way *to believe ;* it was the righteousness of Jesus Christ I needed. Now the whole Bible is not *against me,* as it used to be, but every word is *for me ;* because I see and feel how God can be just, and yet justify an ungodly sinner."

Monday, March 10. This evening, while walking the deck, I happened to cast my eyes into the steerage, and could not refrain wishing, that some of those whose hearts are interested for the salvation of seamen, and who are active in exertions to promote it, could have stood by me for a moment. One person only was there, and, for the time, I wished to see no other; it was C—— eading his Bible. The lamp was suspended from the

upper deck, at too great a height to admit of reading
by it when seated on the floor, and too much fatigued
by a hard day's work to stand, he was kneeling, and
reading with an attention and solemnity that seemed
to absorb every thought and feeling. He did not change
his position in the least, till the bell rang for prayer, a
full half hour from the time I first observed him,
while his attitude, countenance, and whole appearance,
gave strong testimony that he was searching the Scriptures for " the words of eternal life."

K—— and N—— are deeply affected by the change
in their friend G——; and there is a seriousness from
the quarter-deck to the forecastle, that forces itself on
the observation of every one. Even M——, who seemed to be so far given up to evil as to have no one to
care for his soul, is filled with wretchedness as a sinner.
And while conversing with him, I have seen " rivers of
waters" fall from his cheeks into the briny deep, as he
has hid his face on the gunnel of the ship. And what,
my dear M——, shall we say to these things ? Whose
is the power, that has produced such impressions on
the feelings of these hardy sailors ? And what influence, but the breathings of the Holy Spirit, could thus
have melted their hearts into penitence ?

March 12. At two o'clock, P. M. descried a sail ;
and soon afterwards recognized the red banner of Britain. She proved to be the brig Tiber, from Valparaiso,
bound to Valdivia, eight days out. Captain Clasby
asked, before coming up with her, whether any one of
us wished to board her ; but we all declined : which, I
greatly regretted, when after passing, and being nearly

beyond hearing, her commander, in his farewell words, reported, *the U. S. ship Franklin*, 74, *Commodore Stewart, at Valparaiso.* I should have been pleased, in obtaining more particular information from that ship.

Monday, March 24, S. lat. 15°; *W. long.* 96°. In the midst of more important thoughts, I have omitted to mention, that we have entirely left the region of winds and tempest, and long ceased to ride upon " the mountain wave." We are now ploughing a widely extended plain, under a press of sail, at the rate of ten miles an hour; and, instead of the chilling blasts of the Cape, are fanned by a breeze, balmy as the breath of May. When we first sent our top-gallant sails and royals up, and again spread our broad studding-sails to the wind, we almost feared, after seeing the ship so long staggering and reeling to and fro like a drunken man, under close-reefed topsails only, that she could not bear so great an addition of height and breadth; but she hastens on, with all her accustomed stateliness and beauty; and, with so much steadiness, that we are scarce sensible of the slightest motion. The contrast in our whole situation is so great, as to produce a proportionate exhilaration of spirits; and with a sailor's life, in its most favourable aspect, before me, I have been led with Byron to exclaim—

> " Oh who can tell, save he whose heart hath tried,
> And danced in triumph, o'er the water wide,
> The exulting sense, the pulse's mad'ning play,
> That thrills the wand'rer of the trackless way,
> O'er the glad waters of the dark blue sea !"

For some time after entering the Pacific, we almost

doubted the appropriateness of its name : the experience of the last three weeks, however, has fully satisfied us on this point ; but for the deep blue of the surface, we might fancy ourselves to be sailing on the
placid bosom of a lake. We are now off the coast of
Peru ; and have been greatly delighted with the beauty
of the sky and clouds, which is here very peculiar, and
I should think unrivalled in any other part of the world.
Towards evening, and early in the morning, I have seen,
at the same time clouds of almost every colour, in different parts of the heavens ; and of hues I never beheld
there before ; for instance, a rich and perfect green,
amber, and carmine ; while the hemisphere round the
rising or setting sun has been one blaze of glory. Last
night, the tinge on the ocean added greatly to the effect
of the scene ; it was of perfect blood colour, occasioned
by the reflection of a fleecy veil of crimson clouds,
stretched over a greater part of the heavens : the appearance was so extremely singular, as to cause us
almost to shrink from it, as from something supernatural.

Monday, March 31. I never knew a Sabbath on
land, such as yesterday was here. Even the sky was
of a purity I never beheld before ; and the eye, in its
vision, seemed capable of reaching the very limits of
space. About the ship, scarce a sound was heard from
the opening of the morning till the close of day, but the
rippling of the water as we sailed through the deep, or
the voice of worship as we bowed before our God. All
on board appeared to feel, as well as know, that the day
was sacred to its Maker ; and when I viewed the neat-

ness and order of every thing, and witnessed the quiet
and solemnity that prevailed, I could not but fancy
that I saw " HOLINESS TO THE LORD" inscribed on the
cloud of canvass spread to the breeze.   Our public
services were delightful ;—and what Christian would not
have felt them to be so, when the bright tear of rapture
might be seen starting in the eyes of some, and that of
sorrow trembling in those of others ; both of whom, till
of late, " cared for none of these things."

R—— is one of the happiest of creatures.   All he
says, is worth twice its real value, from the manner in
which it is communicated.   He, last night, related to
me a conversation he had with C—— a few days since.
C—— came to him, with a spirit greatly troubled ; and
wished to know in what manner he had obtained the
light and liberty he appeared to enjoy; adding, " I
believe the Bible to be true, and every word of it to be
from God.   I know that I can be saved only by the
redemption of Jesus Christ.   I feel my misery as a sinner—*I believe every thing—but how am I to believe
so as to be saved ?*   I want faith, and how am I to get
it ?"   R—— told him, it was just so with himself once :
" I did not know what faith was, or how to obtain it ;
but I know now what it is, and believe I possess it.   But
I do not know that I can tell you what it is, or how to
get it.   I can tell you what it is not : it is not *knocking
off swearing, and drinking, and such like ;* and it is *not
reading the Bible, nor praying, nor being good ;* it is
none of these; for, even if they would answer for the
time to come, there is *the old score* still, and how are
you to get clear of that ?   It is not any thing you have

done or can do ; it is only believing, and trusting to what *Christ has done;* it is forsaking your sins, and looking for their pardon and the salvation of your soul, because he died and shed his blood for sin ; and it is nothing else." A doctor of divinity might have given poor C—— a more technical and polished answer, but not one more simple or probably satisfactory.

Tuesday, April 8, *N. lat.* 3° ; *W. long.* 115°. We have bidden adieu to the southern hemisphere, most probably for ever. We recrossed the equator on the night of Saturday, 5th instant—three months, to an hour, after having past it in the Atlantic.

The last evening was devoted to the observance of the monthly meeting for prayer, a service not expected to recur again till we shall have left the Thames. It was an exceedingly interesting hour. While the burden of our petitions, in unison with the appointment, was, " *Thy kingdom come !*" the objects, and the end, of the Missionary cause rose with all their moral sublimity on our view, and caused us to sing with delighted animation, the fine hymn—

> " Glorious things of Thee are spoken,
> Zion, City of our God !"

A copy of verses composed by Kristnu, the first Hindoo convert at Serampore, also formed a part of the exercises : and while we chanted its simple stanzas, we could not but hope that similar knowledge and piety might yet characterize the productions of some, who through our instrumentality should be turned " from darkness to light, and from the power of Satan unto God."

Every association connected with the peculiar services

of this day, consecrated as it is by those who look for the salvation of the world, must produce a happy influence on the heart believing that the " fervent effectual prayer of the righteous man availeth much ;" especially on that of the Missionary, who, however unknown, however solitary and destitute, still feels that he is included among the scattered bands for whose special blessing the followers of Christ unitedly—

    " Thus bend the knee, and lift the hand, in prayer."

We were joined in our worship by all the officers and crew off duty, some of whom we trust have found access by the same Spirit to our common Father and God. It was with no ordinary feelings of gratitude we beheld a row of these rough but interesting men uniting with us not only by an external attendance, but, as we believe, in the warm affections of the heart. Often during the evening I saw tears of joy glistening in the bright eye of R—— ; and could easily imagine the language of his soul to be—" If I forget thee, O Jerusalem, let my right hand forget her cunning, if I prefer not thee to my chief joy."

Friday, April 11, *N. lat.* 8° 30′; *W. long.* 134°. This day has been marked by an incident, my dear M——, which to those most intimately connected with us, must take precedence of all others of a temporal nature which I have yet recorded : the birth of a son to our dear H——. It was determined that the young stranger should be by birth as fully an American as possible ; for this purpose the ensign was immediately hoisted ; and Master C—— first saw the light under the proud wavings of our national banner.

April 15. About the period of the last date we entered the north-east trade-winds, and have been rushing onward before their freshness, at the rate of more than two hundred miles a day. Should we continue thus to be prospered, we shall in a very short time make the land of our long expectation.

Thursday, April 24. It is even so—the island of Hawaii is before us. For two or three days, we have had many indications of being in the vicinity of land; several times yesterday, we imagined we could trace the outline of a mountainous coast, but were as often deceived, by the heaping of clouds on the horizon. During most of this morning, we were subject to the same illusions; though the fixedness of clouds and mist, directly before us, seemed to indicate the attraction of high land; and, at three o'clock this afternoon, as this thickness began to rise from the face of the ocean, the broad base of Hawaii, covered with Egyptian darkness, came peering through the gloom. The reality was too certain to admit of a moment's question; and was accompanied by sensations never known before.

In my own heart there was with them a mingling of pain;—it was the signal for separation from those in whom I had become deeply interested; and many of whom were in a state, the issue of which seemed deeply connected with the destinies of eternity. The first tumult of feeling was quickly succeeded by something that insensibly led to solemnity and silence. Several of the crew were seen to brush a tear from heir eyes; and one turned to go below, with the ex-

G

pression, " *Land, indeed it is—and the last and sadest sight I wished to see!*"

The mist and vapour slowly rose higher and higher, disclosing first the cultivated lands along the shore twenty or thirty miles distant, and then woodland regions above, with here and there a projecting cascade. As the scene increased in interest and beauty, the language of our hearts was, " *Hail! and welcome!*" —And after tea, having assembled along the side of the ship next the land, we almost insensibly joined in singing the appropriate hymn—

> " O'er the gloomy hills of darkness
> Look, my soul, be still and gaze."—

We had scarce finished the first line, before we were encircled by the officers and crew, with a seriousness that bespoke a participation of the sentiments on which we were dwelling. Some of their bosoms throbbed, I doubt not, with affections known only to the pious mind. The last rays of a glorious sun were gleaming from the west, and a full-orbed moon rising upon us in the east; before which, the haziness on the land suddenly gave way, without leaving a trace of the gloom, which an hour before had overshadowed the whole island, except a light drapery of clouds on the highest points of the mountains. The change was too sudden and too remarkable not to be noticed; and we could not but hope and pray, that the greater spiritual gloom, which we knew filled the land, might as speedily flee away -before the mild light of the Gospel of Salvation.

CHAPTER V.

HAWAII.

Friday, April 25. The appearance of Hawaii, this morning, was exceedingly beautiful. We were within a few miles of the shore; and the whole of the eastern and northern parts of the island were distinctly in view, with an atmosphere perfectly clear, and a sky glowing with the freshness and splendour of sunrise. When I first went on deck, the grey of the morning still lingered on the lowlands, imparting to them a grave and sombre shade; while the region behind, rising into broader light, presented its precipices and forests in all their boldness and verdure. Over the still loftier heights, one broad mantle of purple was thrown; above which, the icy cliffs of MOUNA-KEA, at an elevation of 17 or 18,000 feet, blazed like fire, from the strong reflection of the sun-beams striking them long before they reached us on the waters below. As the morning advanced, plantations, villages, and scattered huts, were distinctly seen along the shore; and columns of white smoke began to rise here and there, from the early fires of the inhabitants.

At nine o'clock, the breeze being light, a boat was sent off from the Thames for refreshments. Not long afterwards the deck of our ship echoed with the cry, " *A canoe!—a canoe!*"—and one of the rude barks of he natives was seen rapidly approaching us. Every eye was instantly fixed on it with intense observation; and I hastened to assist H—— from her state-room to the cabin windows, to view the uncultivated beings with whom we are to spend our lives. A first sight of these wretched creatures was almost overwhelming. Their naked figures, and wild expression of countenance, their black hair streaming in the wind as they hurried the canoe over the water with all the eager action and muscular power of savages, their rapid and unintelligible exclamations, and whole exhibition of uncivilized character, gave to them the appearance of being half-man and half-beast, and irresistibly pressed on the thoughts the query—" *Can they be men—can they be women?—do they not form a link in creation, connecting man with the brute?*" This indeed seemes to be the general impression; and the officer heading the boat sent to the shore, on his return, exclaimed as he ascended the deck, " Well, if I never before saw *brutes in the shape of men*, I have seen them this morning:" and, addressing himself to some of our company, added, " You can never live among *such a people as this*, we shall be obliged to take you back with us !"

Other canoes soon arrived, and many gathered round us to gratify their curiosity, and dispose of fish, water melons, bananas, sugar-cane, and sweet potatoes.

They remained an hour or two, and, notwithstanding our first impressions, greatly commended themselves to us by their artlessness and simplicity, and an apparent sprightliness and intelligence of mind. They seemed rejoiced to know that more Missionaries had arrived, and on hearing it, addressed one another with great animation, exclaiming, " *Mihanere—maitai, maitai—nui, nui maitai.*" " *Missionary—good, good—very, very good.*" They informed us, that the Missionaries at the islands were all well; and were with the king and chiefs at Oahu.

At twelve o'clock we entered the channel between Maui and Hawaii, and ran close along the north shore of this last island. Every thing here exhibited great poverty. The mountains were covered with clouds, and not a tree or shrub was to be seen. The whole surface of the country was spread with dark rocks; and the little grass perceptible was scorched and sun-burnt. The huts seen scattered along the beach, looked more like the sties and kennels of pigs and dogs, than the abodes of men : and the whole appeared something like the Hawaii I had pictured to my mind's eye, when I first seriously thought of devoting myself to the Missionary work in these islands. Yet the sight made me almost draw back from a home so barren and so miserable.

In the evening Hawaii and Mouna-kea again, at a distance, afforded another of the sublimest of prospects;—while the setting sun and rising moon combined in producing the finest effects on sea and land. The mountains were once more unclouded, and with a glass we could clearly discern immense bodies of ice and snow on their summits.

Saturday, April 26. We sailed rapidly during most of the night, and had the prospect of reaching Oahu early this morning; but our fine wind left us, and we are now slowly advancing along the western sides of Maui, Ranai, and Morokai, with the promontories of Oahu still far before us. All the islands in sight have a mountainous and rocky appearance, not very interesting at a distance, except from the wild and romantic outlines which distinguish some of their number.

Hawaii rises on every side from its broad base in gradual and unbroken ascent, till, like a patriarch, it overlooks the whole cluster to which it gives name. The only irregularity in its outline is occasioned by three wide-spreading pyramids or cones, forming the summits of the same number of mountains—Mounakea on the east—Mouna-roa on the south, and Mouna-Huararai on the west. The height of Mouna-kea has been estimated at 18,000 feet, that of Mouna-roa at 16,000, and that of Huararai at 10,000 feet above the level of the ocean.

The eastern peninsula of Maui forms one unbroken mass, rising 10,000 feet high : but the western end is divided into separate mountains; and though not so lofty as the eastern promontory, is thus in its outline much more romantic and beautiful. We have particularly admired three lofty peaks near this extremity of the island, which the natives on board say are immediately behind Lahaina, one of the most fertile and

beautiful districts in the group, and the proposed site
of a new Missionary station.

Tahurawe is a mass of uninteresting and barren
rock, at an elevation of a few hundred feet only, above
the sea. Ranai is five or six thousand feet high, and
so regular in its contour, that it might be described
by a segment of a circle. While Morokoi immediately
north of it, like the west end of Maui, is broken into
lofty peaks and spurs of mountain, jutting boldly into
the sea, and imparting to the island an appearance of
great wildness and sublimity.

*At anchor off the Harbour of Honoruru, Monday,
April* 28. At twelve o'clock on Saturday night, by
the light of a full moon, we made the south-east end
of Oahu, five miles distant. Nothing can surpass the
wild beauty of the promontories forming the headlands
of this part of the island; and I was detained on deck
for several hours, gazing at them with delight, as the
ship *lay off and on,* waiting the approach of day.

At sunrise we were close under *Diamond Hill,* a
principal point on the south side of the island. It is
the crater of an extinguished volcano, the bare shell
of a decapitated mountain, whose bowels have been
exhausted by fire. It is of a circular form, many
miles in circumference; and rises almost perpendicularly several hundred feet. Its sides every where
look like seared walls; and are fluted and furrowed
from top to bottom by the washings of water-courses,
as if by artificial workmanship. They are also surmounted in many places by a kind of moulding of
equally singular formation; and again by blocks and

piles of jagged lava, having in their elevation, the
appearance of the parapets and battlements of a dila-
pidated castle. A more unique object can scarce be
imagined.

Immediately on rounding this point, the whole of
the south side of Oahu burst on the eye in beautiful
panoramic view; presenting first the bay of Waititi,
encircled by heavy groves of the cocoa-nut, and other
luxuriant trees—then an extensive and perfectly level
plain, stretching four or five miles along the shore,
and a mile or two inland; at which distance a variety
of hills began to skirt its side, rising first in gentle
undulations, and then more abruptly, till they ran off
in lofty and pointed ridges, to a range of mountains
dividing the island in the direction of the coast, and
crowning its centre with two or three elevated peaks.
Some of these hills near the plain were covered only
with a smooth green sward, gleaming in the brightness of the morning with all the softness and richness
of velvet;—others were sprinkled here and there with
single trees and clumps of various coloured foliage
from the darkest of green to that which seemed almost
white; and all, as they rose to the mountains, became
clothed with a rich woodland verdure.

At the farther end of the plain, three or four miles
distant, lay the town of Honoruru: to which a fort
with its floating banner, the American Consulate, the
Mission House, and a cluster of masts in the harbour,
gave something of an aspect of civilization. Directly
in rear of the town, at the foot of the mountains,
another old crater was distinguished, planted with a

battery of guns, from which also the flag of the nation
was waving.   Beyond Honoruru to the west, lay a
wide extent of open country, apparently under good
cultivation ; and terminated at a distance of ten or
fifteen miles, by a noble chain of mountains, the middle
of which is marked by a fine stretch of table land.

At eight o'clock we cast anchor in the open roads,
within a mile of the shore and town : and I had a moment's opportunity for more minute observation. There
was much of natural beauty before us.   All was in a
glow of brightness ; but there was a want of life and
elasticity, that forced itself at once on the notice : a
stillness—not the stillness of the Sabbath, though it
was the day of God—but the stillness of a torrid
clime, whose enervating and depressing temperature
was plainly to be seen in the strong vibrations of a
heated air.   While I gazed on the thickly crowded
huts of the natives,—seeming so many sunburnt ricks of
hay—and saw with a glass their naked inhabitants,
lounging about in listless inactivity, I felt that I had
reached a strange land — a land, far different from
that in which were the habitations of my fathers, and
where till now had been my home.

At nine o'clock, Mr. Bishop, Mr. Richards, and
myself, with the natives William Kamahoula and
Richard Karaioula, accompanied the captain on shore.
We rowed half a mile along the coral reef by which
the coast is here bound, and on which the surf breaks
some hundred rods from the beach, before coming to
the narrow opening forming the channel into the harbour.   The entrance is short ; and we were soon in

the midst of ten or fifteen ships principally American and English whalemen, and some five or six of the native vessels, brigs and schooners, all anchored near to the beach, and some at moorings on the shore. The bay is small, not more than half a mile long and a quarter broad, but deep and perfectly safe.

Perceiving a low stone quay on a point under the fort, and near a cluster of native buildings, we were about to land on it, when a party of islanders exclaimed " *Tabu ! tabu !*" and informed our interpreters, William and Richard, that the largest of the houses was the residence of the king ; and he had prohibited any one from landing at that place William replied, ' *New Missionaries have arrived :*" when they ran to the *palace ;* and a fine looking young female, in a European dress of pink satin, with a wreath of yellow feathers on her head, made her appearance. It was *Tameha-maru*, the favourite queen of Riho-Riho. She expressed her regret that the quay was *tabu ;* and politely requested us to row to a spot on the beach nearer the town, to which she pointed, and where she would meet us.

By this time she was joined by a gentleman, who we afterwards found to be Mr. Jones, the American Consul ; and taking his arm, they proceeded together to the place appointed. On landing, we were introduced to her Hawaiian majesty by this gentleman. She received us very cordially ; and after bidding us welcome to the islands, consigned us to the care of Mr. Jones, and returned to the point. The queen appeared about twenty or twenty-two years of age ; and though well formed, is tall and masculine in figure. Her countenance is open and intelligent, with fine black eyes and hair; but her features are too broad and flat for beauty; and her complexion that of a dark mulatto—the general colour of the islanders.

The news of our arrival soon reached our Missionary friends; and after waiting a few minutes at the Consulate, we had the happiness of receiving the warm salutations of Mr. Loomis, and the Rev. Mr. Ellis, an English Missionary, under the patronage of the London Missionary Society. Mr. Ellis has been many years at the Society Islands, and is but recently established at this group. His experience in Missionary labour, and his acquaintance with the dialects of the South Seas, make him a most valuable accession to the Mission here.

Thronged by a crowd of chattering and noisy natives, who expressed their pleasure at our arrival, by hooting and dancing, and running along our path, we proceeded immediately with these gentlemen to the Mission Houses, situated on the plain, half a mile from the village: here we were introduced to the rest of the family, consisting of the Rev. Mr. Thurston and Mrs. Thurston, Mrs. Bingham, Mrs. Ellis, and Mrs. Loomis. Mr. Bingham was absent at Waititi, three miles distant, attending religious service with a large party of chiefs, at a temporary residence at that place.

At eleven o'clock Mr. Thurston preached in English at the Mission Chapel, to an audience of about one hundred foreigners — sixty of whom were captains, officers, and seamen, from the ships in port. The hour could not be otherwise than deeply interesting to us: the chapel in which we worshipped was the first ever erected on the ruins of idolatry in this land; and though of the simplest and rudest construction, being entirely in the native style, it was on this account beautiful and lovely in our eyes.

We had completed a long voyage, and were permitted to tread the shores of our destination under circumstances of peculiar mercy; and now had the privilege of paying our vows of gratitude to God from one of his peaceful temples, though in the humblest form. I can never forget the excitement with which I entered its lowly roof, trod the matted ground, its only floor, and looked at its unbarked posts and rafters, and coarse thatch of grass: primitive as every thing appeared, I felt that it was a house of God, and one of the happy gates of heaven.

On returning to the Mission House, we had the pleasure of meeting the Rev. Mr. Bingham. The report of our arrival had reached Waititi, and one of the queens of Riho-Riho had been sent with him as a messenger from the chiefs there, to request a visit from us at their afternoon worship: and after dinner we accordingly proceeded to that place.

The queen rode in a light waggon drawn by a troop of natives, who hurried it along with great rapidity; and was followed by a train of attendants, one with a spit box, another with an umbrella, some with fans of cocoanut leaf, &c. &c. Among the rest, one bore two *feathered staffs*, six or eight feet in length, with handles of ivory and tortoise shell—these were carried as badges of rank. We ourselves made the excursion on foot; first over the large open plain to the east, which is entirely without trees or cultivation ; and then through successive groves of the cocoa-nut, and plantations of the banana. We found the chiefs encamped in slight bamboo bowers, under a grove of cocoa-nuts by the seaside, and near the bay of Waititi.

The party consisted of *Keopuolani*, the queen dowager, and mother of the present king ; the Prince *Kauikeaouli*, her son, a lad nine or ten years of age ; the Princess *Nahienaena* his sister, two years younger. *Kaahumanu*, the favourite queen of Tamehameha, and her present husband, *Taumuarii*, king of Tauai and Nihau ; his son *Keariiahonui ;* and *Karaimoku*, or *Mr. Pitt*, as he is usually called, Prime Minister both to the former and present king, with two or three hundred of their favourite attendants and followers. The chiefs were all under one *ranai*, or rude bower, the floor was spread with several thicknesses of mats, on which some were seated, *à là turc ;* others lounging, and some lying down, with their heads resting on round pillows of silk velvet, damask, and morocco. Behind, or near each one, a servant sat or kneeled, fanning his master or mistress with a fan made of the leaves of the cocoa-nut, and holding in the other a small round bowl of dark polished wood, filled with the leaves of an aromatic vine, for a *spittoon*. Another servant sat or stood near each chief with a *kahile* or feathered staff, which he constantly waved, to keep off the flies. They were all dressed in European costume, and each had a small spelling book and slate on his mat with him. They

greeted us with much kindness of expression and manner ; and seemed interested in the improvements they
were making, and in the religious services of the day.
They wrote their own names on their slates, for us to
read, and secure the right pronunciation; and requested
us to leave ours with them, for the same purpose. They
repeatedly shook hands with us, reiterating their joy at
our arrival, saying, they were glad too, that we had
come on the *la tabu*, the Sabbath-day ; appearing to
view this circumstance as a propitious omen.

The servants, and rest of the common people, were
all in the native dress. That of the men consists of a
maro or girdle, eight inches or a foot in width, and
nine or ten feet long, twisted round the loins ; and a
kihei or mantle, usually about six feet feet square.
This article is worn by tying two corners of the same
side together, and then passing the head and one of the
arms through the opening thus made : leaving one arm
and shoulder bare, with the knot resting on the top of
the other, and the folds of the kihei hanging down to
the knee, both before and behind. The drapery thus
formed, is graceful, and not unlike the *toga* of the Romans. The female dress consists of a *pau*, a roll of
cloth, several yards in length, and one in width, worn
in the manner of a petticoat, by wrapping it round the
figure from the hips to the knee ; and of a *kihei* also,
usually of a larger size than that of the men, and worn
as a long shawl, over both shoulders, or over one only
The full costume of maro, or pau, and kihei, forms a
becoming, and in some degree delicate, dress ; but the
kihei is seldom used, except in the cool of the morn-

ings and the evenings ; and as generally seen, without it,
the exposure in both sexes is disgusting.

At sunset we returned to the ship, much gratified
with our trip on shore. We again passed the *palace*
without seeing Riho-Riho: and I am sorry to state the
reason,—he was intoxicated, in which condition he has
been four or five days, since the annual feast in commemoration of the death of his father, and of his own accession to the throne, was celebrated.

Harbour of Honoruru, Tuesday, April 29. The
Thames was towed into the harbour this morning at
sunrise, by twenty well-manned whale boats ; and was
brought to anchor opposite the establishment of the
king, within a stone's throw of the fort. Our companions disembarbed almost immediately, and took possession of native houses, prepared for them in the Missionary enclosure. It is thought most prudent for H——,
to defer removing to a grass hut as long as possible,
and Captain Clasby having kindly insisted on our retaining our accommodations with him, we shall remain
on board the Thames till she is ready to proceed on her
voyage to the coast of Japan.

It was signified early after our entrance into the harbour to-day, that some of our number would be expected
by the king to wait upon him soon at his residence.
Four or five of the gentlemen, including myself, therefore
landed immediately ; and were introduced to his Majesty
and most of his court. Riho-Riho was much indisposed,
being just on the recovery from his late debauch. He
was stretched on a couch of silk velvet, and naked, except
a strip of chints thrown loosely round his waist. Several

servants were fanning him, and one of his queens giving
him a cup of tea. He looked exceedingly stupid; and
so much the worse for his excess, as to be a brutish
object, as he tossed his arms and legs about in all the
restlessness of a fit of nausea. He was too ill to do
more than signify his pleasure at our arrival; and to
request the whole company to call upon him and the
rest of the chiefs, on their way from the ship to the
Mission House.

Accordingly, at eleven o'clock we all went on shore,
for the purpose of a formal presentation to the government. The *palace* stands on a stone quay within a
few feet of the water. It is a large and fine house for
one of the kind; perhaps fifty feet long, thirty broad,
eight feet high at the sides, and thirty at the peak of
the roof. The exterior is entirely composed of a thatch
of grass; and in its whole appearance is strikingly like
the Dutch barns seen in many parts of our country.
There are two large doors, one at each end, and several
windows without glass, but furnished with Venetian
shutters on each side of the house. This is the only
native building in which I have observed windows. The
interior making one apartment only, is neat, well finished,
and elegant, for the Sandwich Islands. All the timbers,
the side posts, a row of pillars supporting the ridge
pole through the whole length of the house, the rafters, &c. &c. are straight and substantial, and all beautifully hewn. The cinet or braid formed from the shreds
of the husk of the cocoa-nut, by which the whole are
fastened together, exhibits both skill and taste in its
manufacture and arrangement. The furniture is rich,

consisting, besides handsome mats with which the ground is every where covered, of three or four large chandeliers of cut glass suspended between the pillars running through the centre of the building; of mahogany dining and pier tables; crimson Chinese sofas and chairs; several large pier glasses and mirrors; some tolerable engravings, principally of naval engagements and battles in Europe, likenesses of distinguished persons, &c. &c.; and two full-length paintings of Riho-Riho taken by an artist attached to the Russian squadron of discovery under the command of Commodore Vaseclieff, which not long ago visited this group.

The king was much in the same state as when I saw him after breakfast. Most of the other chiefs, all the principal personages of the kingdom, including the party from Waititi, having assembled, made a highly respectable appearance; especially the favourite queen Tamehamaru. She was seated on a sofa, at the middle of a long table covered with a superb cloth, having a writing-desk open before her, and a native secretary at each end of the table, recording the names and taxes, of the inhabitants of a district, who were paying tribute. These were entering in single file; and passing along the table on the side opposite the queen, deposited their dollars before her, and left the house at another door. Every twenty or thirty of them were preceded and followed by a couple of the king's body-guard, armed with muskets and a kind of uniform. The only dress of Tamehamaru was a loose pink slip. She left her writing-desk on the entrance of the Missionaries, but immediately after receiving them, resumed her seat, excusing herself from

farther attentions on account of the public business in
which she was engaged. Her manners are dignified
and graceful; and her whole appearance that of a well-
bred woman, having an unaffected expression of con-
scious and acknowledged rank. She is a woman of
business, and appeared well versed in that before her.
She has ordered a roll-book to be opened, in which the
names, residence, and tax of all the nation are to be
registered, and it was the superintendence of this that
so much occupied her attention.

Kaahumanu is one of the most powerful of the female
chiefs, and attracted particular observation. She joined
the company after our arrival, and entered the house
with much of real majesty in her step and manner. She
was dressed in the native female costume. The pau or
under garment consisted of about twenty yards of rich
yellow satin, arranged in loose and graceful folds, with
a full end hanging negligently in front: the upper robe
was of purple satin, in as profuse a quantity. It was
cast over one arm and shoulder only, leaving the other
exposed, and flowed in its richness far on the ground
behind her. Her hair was neatly put up with combs,
and ornamented by a double coronet of the exquisite
feathers so often mentioned in accounts of these islands:
colours bright yellow, crimson, and bluish green. She
appears to be between forty and fifty years of age, is
large and portly, still bears marks of the beauty for
which she has been celebrated, but has an expression of
greater sternness and hauteur than any other islander I
have yet seen.

The young princess Nahienaena came, seated on the

left shoulder of a stout man, her feet resting on his arms,
folded for this purpose across his breast, and having her
right arm round his head and forehead.   This is the way
in which she is usually carried; and she is always followed
by a train of twenty or thirty boys and girls, principally
of her own age.   Her dress, like most of the others, was
in the European fashion; and of black satin trimmed
with broad gold lace, with black satin hat and feathers.
She is a very pretty and well-behaved child, not as an
Indian, but according to our own ideas of the characteristics of childhood.   The prince was also present in
a round coat and pantaloons, of black silk velvet.   They
have both learned to read and write, and are among
the most attentive and docile pupils of the Mission.

My mind had been strongly prepossessed in favour of
Taumuarii, king of Tauai, before I left America.   The
sending of his son George to our country to be educated
at the early period he did, spoke well for his intelligence
and foresight.   The deeply affecting interview, (described in the Journal of the Missionaries,) which took
place between them on the return of the son, after a
protracted absence of fifteen years, and when the father
had long thought him dead; the warm reception given
by Taumuarii to the Missionaries themselves; the active
part he took in the establishment of two of them in his
own island; and the liberality, uniform kindness, and
patronage extended to them afterwards,—had exceedingly interested me.   A knowledge of later events connected with his history, has excited a still deeper interest
for this distinguished chieftain.

Taumuarii, though an acknowledged tributary prince

to Tamehameha, virtually remained the undisturbed
sovereign of Tauai and Nihau, paying only a yearly
tax, of his own levying, to the supreme king. Riho-
Riho, on the death of Tamehameha, felt some uneasiness, lest Taumuarii should throw off his allegiance;
and the apprehension was still farther excited by the
receipt of a latter from George Tamoree, shortly after
his return from America, addressed to him as " *King of
the Windward Islands*"—a limitation of title, by no
means pleasing to his Majesty, the sovereign of the
group.   With characteristic promptness and enterprise,
he immediately determined to visit the " *leeward part
of his dominions :*" and made the voyage to Tauai under
circumstances of singular boldness and intrepidity.

In the August number of the Missionary Herald for
1822, you will find, in a well-written and interesting
journal of Mr. Bingham, an account of this visit; of
the peaceful interview of the kings; and of the Roman
magnanimity exhibited by both, when the sovereignty
of Tauai became the topic of discussion.

It seems, however, that there was a want of sincerity on the part of Riho-Riho, in this apparently ingenuous contest of princely disinterestedness; or at least
circumstances afterwards induced him to change his
views of the subject.   For after being entertained for
several weeks by Taumuarii with great kindness and
hospitality, Riho-Riho invited him, on the arrival, from
Oahu, of his favourite brig the *Haaheo o Hawaii*,
or *Pride of Hawaii*, (the splendid Cleopatra's Barge,
formerly of Salem, Massachusetts,) to go on board of
her for an hour or two one morning; and as soon as

they were well seated in the cabin, secretly gave orders to have the anchor taken, and to bear away for Oahu, thus making a captive of his royal guest! A principal chief in the party of Riho-Riho was left behind, to take the government of Tauai; and Taumuarii, thus treacherously torn from his island and queen Tapuli, to whom he was warmly attached, was compelled by the government, on his arrival at Oahu, in order to throw a veil over the real motives for this procedure, to marry the imperious dowager Kaahumanu. In her chains, and I am told they are far from being silken cords, he is still securely held.

He has a fine figure, though not so large as most of his fellow chiefs, with a noble Roman face, a style of feature very uncommon among the islanders, and when he could feel and exclaim, " *I am monarch of all I survey!*" must have looked indeed like a king. But now the expression of his countenance, and his whole manner indicate a pensive and dispirited mind; he feels himself to be a prisoner of state, and, though still called king of Tauai, knows that he will never again enjoy the government of his favourite island.

The dress of kings will be as interesting to you, as that of queens and princesses; and since Riho-Riho appeared *en sauvage*, I will mention that of Taumuarii. It consisted of a black silk velvet coat and pantaloons, buff kerseymere waistcoat, white silk stockings, splendid gold watch, with seals and rich ornaments, &c. &c.

Karaimoku, or Mr. Pitt, the prime minister, is another individual extensively known to the civilized world. He is a man of very superior powers, and of

great political sagacity. From his youth he has held
a pre-eminent rank in the nation, both as a counsellor
and a warrior. He, too, is a fine-looking man apparently between fifty and sixty years of age; and was
dressed in a suit of lead-coloured silk camlet, with
white Marseilles waistcoat and white stockings.

He has been notorious for his dissipation, especially
for intemperance in drinking; and when intoxicated,
was often guilty of the most wanton outrages of
various character. Happily, through the instruction
and persuasion of the Missionaries, he has of late
entirely abandoned this habit;—it is now many
months since he was known to be in a state of inebriation. He avows his belief in Jehovah as the only
true God; and uses all his influence, as an officer of
the government, in favour of the external observances
of Christanity. By his personal example also, he
supports the Missionaries in their efforts to secure the
moral reformation they are anxious here to achieve.

He is fond of pleasantry, and at times is very playful in his conversation. Not long since, accompanied
by one of his most intimate friends, he took tea with
Mr. Ellis. After partaking to their satisfaction of
this beverage, they both turned their cups upside
down, and placed the spoons across them. Mr. Ellis
asked the reason for this. Karaimoku answered, *" It
is so with the foreigners, when they wish no more ;"*
to which Mr. Ellis replied, *" Perhaps with sailors in
the forecastle it is, but gentlemen merely leave the
spoons in the empty cups."* A few evenings after, the
same two chiefs were at Mr. Ellis's tea-table again.

When Karaimoku had finished, he was careful to leave
his spoon and cup in the manner Mr. Ellis had mentioned, as customary in good society; but his more
negligent friend, forgetting the previous conversation,
arranged his as in the former instance: on which, Karaimoku laughingly said to Mr. Ellis,—" *You see that
fellow still belongs to the forecastle,—he has turned
his cup up again!*"

There were many other high chiefs present: Boki,
governor of Oahu, the brother of Pitt, and Liliha his
wife.   Naihi, the national orator, or hereditary speaker
in the councils of the chiefs; Kaikeoeva, the guardian
of the young prince, with Kapiolani and Keaweamahi
their wives.   Hoapiri, the husband of Keopuolani, and
stepfather of the king.   Naihi Tutui, or Captain Jack,
as he is familiarly called, the commander of the native
fleet, with many other inferior chiefs of both sexes.

We remained more than an hour, during which our
public papers were presented, our commission from the
Missionary Society, instructions, and certificates of
American citizenship: each one of us then made some
present of trifling value, such as a silver pencil-case,
&c. &c. to different individuals in the group; and took
our leave, satisfied with our reception, and the general
kindness manifested towards us.

Friday, May 2.   We have to-day been favoured
with a visit from his majesty.   At one o'clock, Kehikiri,
a chief of rank, and a punahele or intimate companion of
the king, came on board the Thames, to apprize us of
the intended honour.   About two hours afterwards,
Riho-Riho, and Kinau one of his queens, a sister of

Tameha-maru, and Karaimoku, with a crowd of attendants, made their appearance on the stone quay. The
boats of our ship were immediately lowered, and
brought them on board under flying colours and a
salute. I could scarce believe the king to be the same
man, who, as the intoxicated Indian, I had seen with
disgust three days before. He was perfectly sober, and
in fine health and spirits. There is nothing particularly
striking in his countenance, but his figure is noble,
perhaps more so than that of any other chief; his manners polite and easy, and his whole department that of
a gentleman. Both himself and minister were drest in
full suits of handsome broadcloth of navy blue, well
fitted, and fashionably made; with round beaver hats
and Wellington boots. The party remained about two
hours, and, after partaking of some refreshments, left
the ship under another salute. We have also had a
visit from Mr. and Mrs. Ellis, Mr. and Mrs. Bingham,
and Mrs. Loomis.

May 3. The king has very handsomely expressed
his good will to the Mission, by refusing to take the
customary harbour-fees from the commander of the
Thames. Captain Clasby has received the following
letter from him on the subject.

E. CAPT. CLASBY.

Aroha oe.   Eia kau wahi olelo ia oe.
Maitai no oe i kou haavi ana mai i ka kumu hou.
Aore oe e uku i ke ava—aore akahi.

Aroha ino oe.   RIHO-RIHO IOLANI.

To Capt. Clasby.

Love to you. This is my communication to you. You have done well in bringing hither the new teachers. You shall pay nothing on account of the harbour—no, nothing at all.

Grateful affection to you.

Riho-Riho Iolani.

He remitted the harbour-fees in like manner on the arrival of Mr. Ellis from the Society Islands; making a sum of £160, which in the course of three months he has generously relinquished from a regard to the Mission. *Iolani* is a favourite name, which he often attaches to his common signature.

Monday 5. The Sabbath was distinguished by the reception of the reinforcement into the Mission Church; by the administration of the Lord's Supper; and by the baptism of our son. The hours for public worship with the natives are ten o'clock in the morning, and four o'clock in the afternoon. Mr. Ellis preached in the native language in the morning to a crowded congregation, including the king and all the chiefs, from the text " How beautiful upon the mountains are the feet of him that bringeth good tidings—that publisheth peace—that bringeth good tidings of good, that publisheth SALVATION." At eleven o'clock when the services mentioned above took place, Mr. Richards preached in English to a large congregation, from the words, " The God of heaven, he will prosper us, therefore we his servants will arise and build." The chapel was

I

thronged with the chiefs in rich dresses of silk velvet, damask, satin, crape, &c. who seemed interested in the ceremonies, though scarce any of them understand a word of English.   There were a large number of respectable looking foreigners also present—the whole audience making not less than four hundred—gathered to this humble temple, by the sound of the "*church-going bell*," which, till within the last three years,

"These valleys and rocks never heard."

Riho-Riho attended all the services of the day.   He was still sober, and when so, I can readily believe what is said of him to be true—that he is one of the most interesting characters in the nation.   He looked remarkably well, and spent half an hour at the Mission House before the worship in the chapel began.   In a suit of dove-coloured satin, with white satin waistcoat, silk stockings and pumps, he appeared both in dress and manners the perfect gentleman.   I have been led to notice the dress of the chiefs, more particularly than I should otherwise have done, from my surprise at finding such richness of material, such variety of changes in their wardrobes, and such taste in the selection and arrangement of colours: I doubt not it will be equally a surprise to our American friends.

Tameha-maru saw H—— and C——, for the first time yesterday: she claimed C—— as her son immediately, and would let no one take him from her arms during the time she remained.   She has been to see them on board the Thames already this morning; and amused herself and us, by writing and reading both in English and in the Hawaiian tongue.   She does not understand English, but has learned to pronounce and read it with tolerable accuracy. She is fond of study ; puts her knowledge of writing to daily use, in sending notes and letters to the different Missionaries, and such of the chiefs as have learned to write ; and is very assiduous in her efforts to make greater attainments than she has yet secured.

Mission-House, Monday, May 12*th.* Early this morning, the ship, so long our happy home, cleared the harbour, and bore away upon the open sea. We watched the receding sail with sensations of deep feeling, till she became a speck in the horizon ; and, for myself, I may say, till that speck wavered against the sky in the uncertainty of the distance, and was at last lost to my sight in the starting tear of a farewell benediction.

We ourselves disembarked on Saturday, and became the inmates of an Indian hut within the Missionary enclosure. Our friends would probably think our situation worthy of deep commiseration, could they see us as we are. Our house might easily be erected in the smallest room in yours, my dear M——; it being only fourteen feet long, and twelve broad ; three feet high at the eaves, and nine feet at the peak of the roof. It is composed of poles and a thatch of grass, in the native manner, having no floor, but the ground spread with mats : for windows, three holes cut through the thatch, without sash or glass : and a door, without bolt, lock, or bar. In this little cabin, H—— and myself, C—— and B——, with all our personal luggage, are stowed : the trunks and boxes containing the latter are rather a convenience, however, than an incumbrance ; for, with the exception of a bedstead and a cot, they constitute the whole of our furniture, and form our only tables and chairs, articles of which, *in propriâ formâ*, we have neither. Still, I can assure you, we are truly contented, and feel ourselves even more comfortably accommodated than we could have anticipated on first landing in this heathen country : if light hearts and bright faces are signs of happiness, we are not without good proof that with us there is, at present, a fulness of that blessing.

Yesterday I preached my first sermon in these distant islands, to a large and attentive audience; among whom were most of the officers and crew of the Thames. Some of those, of whose serious impressions on our voyage we thought favourably, much to our sorrow have shewn, since our arrival in port, that "the root of the matter" was not in them. Their goodness, " *as a morning cloud, and as the early dew,* disappeared under the influence of temptation, and the power of sin. Among the number, however, there is one only in whose moral integrity we had placed confidence. The rest, by their steadfastness in the midst of a licentiousness that can scarce have a parallel, and which is so universal in its influence, as almost, without an exception, to sweep into its deadly vortex visitors of all ranks and of every age—have greatly rejoiced our hearts ; and encouraged us with fresh confidence to commend them to the love of God, and to the word of his grace ; hoping, that ever after, as now, they will be kept from the evil that is in the world, and eventually attain unto everlasting life.

Before Captain Clasby took his leave, the passengers of the Thames addressed a letter to him and to his officers, expressive of their gratitude for the unwearied kindness and attention received from them during the voyage. They were richly entitled to this mark of respect and good will.

May 14. It has been determined in a full meeting of the Mission, that before occupying any new station, an exploring expedition shall make a tour through the island of Hawaii; visiting every place of importance, and bringing a report to the Mission at Oahu.— The Rev. Mr. Ellis, Rev. Mr. Thurston, Rev. Mr. Bishop, Mr. Goodrich, and myself, form the deputation appointed for this purpose. We are to embark in the first vessel that sails for that island; and as that may be in a day or two, with the information of this appointment, I will close the journal of my voyage to the islands.

CHAPTER VI.

Mission House at Oahu, May 15. A scene was acting at the time of our arrival, to which I would for a moment revert : an annual feast in commemoration of the death of Tameha-meha, and of the accession of Riho-Riho to the throne. My notice of it, however, must be principally from the statements of others ; it having commenced three days before the Thames reached Oahu, and though it continued for a fortnight, the only day afterwards, distinguished for much parade, was one of special religious observance at the Mission House.

On the first day previous to our arrival, the king gave a very large dinner, well served in a *ranai* or bower, where tables were laid for two hundred persons. The Missionaries were invited; and Mr. and Mrs. Bingham, Mr. and Mrs. Ellis, and Mr. Loomis, attended. The foreign residents of respectability, and the officers of the numerous ships in port, were also of the party. All the natives present wore the European costume. Black had been given out as the *court dress,* and every article of that hue in the place, satin, silk,

crape, velvet, and cloth, was immediately bought: and
those who were not fortunate enough to secure any of
these, purchased pieces of black silk handkerchiefs, and
had them made into dresses.

Tameha-maru in satin and lace sustained the part of
mistress of ceremonies. She personally saw that no
one of the company was in any degree neglected;
and extended her kindness even to those who had no
claim to special civility. For instance, seeing a crowd
of American seamen without the guard, who to the
number of two hundred surrounded the bower, she immediately gave orders to have refreshments served to
them.

While at table, a procession of four hundred natives,
the inhabitants of eight districts of Oahu, passed before
the party, and deposited a tax, *in kind*, at the feet of the
king. They were all dressed in white native cloth, and
made a handsome appearance as they marched in
single file ; each district led by its headman, or overseer, carrying a large torch of the *tutui* or oil nut ; and
all bearing before them various articles, the produce of
their plantations, neatly wrapped up, and tastefully ornamented with green leaves. This procession was the
only thing in the entertainment, not designed to be in
imitation of foreign customs ; such as the style of dress,
manner of cooking and serving up the provisions, the
discharge of cannon, music, &c.

The ceremonies of the last day were altogether
Hawaiian in their character ; and highly interesting
as an exhibition of ancient customs, which it is probable
will soon be lost for ever in the light of civilization and

Christianity, now rapidly dawning on the nation. The most intelligent and influential of the chiefs and people, already speak of the *"time of dark hearts;"* and I believe are sincerely desirous of abolishing every unprofitable practice which had its birth in the ignorance of former days. In this abolition, much connected with the late celebration will be included : a fact which gives a double interest to its scenes, and leads us to catch at them as at the relics of paganism. There is much reason to believe, that a taste for these ceremonies among the chiefs will be so far lost, even before the lapse of another year, that they will never be repeated; and that the notes now taken of them, will prove to be a record of the last striking features of heathen usages at the islands on such occasions.

Tameha-maru on this day was, as usual, a conspicuous object. The *car of state,* in which she joined the processions passing in different directions, consisted of an elegantly modelled *whale boat,* fastened firmly to a platform or frame of light spars, thirty feet long by twelve wide ; and borne on the heads or shoulders of seventy men. The boat was lined, and the whole platform covered, first with fine imported broadcloth, and then with beautiful patterns of tapa or native cloth, of a variety of figures and rich colours. The men supporting the whole were formed into a solid body, so that the outer rows only at the sides and ends were seen ; and all forming these, wore the splendid scarlet and yellow feather cloaks and helmets, of which you have read accounts ; and than which scarce any thing can appear more superb.

The only dress of the queen was a scarlet silk *pau*, or native petticoat, and a coronet of feathers. She was seated in the middle of the boat, and screened from the sun by an immense Chinese umbrella of scarlet damask, richly ornamented with gilding, fringe, and tassels, and supported by a chief standing behind her in a scarlet maro or girdle, and feather helmet. On one quarter of the boat stood Karaimoko the prime minister; and on the other, *Naihi* the national orator; both also in maros of scarlet silk and helmets of feathers, and each bearing a kahile or feathered staff of state, near thirty feet in height. The upper parts of these kahiles were of scarlet feathers, so ingeniously and beautifully arranged on artificial branches attached to the staff, as to form cylinders fifteen or eighteen inches in diameter, and twelve or fourteen feet long; the lower parts or handles were covered with alternate rings of tortoise shell and ivory, of the neatest workmanship and highest polish.

Imperfect as the image may be which my description will convey to your mind, of this pageant of royal device and exhibition, I think you will not altogether condemn the epithet I use, when I say it was *splendid*. So far as the feather mantles, helmets, coronets, and kahiles had an effect, I am not fearful of extravagance in the use of the epithet. I doubt whether there is a nation in Christendom, which at the time letters and Christianity were introduced, could have presented a *court dress* and insignia of rank so magnificent as these : and they were found here in all their richness, when the islands were discovered by Cook. There is

something approaching the *sublime* in the lofty nod-
dings of the kahiles of state, as they tower far above
the heads of the group whose distinction they proclaim :
something conveying to the mind impressions of greater
majesty than the gleamings of the most splendid banner I ever saw unfurled.

The queens Kinau and Kekau-onohi presented themselves much in the same manner as Tameha-maru ; but
instead of whale boats, had for their seats *double
canoes.* Pau-ahi, another of the wives of Riho-Riho,
after passing in procession with her retinue, alighted
from the couch on which she had been borne, set fire to
it and all its expensive trappings, and then threw into
the flames the whole of her dress, except a single handkerchief to cast around her. In this she was immediately
imitated by all her attendants : and many valuable
articles, a large quantity of tapa, and entire pieces of
broadcloth, were thus consumed. This feat of extravagance was induced, however, by a nobler motive than
that which once led a celebrated and more beautiful
queen to signalize a festival by the *drinking of pearls.*
It was to commemorate a narrow escape from death by
fire, while an infant : a circumstance from which she
derives her name— " *Pau,*" *all* or *consumed* — and
" *ahi,*" *fire.* Her house was destroyed by an explosion
of gunpowder, which became accidentally ignited. Five
men were killed by it, and Pauahi herself was much
burned.

The dresses of some of the queens-dowager were expensive, and immense in quantity. One wore *seventy-
two* yards of kerseymere of double fold : one half being

scarlet, and the other orange. It was wrapped round her figure, till her arms were supported horizontally by the bulk; and the remainder was formed into a train supported by persons appointed for the purpose.

The young prince and princess wore the native dress, maro and pau, of scarlet silk. Their *vehicle* consisted of *four field-bedsteads* of Chinese wood and workmanship, lashed together side by side, covered with handsome native cloth, and ornamented with canopies and drapery of yellow figured moreen. Two chiefs of rank bore their kahiles: and Hoapiri and Kaikioeva, their stepfather and guardian, in scarlet maros, followed them as servants: the one bearing a calabash of *raw fish*, and a calabash of *poe*, and the other a *dish of baked dog*, for the refreshment of the young favourites.

From the parts I myself saw, I can readily believe that the whole procession, from the richness and variety of dress and colours, wreaths of flowers, evergreens and feathers, cloaks, helmets, kahiles, and splendid umbrellas, must have formed an interesting spectacle, even to visitors from civilized and polished countries.

The king and his suite made but a sorry exhibition. They were nearly naked, mounted on horses without saddles, and so much intoxicated as scarce to be able to retain their seats as they scampered from place to place in all the disorder of a troop of bacchanalians. A body-guard of fifty or sixty men, in shabby uniform, attempted by a running march to keep near the person of their sovereign, while hundreds of ragged natives, filling the air with their hootings and shoutings, followed in the chase.

Companies of singing and dancing girls and men, consisting of many hundreds, met the processions in different places, encircling the highest chiefs, and shouting their praise in enthusiastic adulations. The dull and monotonous sounds of the native drum and calabash, the wild notes of their songs in the loud choruses and responses of the various parties, and the pulsations, on the ground, of the tread of thousands in the dance, reached us even at the Missionary enclosure. But they fell on the heart with a saddening power; for we had been compelled already from our own observation, as well as from the communications of others, necessarily to associate with them exhibitions of unrivalled licentiousness, and abominations which must for ever remain untold.

I can never forget the impressions made upon my mind, the first few nights after coming to anchor in the harbour, while these songs and dances were in preparation by rehearsal and practice. With the gathering darkness of every evening, thousands of the natives assembled in a grove of cocoa-nut trees near the ship; and the fires round which they danced, were scarce ever extinguished till the break of day, while shouts of revelry and licentiousness, shouts of which till then I had no conception, and which are heard only in a heathen land, unceasingly burst upon the ear.

The necessary and frequent recurrence in my writing, of the names of persons and places, and other words, in the native tongue, leads me to anticipate the perplexity you may feel in the pronunciation of them. A remark or two on the principles of the language, and a few hints on its orthoepy, will enable you with facility rightly to pronounce any word or phrase that may be introduced.

The language, as you know, was exclusively oral till after the arrival of the American Missionaries : a first effort by them, was the reduction of it to a written form. They found it to be simple in its elements, and capable of being represented in its sounds by a selection of letters from the Roman alphabet. Its peculiarities consist in a predominance of vowels, an entire rejection of double consonants, and of all sibilant, nasal, and guttural sounds, and the invariable termination of every syllable and word by a vowel.

The Hawaiian alphabet consists of seventeen letters : five vowels, a, e, i, o, u, and twelve consonants, b, d, h, k, l, m, n, p, r, t, v, and w. That no letter should be silent, and that every letter should have one undeviating sound, were made radical principles in the written language. The English sounds of the consonants were retained : but important advantages led to the adoption, for the vowels, of the sounds given to them in the principal languages of the continent of Europe. To pronounce any word in their tongue correctly, therefore, it is necessary only to learn the proper sounds of the vowels and diphthongs.

a is sounded ah, as in man, mat, marry.

e has the sound of a in fate, mate, date.

i has the sound of ee in bee, or i in marine, machine.

o is sounded as in no, note, mote.

u has the sound of oo as in rude, rule, and ruin.

K

The principal diphthongs, are

   ai, sounded as in aisle.

   au, sounded ow, as in vow.

   oi, sounded as in oil.

   ou, sounded like o followed closely by oo.

By way of illustration, I will add the correct orthography and orthoepy of the names of the Islands, and places of the present, and contemplated Missionary stations.

Names of the Islands.

Spelled.	Pronounced.
HA-WAI-I,	Hah-wye-e.
MAU-I,	Mow-ee.
MORO-KINI,	Moro-keenee,
TAHU-RAWE,	Tah-hoo-rahway.
RA-NAI,	Rah-nye.
MORO-KAI,	Moro-kye.
O-A-HU,	O-ah-hoo,
TAU-AI,	Tow-eye.
NI-HAU,	Nee-how.
TAU-RA,	Tow-rah.

Missionary Stations.

HONO-RURU,	Hono-rooroo.
WAI-MEA,	Wye-mayah.
LA-HAI-NA,	Lah-hye-nah.
KAI-RUA,	Kye-rooah.
KA-AVA-ROA,	Kah-ah-vah-roah
WAI-A-KEA,	Wye-ah-kayah.

The name of the largest island is not Owhyhee, as generally written since the time of Cook, but Hawaii. The O is satisfactorily ascertained to be the sign of a case only, and not a part of the proper name. The Islanders say, *No Hawaii, I Hawaii, Mai Hawaii,* as well as, *O Hawaii :* forming the regular declension of the noun Hawaii.

Nom.	O Hawaii,	Hawaii.
Poss.	No Hawaii,	Of Hawaii.
Obj.	I and mai Hawaii,	To and from Hawaii.

The language is radically the same as that spoken at the Marquesas, Society, and Friendly Islands, and at New Zealand. It is soft and harmonious in its sounds, and, so far as a knowledge of it has been acquired by the Missionaries, has proved more copious, forcible, and systematic in its construction, than had been expected.

May 18. Our constant intercourse with the king, and chiefs forming his court, will make an outline *of the peerage of Hawaii* desirable, if not indispensable to a right understanding of the relative rank, situation, and offices of different individuals.

The whole body of chiefs may be divided into three classes or grades of rank : *the first* embracing the royal family, and those most intimately connected with it : *the second,* those holding hereditary offices of power, and the governors of the different islands : and *the third,* the rulers of districts, and all inferior chiefs. Those included in the two first grades are usually called *high chiefs ;* and those of the third, *small* or *low.* The high chiefs are few in number, and closely allied both by blood and marriage; forming in fact but one family. Still they are filled with the pride of birth; and even the highest, tenaciously prefer the slightest grounds of precedence.

Rank, as a right, is hereditary in the male and female line. The dignity of the mother, as well as that of the father, fixes the grade of the child. The individual who in rank at the present time takes precedence of all others is a female, Keopuolani, the queen-dowager, and mother of Riho-Riho, who both by father and mother is the last lineal descendant of the ancient kings of Hawaii and Maui; and boasts the unmingled blood of royalty immemorial. She was made captive by Tamehameha in his usurpation; and espoused by him, principally from a motive of policy, that his children might have an hereditary right to the throne from their mother, as well as a right by conquest from their father.

The following scale will present the number, grade, and office of the generation of chiefs now living.

Chiefs of the first rank.

The mother Queen, Keopuo-lani, a wife of the late Tameha-meha.

The King Riho-Riho.

The Prince Kauike-aouli.

The Princess Nahi-enaena—children of Keopuolani by Tameha-meha.

Queens of Riho-Riho—Tameha-maru, Kinau, Kekau-ruohi, Pau-ahi, and Kekau-onohi. The first three are daughters of Tameha-meha by Kala-kua of the former royal family of Maui. And the fourth, Kekau-onohi, a niece of Karaimoku the prime minister.

Queens-dowager, the Wives of Tameha-meha—Kaahu-manu, Kalakua, and Nama-hana, three sisters of the former royal family of Maui.

Royal Family of Tau-ai—The Ex-King Taumuarii, Ex-Queen Tapuli, Kearii-ahonui, son of Taumuarii, (and a husband, as well as his father, of Kaahu-manu,) and Wahine-nui a sister of Taumu-arii. (The mother of George Tamoree, the oldest son of the king, being only a woman of ordinary rank, the title that George held as prince was only through courtesy; and having from dissipation and ill conduct forfeited the favour of his father, he is reduced to the grade of a commoner; and now lives in comparative obscurity on his plantation at Tau-ai.)

The Prime Minister—Karai-moku, or Mr. Pitt. This chief originally belonged to the third grade. But now ranks with the royal family, and indeed is virtually king.

Lealea-hoku, infant son of Karai-moku.

Chiefs of the second rank.

The Guardian of the Prince—Kaiki-oeva; and Keawea-mahi his wife.

The Guardian of the Princess—Hoa-piri, the present husband of Keopuo-lani.

The hereditary Orator of State—Naihi; and Kapiolani his wife. These chiefs Kaiki-oeva and Naihi with their wives, and Hoa-piri, are the descendants of leading families under the ancient kings of Hawaii; and have

K 2

at present large possessions in land, and are of great influence.

Governor of Hawaii—Kua-kini, or John Adams, son of Keeaumoku, a chief of Hawaii, prime minister, and a brother of the queens-dowager of Tameha-meha. The name of Adams was given to him when a child, at the time the presidential chair of the United States was occupied by our venerable countryman of Quincy. He considers the name a great honour, and prefers it, in being addressed, to any other.

Governor of Maui—Keeau-motu, or Cox, a brother of Governor Adams and the queens-dowager. Tahu-rawe, Ra-nai, and Moro-kai, are dependencies of Maui, and subject to its governor.

Governor of Oahu—Boki, brother of Karai-moku the prime minister.

Governor of Tau-ai and Ni-hau—At present, Wahine-nui, the sister of king Taumu-arii. Wahine-pio, a sister of Karai-moku, and mother of Kekau-onohi, one of the wives of Riho-Riho, belongs to this grade of chiefs ; and also Kaha-laia, a young chief, her son by a brother of Tameha-meha.

Chiefs of the third rank.

The Captain of the king's vessels—Kapihe, or Nai-hi-tutui, familiarly called Captain Jack.

Superintendent of Sandal wood, and King's Treasurer—Kekua-naoa.

Governors of important districts—Hanau-maitai, of Waititi at Oahu. Keo-ua of Lahaina, and Auae of

Wai-ruku, at Maui. Kama-kau of Kaava-roa, and Maa-ro of Wai-akea, at Hawaii, &c. &c.

Chiefs without particular offices, but of the same rank as the preceding.

Kaiko and Kehikiri, brothers descended from the king of Maui : the last Kehikiri is the husband of Wahine-pio, Mr. Pitt's sister. Both are puna-hele or bosom companions of the king ; by which distinction Ii, Karai-koa, Hinau, Puaa, &c. &c. of this grade, are also known. To this grade, Laa-nui, an interesting young chief, husband of Nama-hana, one of the former wives of Tame-hameha, also belongs ; and many others, who are known only as *small chiefs.*

The chiefs of the last rank are the most numerous, but are as inferior in consequence to those of the two former, as an English esquire or baronet is to a royal duke, or noble earl, or marquis.

All the persons included in this catalogue have a variety of names—here, the substitute for a string of titles. I have used the most favourite too and those by which the respective individuals are commonly addressed. The chiefs frequently change their names, or assume new ones from passing circumstances. For instance, Paa-lua, " *twice blind,*" is now a name of Karai-moku, often used by himself and others, and perhaps that to which he is most partial. It was assumed in the following manner ; When Tameha-meha died, the prime minister expressed his loss in the death of his friend by saying that he had lost an eye—*paa-kahi*—blind in one eye, or once blind, and chose that word for a name. Within the last year a favourite wife, the daughter of Kaiki-oeva, died : when he proclaimed himself *paa-lua,* blind in both eyes *or twice blind,* and he is now known throughout the nation by the name of Paa-lua.

All names of persons are significant. Keopuolani is literally " *The gathering of the heavens,* or, *of the clouds of heaven.*" Tameha-meha " *The lonely one.*" Tameha-maru, a name assumed by the queen after the death of her father—" *The shade of the lonely one.*" Kaahu-manu—" *The feather mantle.*" Kalakua—" *The way of the gods.*" Kapio-lani—" *The captive of heaven.*" Lealea-hoku—" *The necklace of stars,* or, *the starry necklace,*" &c. &c. The names of the chiefs are pro-hibited, or tabu, to the commoners.

The motives which lead to a choice of names for their children, among the common people, may be estimated by the following fact. One of the pupils of the Mission belonging to the family of a chief is named *Wai-lepo-lepo.* His father was a personal attendant of Tameha-meha. The king called on him one day for a drink of water; the man, in his haste to procure it, took into the calabash that which was not perfectly pure; and the king, as soon as he tasted it, dashed the whole calabash and all at the head of the fellow, exclaiming " *wai-lepo-lepo !*" " *dirty—dirty water !*" On going to his house, the servant found a new-born son, which he immediately named Wai-lepo-lepo; a phrase not likely to be for-gotten by him, even without such means of remem-brance.

From the schedule of rank given, the complicated,

and in some instances shocking affinity of the chiefs may
be learned. All of the first grade, except the prime
minister, besides their present relations, are cousins to
each other by blood. Keopuo-lani was at once the
cousin, niece, and wife of Tamehameha. Three of the
wives of Riho-Riho are his half-sisters; and one was
also the wife of her stepfather, and his own father Tamehameha: and Taumuarii, the king of Tauai, and his son
Keariia-honui, are both at present the husbands of Kaahumanu. Kapiolani also has two husbands.

There appears ever to have been 'close alliances by
marriage among the chiefs of the whole group: but till
the conquest of Tamehameha, each island, and often
different districts of the same island, were subject to
separate and independent kings, and the whole government was more of the feudal form than it now is. All
the chiefs being descended more or less directly from
former kings, the jealousy and rivalry peculiarly incident
to an uncivilized state, might make the stability of the
present dynasty doubtful, but for a balance of power
kept by the opposing ambition and conflicting interests
of the two connexions next in rank and influence to the
reigning family: those of the Maui, or Adam's family
as it is sometimes called—consisting of the governors of
Hawaii and Maui, and the queens dowager, and the prime
minister or Pitt family. These share equally in the
favour of the king, and in the honours of the nation;
and such is the equality of their power, that an attempt
at revolt or usurpation by either, could not be successful
so long as the other remained faithful to the king.
That they should combine to overthrow the royal family,

is scarcely possible : for though in such case they might be successful, the interests of one only of the parties could be promoted, while the other would have hazarded every thing without the prospect of an advancement. The certainty therefore is, that they will both remain loyal ; and so long as that is the case, the present government must be permanent.

This balance of power we consider a happy circumstance ; for by it far greater facilities for the achievement of our enterprise are afforded, than could otherwise be secured. The most formidable impediments yet experienced to the success of Missions in the Polynesian Islands, have arisen from the rivalship and wars of the petty kings of independent districts and islands.

The government is a despotism ; and the rank of the king and of the chiefs, hereditary. All rights of property and power are vested in the throne, and are at the disposal of the king, whose will and word alone are law : though in important measures he usually takes the sentiment of the chiefs in council. The appointments of office, such as governors of islands and districts, commanders of forts, &c. &c. are made only by the king.

The support of the king is by an annual tribute from all the islands, rendered at different periods by different districts and islands, as his majesty may direct. It consists of the produce of the country ; hogs, dogs, fish, fowl, potatoes, yams, taro, bananas, melons, &c. &c. —of articles of manufacture, canoes, fishing-nets, tapa, mats, bird's feathers, unwrought hemp, &c. &c.; and, since the introduction of trade with foreigners, of sandal wood, and occasionally of specie. Besides this tribute,

however, the king has power to levy any extra tax he
pleases, and even to appropriate to his own use, by direct
and unintimated seizure, any personal possession of a
chief or other subject: and not unfrequently the whole
growth of a plantation is thus borne off by the servants
of his household, without the slightest apology or com-
pensation.

The revenue of the throne has been greatly augmented of late years, by the charges placed on the port
of Honoruru. The pilotage both on entering and leaving
is one dollar a foot on the draft of each vessel; for
an anchorage in the outer harbour sixty, and in the
inner harbour eighty dollars. Since the visit of the
Blonde, it has been considerably reduced.

The exaction of harbour fees originated in a circumstance somewhat peculiar. Tameha-meha in his shrewd-
ness early discovered that the foreign merchants trading
with him were making large profits on the sandal wood
shipped by them from the Islands for the Chinese market:
and determined himself to send a cargo of wood to Canton, in a ship he had just purchased. She was laden
with a large quantity of this article; and despatched
under the command of English officers with a native
crew, and Kapihe, or Captain Jack, as supercargo. It
was not for the interest of foreigners that the voyage
should prove successful; and by some means, fair or
foul, when the ship made her appearance off the Islands
on her return—(the broad pennant of her commander,
and the Hawaiian flag floating as triumphantly in the
breeze as if she bore the richest freight of damasks, and
crapes, and nankeens and china)—and the king in his

gladness quickly boarded her, all her cargo was found
to be a bill of charges amounting to 3000 dollars! In
the items of the bill were *pilotage and anchorage*, and
custom-house fees to a large sum; and when told that
maritime states in other countries derived large revenues
in this manner, he immediately said " Well then, I will
have fees for my harbour too;" and from that time the
harbour at Oahu has been taxed in the amount mentioned.

The king and highest chiefs have a singular mode of
raising money, and one I presume entirely peculiar to
themselves.   It is by building a fine new house; and on
taking possession of it, to refuse an entrance to any one
without a present in cash, proportionate to the rank and
property both of the giver and receiver.   The *tabu* on
the house of the king at the time of our arrival was of
this nature.   Many of the chiefs presented fifty, sixty,
and eighty dollars; merchants, sea captains, and foreign
residents, twenty and thirty; and every servant of the
household, even his pipe-lighter, at least two dollars
The whole sum thus collected amounted to several thousand dollars.   A few months ago the mother-queen
raised eight hundred dollars in the same manner.

The governors of islands and chiefs of districts are
entitled, by their offices, to an exercise of all the pre-
rogatives of royalty in their respective limits.   They
each, like the king, have their annual tribute from the
people; and, like him, hold the lives and property of all
under them at caprice.

All the chiefs have large landed estates under the
king; and derive their support from yearly taxes upon

them.   Like the king and governors, they have every
right, even to that of life, over the occupants of their
plantations, and all their people.

The nobles of the land are so strongly marked by their
external appearance, as at all times to be easily distinguishable from the common people.   They seem
indeed in size and stature to be almost a distinct race
They are all large in their frame, and often excessively
corpulent; while the common people are scarce of the
ordinary height of Europeans, and of a thin rather than
full habit.   Keopuolani, the mother of Riho-Riho, and
Taumuarii, king of Tauai, are the only chiefs arrived at
years of maturity, I have yet seen, who are not heavy,
corpulent persons.   The governess of Tauai, the sister
of Taumuarii, is said to be remarkably so; Namahana,
one of the queens of Tamehameha, is exceedingly corpulent; her sisters Kaahumanu and Kalakua nearly the
same; and her brother Kuakini, governor of Hawaii,
though little more than twenty-five years old, is so remarkably stout, as to be unequal to any exertion, and
scarcely able to walk without difficulty.   This immense
bulk of person is supposed to arise from the care taken
of them from their earliest infancy; and from the abundance and nutritious quality of their food, especially
that of poe, a kind of paste made from the taro, an esculent root, a principal article of diet.   They live on the
abundant resourses of the land and sea, and, free from
all toil and oppression, their only care is " *to eat, and
to drink, and to be merry.*"

Many of those whose corpulency does not amount to
deformity, are among the noblest figures imaginable.

L

Kehikiri, or " *The thunder*," a chief of the Maui family, though a savage in countenance, in form and muscle is a perfect Hercules.   Kearii-ahonui, of Tauai, has a handsome face, and in the classic drapery of a yellow satin maro and purple satin kihei, presents as perfect a model of manly beauty as ever challenged the efforts of pencil or chisel.   Many of the common people too have great beauty of person, though on a less noble scale. Only a few mornings ago, in walking on the plain, I met a young man, eighteen or twenty years old, whose figure struck me as one of the most admirable I ever beheld. His black eye sparkled with youth and spirit; and every motion was free as the wind, in which his light mantle flowed gracefully from his shoulder.   As with firm and elastic tread he hurried past, a bright smile accompanied his salutation—" *Aroha oe*"—*Love to you:* in returning which I almost involuntarily said, " *Aroha no ia oe, e Apollo*"—*Love indeed to you, thou Apollo !*

Besides a profusion of melons, cocoa-nuts, bananas, sugar-cane, &c. &c. some of which they are almost constantly eating, the chiefs have regular meals of baked dog, or pig, and pickled or raw fish and poe, four times a day; one as soon as they rise in the morning; another at ten or eleven o'clock, A. M.; a third about four in the afternoon; and a fourth at nine or ten in the evening

Their food was formerly served in wooden dishes and calabashes; but now generally on china brought by the merchants from Canton.   It is placed on the ground, before the group for whom it is designed, who, lounging on their mats in the attitude of the ancient Romans, partake of it with one hand, while they recline upon the other. Servants separate the meat with their hands, wiping them occasionally *in their mouths or on their naked arms or legs;* after which, all eat from the same dishes, using their fingers in place of forks and spoons.

Whatever pets the ladies may have, whether pigs or dogs, and most have one of either, share from the common dishes without disturbance, unless perhaps they should be so ill-bred as to put their *forefeet,* as well as their *noses,* into the food, when a gentle tap may remind them of better manners.

The pets of the nobles, of whatever kind, have in many cases uncontrollable privileges. There is at present attached to the palace, a hog of this character, weighing four or five hundred pounds, called "*Kaahumanu,*" after the haughty dowager of that name, which is permitted to range at pleasure, within doors as well as without; and not unfrequently finds a bed among the satins and velvets of the royal couches.

The chiefs, male or female, are at once known, not only by their size, but by their walk, general air, and manners. In these respects there is as marked a difference between them and the "*Maki ainana,*" or ignoble *vulgus,* here, as there is between the courtiers of St. James and Versailles, and the peasantry of England or France. A consciousness of natural superiority, and the pride of adventitious distinction, imbibed and nourished from their earliest childhood, give them an ease of action, and an unaffected dignity of deportment, that would distinguish them as persons of rank, in whatever company they might appear. You must not understand from this, however, true as it is, that there is any thing Chesterfieldian, or artificial, in their breeding. They are still uncivilized heathen, living not only in all the simplicity, but in all the vulgarity, of untutored nature:—and while I can sincerely say, that in them "*I see much that I love, and more that I admire*,"—I must in candour add,—"*and much, if not all, that I abhor.*"

Many of them, besides large landed possessions, have considerable wealth in money, accumulated by the sale of sandal wood; and in large quantities of rich foreign manufacture. When the Missionaries arrived in 1820, the usual, and indeed only dress, except in the case of one or two individuals, was the native costume; but now most of the chiefs constantly wear a part or whole of the European dress:—the females, on ordinary occasions, a loose slip with the native pau or petticoat over it; and the men, a shirt or wrapper.

On Sundays and holidays, and all occasions of ceremony, they appear in full dress, according to our fashion, and frequently of the richest material. There are several good tailors among the foreign residents, and the clothes of the men are generally well and fashionably made. The men also often send their measures, by the trading ships, to Canton, and have ready-made dresses brought back to them. Only a short time since, the king received four hundred garments at one time, in this way.

The females do not look so well, or so much at ease in their dresses, as the men: though the ladies of the

Mission have much of their leisure occupied in sewing for them, and in teaching them to cut and sew for themselves. Tameha-maru has become quite skilful in this respect; and I doubt not that others will imitate her example, and here, as in other parts of the world, the sex will claim its prerogative to precedence in all matters of taste and fashion. Some of the ladies of the court, I am told, have talked already of *eating less poe* than they have done, that their persons may be more delicate, and *their clothes sit better*.

The houses of the chiefs are generally large, for the kind of building,—from forty to sixty feet in length, twenty or twenty-five in breadth, and eighteen or twenty in height at the peak of the roof. The sides and ends, as well as the roof, are of thatch, and the whole in one apartment. They are generally without windows, or any opening for light or air, except a wide door in the middle of a side or end. In the back part of the house, the personal property and moveables, such as trunks, boxes, calabashes and dishes for water, food, &c. &c. are deposited; while the mats for sitting, lounging, and sleeping, are spread near the door.

Every chief has from thirty to fifty and an hundred personal attendants, friends and servants, attached to his establishment; who always live and move with him, and share in the provisions of his house. All these, except the bosom friends, or *punahele*, have different offices and duties:—one is a pipe lighter, another a spittoon carrier, a third a kahile bearer, &c. Others, with their families, prepare, cook, and serve the food, &c. All the former, from the bosom friend, or punahele, to the pipe lighter, eat from the same dishes and calabashes with their master; and form, at their meals, a most uncouth and motley group. In every respect, indeed, as well as in that of eating, the household servants of the whole company of chiefs, from the king to the petty headman of a village, seem to enjoy a perpetual *saturnalia.*

The formation of this establishment takes place immediately on the birth of a chief, whether male or female. A *kahu* or nurse is appointed, who assumes all the care of the parent, and directs the affairs of the child, till he is old enough to exercise a will of his own. Thus, often, very little intercourse takes place between the parents themselves, and the young chief: the former not unfrequently residing at a different district, or on a different island. The present prince and princess, who are both children, have each separate houses, and a large train of attendants: and though their guardians of state reside near them, they are left very much to their own will, or to that of their *kahus* or nurses.

I have seen a young chief, apparently not three years old, walking the streets of Honoruru as naked as when born, (with the exception of a pair of green morocco shoes on his feet,) followed by ten or twelve stout men, and as many boys, carrying umbrellas, and kahiles, and spit boxes, and fans, and the various trappings of chieftainship. The young noble was evidently under no control but his own will, and enjoyed already the privileges of his birth, in choosing his own path, and doing whatever he pleased.

This portion of the inhabitants spend their lives pincipally in eating and drinking, lounging, and sleeping; in the sports of the surf, and the various games of the country; *at cards,* which have long been introduced; in hearing the songs of the musicians, a kind of recitation, accompanied by much action; and in witnessing the performances of the dancers. They are not, however, wholly given to idleness and pleasure. It is customary for the male chiefs to superintend, in a degree, any work in which their own vassals, at the place where they are residing, are engaged, whether of agriculture or manufacture: and the female chiefs, also, overlook their women in their appropriate occupations, and not unfrequently assist them with their own hands.

A great change appears about to take place among the chiefs, in the general manner of employing time. The *palapala* and the *pule, letters* and *religion,* as presented by the Missionaries, are happily beginning deeply to interest their minds; and books and slates, I doubt not, will, as is the fact already, in individual cases, soon universally take the place of cards and games, and every amusement of dissipation.

These general and desultory remarks will give you, my dear M——, some idea of the external character and state of the nobler part of the nation, for whose benefit H —— and myself have sacrificed the innu merable enjoyments of home.   As to their qualities of heart and mind, they in general appear to be as mild and amiable in disposition, and as sprightly and active in intellect, as the inhabitants of our own country. Ignorance, superstition, and sin, make all the difference we observe : and though that difference is at present fearful indeed, still we believe, that, with the removal of its causes, it will be entirely done away.

Notwithstanding the dreadful abominations daily taking place around us, drunkenness and adultery, gambling and theft, deceit, treachery, and death, all of which exist throughout the land to an almost incredible degree, such has already been the success attending the efforts at reformation, made in the very infancy of the Mission, that we are encouraged by every day's observance, with fresh zeal to dedicate ourselves to the work of rescue and salvation. No pagan nation on earth can be better prepared for the labour of the Christian Missionary; and no herald of the cross could desire a more privileged and delightful task, than to take this people by the outstretched and beckoning hand, and lead their bewildered feet into paths of light and life, of purity and peace; nor a greater happiness than to be the instrument of guiding, not only the generation now living, in the right way, but of rescuing from wretchedness and spiritual death, millions of the generations yet unborn, who are here to live, and here to die, before the angel " *shall lift up his hand to heaven, and swear that there shall be time no longer !*"

CHAPTER VII.

POVERTY OF THE COMMON PEOPLE.

Thursday, May 20. An opportunity of making our voyage to Hawaii has not yet been presented. I am anxious to commence the contemplated tour, though every day more and more persuaded, from what I find to be the state of the common people, that it will be attended with great privation, and with much to shock and to disgust.

This class of the inhabitants constitutes at least one hundred and forty-nine thousand, of the hundred and fifty thousand supposed at present to be the population of the group. In external appearance, and manners and habits of life, the kanakas, or common natives, present a strong contrast to the chiefs; and are, indeed, a wretched people—subject, not only to a total blindness of mind and heart, but also to the most abject poverty. If the former are the objects of an interest, to the Missionary, approaching to admiration; the latter are, of a compassion that sometimes borders on agony; and in beholding their degradation, and the near approach they make to the level of the brute, I am often ready " *to blush, and hang my head, to think myself a man.*"

The greatest wealth they can boast consists of a mat on which to sleep—a few folds of tapa to cover them;—one calabash for water, and another for poe —a rude implement or two for the cultivation of the ground—and the instruments used in their simple manufactures.   Taro, potatoes, and salt, with occasionally a fish, constitute their general food; while all else that they grow, or take, and every result of their labour, goes to meet the series of taxes levied by the king, and his governors, and their own respective chiefs.

The spontaneous production of the islands is very limited; and labour at all times of the year is necessary to the support of life.   In this respect this group differs widely from the Society and other islands of the South Seas, where, eight months in twelve, the natives have only to pluck their food, principally bread-fruit, from the trees overhanging their habitations.   The growth of the bread-fruit here, is confined to a few districts on one or two islands, and, where found, yields a very partial supply of food, at any season.

Taro, an article which I have repeatedly mentioned, is the principal food of the Sandwich Islanders, and to the whole nation answers the double purpose of vegetables and bread.   The genus of plant to which it belongs, is the arum ; a root growing in many parts of America, and generally known by the names of the wild Indian, and French turnip.   The taro is the *arum escu-*

lentum of botanists; and is used in many other warm
climates as a vegetable.

It here occupies most of the cultivated ground, especially such as is capable of being overflown by water;
and the planting, irrigation, and necessary care of it,
forms the most laborious part of the native farming.
The islanders have arrived at great skill in the cultivation of this plant; and perhaps their mode of growing
it, considering the general face of the country, scarce
admits of improvement, unless it be in the implements
with which they work. The beds in which the taro
stands are usually square or oblong, of various sizes,
from that of a few yards to half an acre. These are
formed with great care; first by excavating the earth
to a depth of two or three feet, and converting the dirt
thrown out into strong embankments on every side.
The sides and bottom are then beaten with the woody
ends of the cocoa-nut leaf, which are broad, and, when
dry, exceedingly hard, till they are impervious to water:
after which, the tops of the ripe root, by which the plant
is propagated, cut off just below the formation of the
leaves, are set out eighteen inches or two feet apart, in
a thin layer of soil and dried grass, and the water let
upon them till the leaves float on its surface. The
roots are kept thus covered with water, till they become fit to eat: a period of from nine to fifteen months,
though they continue to grow for two years or more,
and improve in quality to the end of that time.

The leaves of the taro are large and heart-shaped,
and of a light green colour. The root is of a regular
oval form, from four to eight inches in length, and from

six to twelve in circumference. In its natural state, whether ripe or unripe, both the leaves and root have all the acrid pungent taste of the genus of plants to which it belongs; but on being thoroughly cooked, either by baking or boiling, it becomes mild and palatable, without any peculiarity of taste, more than belongs to good bread. It is compact, and, both before and after cooking, white, with a slight tinge of purple on the exterior; when poor, or unripe, the colour throughout is a dull lead.

The natives prepare it for use, first, by baking it, in the only manner practised among them. This is, by digging a hole in the ground a foot or two deep, and five or six feet in circumference, and placing a layer of stones on the bottom, upon which light wood is placed and a fire kindled. Other stones are laid upon the fire, and by the burning of the wood the whole become signited. Those on the top are then drawn off, and the taro, or potatoes, or fish, pig, or dog, &c. closely wrapped in the leaves of the banana, or of the *ti, (dracæna terminalis,* growing in great abundance here,) is laid on the hearth of stones still remaining at the bottom, and immediately covered with the rest. A little water is poured on the pile to create a steam, and the whole hastily buried with earth, by which the heat and steam are kept from escaping, and the article in the *umai* or *oven,* becomes baked.

The taro, after being thus cooked, is in the next place made into the favourite *poe.* The process in this is simple, though so laborious as to be performed by tne men. It is merely by beating the taro upon a short plank of hard wood, slightly hollowed in the middle like a tray, with a stone something in the shape of a thick and clumsy pestle, wetting it occasionally with water, and moulding it till it becomes an adhesive mass like dough. It is then put into a calabash, diluted with water till of the consistency of paste, and set aside for fermentation. This soon takes place, and the poe is fit for use in a day or two, though preferred when four or five days old. It is eaten by thrusting the fore-finger of the right hand into the mass, and securing as much as will adhere to it in passing it to the mouth, with a hasty revolving motion of the hand and finger. The only name of the fore-finger is derived from this use of it, "*Ka rima poe*," "*the finger poe*, or *poe finger*." The second finger is often also used; and not unfre-quently the thumb at the same time. This is the usual mode of eating it—a dozen or more from one calabash; but I have seen the calabash taken up with both hands, and applied to the mouth as in drinking; and thus passed from one to another, round the whole group.

Hard or dry poe is taro baked and beaten in the manner described, but not moistened with water. It is not much eaten in this state; but is packed in small bundles, and bound in leaves, to be diluted and formed into soft poe at pleasure. In this manner it will keep without injury for months; and makes a principal article in the sea stores of the native vessels.

We find taro a pleasant vegetable. It is most ex-cellent when cut into slices and fried, after being baked or boiled, though less nutritive than in the form of poe.

Next to taro, the sweet potatoe is a principal article

of cultivation. The yam also is grown; but chiefly at the leeward islands, Tauai and Nihau. Indian corn has been introduced, and will probably become extensively an article of food. Other esculent plants, cabbages, onions, pumpkins, squashes, cucumbers, beans, radishes, &c.—the seeds of which have been brought by the Missionaries and other foreigners, are becoming abundant: but they are cultivated almost exclusively for the refreshment of ships, and the tables of foreign residents. Sugar-cane, and a great variety of the plantain and banana, are indigenous, and occupy a considerable portion of every plantation. The cane, however, is used by the natives only as a fruit. Water melons and musk melons were introduced by Vancouver, and are now abundant every where.

In the cultivation of the ground, the making and care of artificial fish-ponds, a part of the possessions of every chief, may be included. These are constructed much in the manner of the taro plantations; and after the water is let into them, are filled with young fish from the sea, principally the fry of the grey mullet, a fish of which the chiefs are particularly fond.

The building of houses, construction of canoes, making of fishing nets, wooden dishes and bowls, &c. are labours assigned to the men; while the manufacture of cloth in all its processes, and the platting of mats, &c. fall to the department of the women.

The cloth is of tedious manufacture. It is formed from the inner bark of the *morus papyrifera*, or paper mulberry, here called *wauti*, and cultivated for this purpose, in regular groves on every farm. The plant is kept trimmed to a single shoot, from its earliest growth, to secure a stem unbroken by branches ; and when it has attained the thickness of an inch or two, and the height of ten or twelve feet, is cut down for use.   The bark is taken off in a single piece, by a longitudinal incision from end to end; the exterior coat scraped off ; and the interior of each piece spread out, and rolled together in its length, and left till it has acquired a flat surface.   The whole is then placed in water, till it becomes covered with a mucilaginous substance : after which it is laid on a plank, and beaten with a short square stick of hard wood, to the tenuity desired.   Its length and breadth are increased at pleasure by the addition of the bark; and should any part become too thin before the whole has received an even texture, the difficulty is obviated in the same way.   After the whole is of the texture and size required, it is laid in the sun to bleach and dry.

The wooden sticks or mallets, used in beating, have one side smooth, another coarsely grooved, the third very finely furrowed in the same manner, and the fourth more or less closely checked in squares or diamonds : and thus, according to the side used in beating, a corresponding figure is given to the body of the cloth. That beaten with the plane side, is smooth like paper ; that with the coarse groove, has something of the appearance of dimity ; that with the close, more like corded muslin ; and that with the check, like the web of fine diaper.

The thickness of the different kinds of cloth is various.   I have seen females with mantles of it, as

thin and transparent as Italian crape; which, at a
short distance, it greatly resembled. That generally
used for *maros* and *paus*, is more compact, like paper.
The *kiheis* of the men and covers for sleeping, are still
firmer and thicker; and are composed of several sheets
of the former, spread with a gelatinous wash made
from the gum of a tree, and then beaten together.
There is a kind still superior in texture and beauty,
worn by the chiefs both for maros and paus: it is
made of the best bark, and is as thick as morocco,
to which, stamped with the brightest colours, and
glazed with a composition having the effect of varnish,
it bears a striking resemblance. The *tapa moe*, or *cloth
for sleeping*, is the largest in size; each sheet, ten of
which, fastened together at one end, form a bed-cover,
being as large as an ordinary counterpane.

The tapa is naturally of a light colour, and capable of
being bleached till perfectly white. Much of it is worn
in this state; but the greater portion is stained with a
variety of dies, extracted with much skill from different
indigenous plants. The colours are often very beautiful, principally green of every shade, from the lightest
to the darkest; yellow, from a dark salmon to straw
colour; red, from a rich crimson to a delicate blossom
purple, from a dark plum through all the hues of lilac
to a light dove; brown, from chocolate to fawn; and
black and white. The cloth is dyed with one of these
plain throughout, and worn thus, or is again stamped
with several others, in an endless variety and combination of figures. These they devise with much ingenuity and
taste, or imitate skilfully from those on imported articles.

The pattern intended to be impressed upon the cloth is cut on the inside of a piece of bamboo. The bamboo is then dipped into the colour prepared, carefully transferred to the tapa, and pressed closely upon it with the fingers and hand: it is then returned into the die again, and again placed upon the cloth, till the whole piece is covered with the figure and colour or colours.

The best made and coloured tapa is little inferior in beauty to most common calicoes and chintzes, but so perishable in its quality, as to be an expensive article of clothing. Some kinds are saturated with the oil of the cocoa-nut, to make them more durable, and to shed water; but even these quickly wear out, and require to be renewed every few weeks. That which is not oiled does not allow of being washed; and a new suit is necessary once a month. An immense deal of time and labour must therefore be requisite, to meet the demands of the whole population.

The manufacture by the females, next in importance to the making of tapa, is that of mats, which form the seats of the islanders in the day, and their beds at night. The lounges and beds of the chiefs are generally eight or ten feet square, and consist of many thicknesses of these, from a dozen to thirty and forty, and even a greater number. The materials of which they are made are of two kinds; one a species of rush, and the other the leaves of the *hala,* a palm, *the pandanus odorotissimus.* Those of the last article are most valuable, as they are much the most durable, and admit of frequent washing, which the rush mats do not. Both kinds are woven or braided by hand, without the aid of frame or instrument: and though often twenty feet square, and even larger, are finished with great evenness of texture and regularity of shape. Some of the hala mats are very course; and others of various braid, to the very finest and most beautiful specimens of matting I ever saw. These last, however, are generally small; finished with a deep fringe at the ends; and carried on the arm of a servant, after his chief, to be spread on other mats, on which he may choose to sit. I have observed one of this kind in the train of the young princess, of a braid almost as delicate and even as that of a Leghorn hat, and of the most beautiful whiteness.

The rush mats are soft and pleasant, and many of them very fine. The Leeward Islands, Tauai and Nihau, are most distinguished by the manufacture of these. They are there ornamented with much taste and ingenuity by stained grass, of a rich and glossy brown, interwoven with the body of the mat, or wrought on its upper surface, in the manner of embroidery, in a variety of figures, such as diamonds, stars, stripes, waving lines, &c. &c

Besides being engaged in these manufactures of cloth and mats, the females, especially those attached to the households of the chiefs, spend much time in making articles of ornament; in the braiding of human hair for necklaces; trimming and arranging feathers for wreaths and kahiles; polishing tortoise shell and the ivory of whale's teeth, for finger rings, and the handles of feathered staffs, &c.

Notwithstanding the variety of apparently necessary

employment falling both to men and women, few of either sex devote more than four or five hours of the twenty - four to work. Though unavoidably more laborious than many other Polynesians, they partake of the indolence of character incident to the inhabitants of tropical climates, and sleep and lounge away more than half their time, while much of the remainder is given to amusement and pleasure. It is, however, difficult to determine how far the Sandwich Islanders partake of this indolence, from the fact that there is no motive for industry presented to them, beyond the fear of starvation, and a dread of the displeasure of their chiefs.

One of the strongest inducements to exertion— that of a right of property—is entirely unknown. Were not this the case, the profit which every farmer might derive from the visit of ships for refreshment, would soon cause the face of the country to assume a new aspect. But this means of emolument is a monopoly of the king and chiefs; and only proves a new source of oppression to the people, by increasing their toil, without adding to their possessions. Two-thirds of the proceeds of any thing a native brings to the market, unless by stealth, must be given to his chief; and, not unfrequently, the whole is unhesitatingly taken from him. In two or three instances, when conversing on the beach with the officers of ships, I have seen money just put into the hands of a native, by them, for a bunch of fruit slipped from under his kihei into their boat, taken directly, and openly, away, by some one appointed to detect any traffic of the kind;

and whose proceeding was not, for a moment, to be questioned or resisted.

Nor is there greater inducement to industry, from motives of immediate personal enjoyment. Any increase of stock, or growth of a plantation, beyond that necessary to meet the usual taxes, is liable to be swept off at any hour; and that, perhaps, without any direct authority from king or chief, but at the caprice of some one in their service. An instance of this kind lately occurred at Oahu, which will shew the extremity, if not the extent, of these depredations. The poverty of many of the people is such, that they seldom secure a taste of animal food, and live almost exclusively on taro and salt. A poor man of this description, by some means obtained the possession of a pig, when too small to make a meal for his family. He secreted it at a distance from his house, and fed it till it had grown to a size sufficient to afford the desired repast. It was then killed, and put into an oven, with the same precaution of secrecy; but when almost prepared for appetites, whetted by long anticipation to an exquisite keenness, a caterer of the royal household unhappily came near, and, attracted to the spot by the savoury fumes of the baking pile, deliberately took a seat till the animal was cooked, and then bore off the promised banquet without ceremony or apology !

Such is the civil condition of the mass of the nation. Their only birthright is slavery; and its highest immunities cannot secure to them a right of life, much less any inferior possession. Surely to such, the messages of salvation must prove indeed " *glad tidings of great joy.*" May they receive them with thanksgiving; and, through them, become free in the spirit of the gospel, and rich in the inheritance of eternal life!

May 22. Last night I strolled a mile through the marshes and fish-ponds, along the beach south of the Mission House. In attempting to give you a sketch of my walk, you will almost think me sporting with your credulity, by a picture of poverty and filthiness too degrading to be real. The largest hut I passed was not higher than my waist; capable only of containing a family, like pigs in a sty, on a bed of dried grass, filled with fleas and vermin. Not a bush or shrub was to be seen around; or any appearance whatever of cultivation. It was the time of their evening repast; and most of the people were seated on the ground, eating *poe* surrounded by swarms of flies, and sharing their food with dogs, pigs, and ducks, who helped themselves freely from the dishes of their masters! The *tout ensemble* was almost too disgusting to be witnessed; and while I gazed I could but exclaim—

> "———— Can this be man ?—
> Bone of the bone, and flesh of the flesh, of him,
> Whose majesty dignifies and crowns creation's plan,—
> And without whom, 'twere wild profusion all,
> And bootless waste?"

The hope of enlightening and elevating such, seemed almost rashness; and I turned from them, more than ever persuaded, that nothing less than the power which first spake light from darkness, can scatter the gloom in which they are enveloped.

I should be doing injustice to your wish and expectations, of having the manners and habits of the people, on points capable of being touched, and there are not a few, that can never be mentioned, presented to you " *living as they rise*," were I to pass in silence, subjects, which, though not the most pleasant that might be selected, daily and hourly obtrude themselves on the observation. Among these, is the prevalence of *a most infective and loathsome cutaneous disease :* not altogether unknown in our own country. This contagion is so common, and I might say universal here in all ranks, as to be without reproach, except in the eyes of a foreigner. I was somewhat startled, a day or two after our arrival, to have the question put to me, " *Whether I had any thing to cure the itch ?*" immediately, after shaking hands with a high chief, whom I at once perceived to be greatly infected with it. The etiquette of the court seemed to require this manner of salutation ; and I thought it would be impossible for me to escape the disorder, even for a week. I learned from the older Missionaries, however, that they had shaken hands with thousands with perfect impunity ; and thus far, I have myself been equally fortunate.

It must be less contagious, than the disease known in America by the same name ; and appears also to be less irritable and troublesome. Most of the chiefs are at present free from it, but the common people are every where greatly infected. Few seem to regard it as an evil, or take any measure to divest themselves of it. Like most other diseases, its introduction is attributed, by the natives, to foreigners; though, I suspect it has existed among them to "a period to which the memory of man runneth not contrary."

Not to mention the frequent and hideous marks of a scourge, which more clearly than any other proclaims the curse of a God of purity, and which, while it annually consigns hundreds of this people to the tomb, converts thousands, while living, into walking sepulchres; the inhabitants, generally, are subject to many disorders of the skin. The majority are, more or less, disfigured by eruptions and sores; and many are as unsightly as lepers. The number of either sex, or of any age, who are free from blemishes of the kind, is very small; so much so, that a smooth and unbroken skin is far more uncommon here, than the reverse is at home.

I am not physiologist enough to say to what cause this fact it attributable:—perhaps to a very free use of salt in eating, in conjunction with the habit of constant sea-bathing. Taro, too, when in the form of poe, though of easy digestion, has probably a great tendency to grossness of blood. Whatever the cause or causes may be, the effect certainly detracts much from the good appearance of the people.

Another subject, which I would notice from the same reason that led to the introduction of the preceding, is nearly allied to it, according to our ideas, in point of offensiveness. A clue to it may be given,

without a mention of names, by referring you to the
spirited effusion of a genius, beginning

    " Ha, whare ye gaw'n, ye crawlin ferlie ?"

Had the bard of Ayr lived on these coral-bound
shores, the novelty of the sight, at least, would never
have induced him to immortalize by song, the excur-
sions of one of that disgusting race. In our humble
kirk, in place of one on " *Miss's bonnet*," dozens
may, at any time, be seen sporting among the deco-
rated locks of ignoble heads ; while, not unfrequently,
a privileged few wend their way through the garlands
of princes of the blood, or triumphantly mount the
coronets of majesty itself!

As to the servants of the chiefs, and the common
people, we think ourselves fortunate indeed, if, after a
call of a few minutes, we do not find living testimonies
of their visit, on our mats and floors, and even on our
clothes and persons ! The bare relation of the fact,
without the experience of it, is sufficiently shocking.
But the half is not told ; and, I scarce dare let truth,
here, run to its climax. The lower classes, not only
suffer their heads and tapas to harbour these vermin ;
but they openly, and unblushingly, *eat them !* Yet so
fastidious are they, in point of *cleanliness*, than an
emetic could scarce be more efficaciously administered,
than to cause them to eat from a dish in which a fly
had been drowned ! So much for the force of custom,
and the power of habit.

They have, by some, been called a cleanly people,

in their persons, and food; but, with these facts, which cannot be denied, in view—and, to which may be added, long and dirty nails, like the talons of birds, &c.—it is difficult to allow them a right to the epithet, notwithstanding the practice of spending hours together in the foamings of the surf, or the dashings of the mountain torrent; and the punctilious observance of the ceremony of washing, at least the fingers, before and after their meals.

May 24. When last in Schenectady, I was particularly requested to make inquiry respecting Anthony Allen, an African, residing on this island, once the servant of a gentleman of that city. He is quite a respectable man; and has a very neat establishment, consisting of a dozen houses built in the native manner, and covered with mud : one for sitting and sleeping, one for eating, another for a storehouse, another for milk, a kitchen, blacksmith's shop, &c. &c. He owns large flocks of goats, and a few cows; and supplies the tables of many of the residents with milk. He also keeps a kind of boarding-house for seamen; by these means, and the cultivation of a small farm which he holds under Hevaheva, the ex-highpriest, he obtains a comfortable support for himself and wife, a modest native, and three children. He has been very kind to us in sending melons, bananas, several kids, and a regular daily supply of milk from his goats.

His plantation is two miles from the Mission House on the plain, towards Waititi. The road to it, although the plain is uncultivated and entirely unshaded, affords the most pleasant walk in the immediate vicinity of Ho-

noruru.   The mountains are too distant to be reached
in an hour's ramble ; and the shore is lined only with
fish-ponds and marshes.   Every thing short of the
mountains is sunburnt and dreary.   There is not a tree
near us, much less groves, in whose shade we might
find shelter from the heat of a torrid sun : no babbling
brooks, no verdant lawn, no secluded dell or glade, for
the enjoyment of solitude and thought ; indeed, nothing
that ever formed part of a scene of rural delight.

The number of foreigners residing at the islands is
far greater than I supposed.   Four American mercantile houses—two of Boston, one of New York, and one
of Bristol, Rhode Island—have establishments at this
port, to which agents and clerks are attached.   Their
storehouses are abundantly furnished with goods in demand by the islanders ; and, at them, most articles contained in common retail shops and groceries, in America,
may be purchased.   The whole trade of the four, probably amounts to one hundred thousand dollars a year :
sandal wood principally, and specie, being the returns
for imported manufactures.   Each of these trading
houses usually has a ship or brig in the harbour, or at
some one of the islands ; besides others that touch to
make repairs, and obtain refreshments, in their voyages
between the North-west, Mexican, and South American
coasts, and China.   The agents and clerks of these
establishments, and the supercargoes and officers of the
vessels attached to them, with transient visitors in ships
holding similar situations, form the most respectable
class of foreigners with whom we are called to have
intercourse.

There is another, consisting of fifteen or twenty individuals, who have dropped all connexion with their native countries, and become permanent residents on different islands; and who hold plantations and other property under the king and various chiefs. Of these, Marini, a Spaniard, interpreter for the government; Rives, a Frenchman, private secretary to Riho-Riho; Law, a Scotchman, the king's physician, all of Oahu; Young, an Englishman; and Parker, an American, of Hawaii; and Butler, an American, of Maui, are the principal and most known. Marini and Young have been at the islands more than thirty years; and were companions and counsellors of Tamehameha. The former has accumulated much property, holds many plantations, and owns extensive flocks of goats, and herds of cattle; and is said to have money in fund, both in the United States and in England.

He has introduced the grape, orange, lemon, pine-apple, fig, and tamarind trees, but to a very limited extent; and seemingly from a motive entirely selfish: for he has perseveringly denied the seeds, and every means of propagation, to others, and been known even secretly to destroy a growth that had been secured from them without his knowledge. A considerable quantity of wine is yearly made from his vineyard; and his lemons and pines, by sales to ships and in the town, bring quite an income. He has a numerous breed of mules; and several horses, some twenty or thirty of which have within a few years been brought from the coast of California, and are now rapidly increasing. Flocks of beautiful doves, also an importation, are domiciliated at his establishment; and some few miles from the town, along the coast, there is an islet, covered with the burrows of English hares, belonging to him.

Besides this class of foreigners, there are between one and two hundred runaway sailors and vagabonds, scattered through the group, wanderers on the earth, the very dregs and outcasts of society. These, and, I am sorry to say, too many others, who, from their birth and education in a Christian land, ought to be examples of rectitude and morality, are the greatest corrupters of this wretched people; and present the most formidable of obstacles to the moral influence of our teaching. Fancying themselves, in this remote part of the world, free from every restraint of God and man, instead of attempting to turn the heathen from their darkness, they encourage them in sin; even become pioneers in iniquity; and the instruments of doubly sealing them, as we fear, in the gloom of spiritual and eternal death.

When the first Missionaries reached the Sandwich Islands, in the spring of 1820, an effort was made by some of the foreigners, to have their landing and establishment at the islands forbidden by the government. With this view, their motives were misrepresented by them, to the king and chiefs. It was asserted, that while the ostensible object of the mission was good, the secret and ultimate design was the subjugation of the islands, and the enslavement of the people: and by way of corroboration, the treatment of the Mexicans, and aborigines of South America and the West Indies, by the Spaniards, and the possession of Hindostan by the British, were gravely related. It was in consequence

of this misrepresentation, that a delay of eight days occurred before the Missionaries could secure permission
to disembark.

In answer to these allegations, the more intelligent
of the chiefs remarked, " *The Missionaries speak well:
they say they have come from America, only to do us
good: if they intend to seize our islands, why are they
so few in number? where are their guns? and why have
they brought their wives?*" To this it was replied, " It
is true, their number is small : a few only have come
now, the more fully to deceive. But soon many more
will arrive, and your islands will be lost !" The chiefs
again answered, " *They say that they will do us good;
they are few in number; we will try them for one year,
and if we find they deceive us, it will then be time
enough to send them away.*" And permission to land
was accordingly granted. Mr. Young, I am told was
the only foreigner who advocated their reception.

The jealousy of the government was, notwithstanding,
greatly awakened ; and all the movements of our friends
were closely watched : the king was even led to believe
that the digging of the cellar, and the laying of the
foundation, of the Mission House, was the commencement of a fortification, of which the spaces left for windows were the embrasures.

By the close of the first year the Missionaries had so
far proved to the government the purity of their motive,
and the integrity of their character, that the question
of their longer continuance was not agitated. Some of
the chiefs had already become interested in the instructions commenced in English, and in the services of

Christian worship, regularly observed on the Sabbath, and occasionally at other times. The partial acquisition of the language of the country—the formation of an alphabet for the native tongue—the elementary lessons in reading and writing which immediately followed—and chiefly perhaps the PREACHING OF THE GOSPEL—had by the end of the second year confirmed to the Missionaries the confidence of the rulers, and began to secure to them decided marks of friendship.

A first effort at opposition having proved thus unsuccessful, another soon made its appearance. The object in this case, was the defeat of the moral influence of Christianity : and the extremity to which some of the foreigners pushed their point, and of the means resorted to for its accomplishment, you may judge from the fact, that the pupils of the first female school collected at this place, by Mrs. Bingham—after being clothed, and brought with much care and attention to habits of neatness and propriety in their persons, and made themselves to be deeply interested in various useful instruction—were borne off openly and forcibly by them, to become their mistresses, while the instructress herself could answer the appeals made to her for protection, only *by her tears !*

Still the moral influence of Christianity has been felt : and I am persuaded its glorious progress cannot now be stayed. A chief object at present with those opposed to the Mission, is the blasting of its character abroad. A vessel scarcely comes to anchor, before the ears of those attached to it are filled with slander and falsehood, in reference to the influence exerted by us. Even Captain Clasby had scarce reached the shore, before he heard the lowest abuse heaped on our associates ; and was told by a leading resident, that his passengers *should not be permitted to land :* that the nation was already nearly ruined *by the worthless set of fellows* we had come to join !

When a strange ship arrives, and the officers complain of the extravagance of the harbour-fees, this impost is immediately declared to be exacted by the advice of the Missionaries : the high prices of articles of refreshment in the market, is assigned to the same cause : though we ourselves are now living almost exclusively on *sea biscuit, salt beef, and pork,* brought from America, two or three years old, and scarce ever taste a banana or melon, because we do not feel at liberty to purchase fresh provisions and vegetables—much less fruit—at the price demanded by the chiefs.   Equally untrue is a whole catalogue of charges, by which we are represented as the worst enemies of our countrymen, and of all foreigners ; and the basest of men, both in principles and morals.

The minds of many visitors at the islands are by these means so strongly prejudiced against us, that they do not call at the Mission House ; and in some instances, after a casual introduction, have, on meeting us in the street passed in haughty silence, and even betrayed a sneer of contempt.   And when they take their departure, they bear with them to the coasts of Mexico and Peru and Chili, or to Canton, England, and America, the most erroneous impressions of our influence here, and not unfrequently the lowest slanders of our character.

When I speak thus of the opposition with which we are obliged to contend, you are not to understand that all foreigners—residents or visitors—are of the character represented. Some of every class are warmly and decidedly our friends, and have our high respect for the rectitude of their character, and our sincere gratitude for many favours : and, inconsistent as it may appear, even those most embittered in their feelings against our object, treat us personally with respect, and often with great kindness. Scarce a week passes, in which donations of a liberal and important character are not conferred on one or another of the family ; and we are often made to feel the obligation of civilities, which we have not the means of returning.

The scale of prejudice which was made to bear so heavily against the Missionaries on their arrival, has now not only gained its balance, but is beginning to settle with ominous bearing against those who attempted by it to prevent the establishment of the Mission. The haughty and powerful queen Kaahumanu was at first exceedingly jealous of the teachers ; and it is only within the last few months, that she has paid a regard to instruction of any kind. She long persisted in her refusals to attempt to learn to read and write, and was but recently induced for the first time to lay aside her cards for a few minutes, and to repeat the alphabet after a Missionary : since then, she has, however, become an assiduous scholar ; and has made her books and slate the principal sources of amusement.

Within a day or two, I called upon her in company with Mr. Ellis. Soon after entering, she asked Mr.

Ellis for a blank book he had promised to give her:
he was obliged to tell her he had not yet made it; and
added, " I fear you will think *I am deceiving you*, by
delaying so long to fulfil my promise"—when she hastily
interrupted him, saying—" *Aore !—aore ! ua pau koma-
kou manao ino i ka poe Mikanere—ka wahahe wale
no kahaori !*"—" No ! no !—ended are our evil thoughts
of the company of Missionaries—false or deceitful only
are the foreigners !"—meaning by foreigners, those who
had originally misrepresented and traduced the character
of the Missionaries.   She expressed her full determination to serve Jehovah and to keep his law : in the course
of the conversation, she requested Mr. Ellis to write her
a form of prayer for grace at meals, adding, " I know
that all things are from Jehovah—and it is well to give
thanks to him for every favour, but without some direction I shall perhaps make *crooked work of it.*"

The same morning we for a moment visited Kapiolani.
She is an exceedingly interesting character : and from
having been addicted to the grossest intemperance and
dissipation, has become perfectly correct in her habits ;
and is invariably serious and dignified in her deportment.   I first saw her at the Mission House on the
morning of our arrival ; and was so forcibly impressed
with the neatness of her dress, and the propriety of her
whole appearance, as to be led to inquire who she was,
and whether she could be a Sandwich Islander.   She is
deeply interested in the success of the Mission ; is herself an indefatigable scholar ; and shewed us a very
handsome writing-desk and table, for which she had just
given seventy-five dollars.

Monday Morning, 26. The Sabbath here is a most interesting day to the Christian and Missionary. The number of decently dressed heathen who flock to the humble temple of the only true God; the attention and seriousness with which many of them listen to the words of eternal life proclaimed in their own language, by the ambassadors of Jesus Christ; the praises of Jehovah chanted in this untutored tongue—necessarily produce a lively and joyful impression on the pious mind. Of this I saw a pleasing instance only two.Sabbaths since. An officer from one of the ships in port—a serious young young man, spent the interval between the English and native services with me at the Mission House. As the congregation began to assemble, he accompanied me to the door of the chapel, intending to take leave when the exercises should begin, as he was unacquainted with the language, and had been already longer from his ship than he designed; but after standing a few minutes, and seeing hundreds of natives assembling quietly and seriously from various directions; he suddenly exclaimed, while tears glistened in his eye, " *No !—this is too much—I cannot go till I worship with these heathen.*"

It is also an interesting day to the passing stranger; —for on the Sabbath, the real state of the people, struggling from barbarity to. civilization, is more observable than at any other time. Any one of the fabled beings, represented as half *man* and half *beast,* would be an appropriate emblem of the present national character; and an emblazoned *Centaur* would, in the view of a herald, furnish his Hawaiian majesty with a very intelligible coat of arms.

Recollecting of how late a date the first improvements here are, there is certainly much to admire; but more, in one sense, *at which to laugh.* This fact is conspicuous to the simple *looker-on,* in nothing more than in dress—the variety and grotesque mixture of which is indescribable. The king, queens, prince, princess, and all the highest chiefs, are, at church, always well, and often richly and fashionably, dressed. But when grouped—which is always the case—with the *" Royal Guards,"* and the several retinues of the chiefs, they present a most incongruous and ridiculous spectacle. The dress of the *guards,* which is intended to be a *" uniform,"* appears to be the cast-off regimentals of half a dozen different nations, and, I had had almost said, of as many different centuries. Some suits I think bear strong evidence, *prima facie,* of having passed through the honourable hardships of the *Revolutionary War;* and I have been half-tempted to recognize in others, the parade clothes of the *" Bowerstown Artillery,"* the objects of general admiration, when, as a boy, I first visited the wilds of Otsego. You may judge how these, or *the like,* would appear,—a coat and cocked hat, for instance, on a native *" sans culotte;"* or a hat and pantaloons without a coat or shirt, or a hat and shirt alone; all of which varieties may be seen. Some of the officers, however, appear very well, in full new suits of blue, with lace and epaulettes of gold.

There is sometimes, also, an odd mixture of materials in the dress of the chiefs; for example, a rich suit of Canton crape, satin or silk velvet, with a sai-

lor's check or red flannel shirt, and parti-coloured
woollen cap, and perhaps one coarse stocking and
shoe. I have seen a female, of high rank, and mon-
strously large, going to church in a loose slip of white
muslin, with thick woodman's shoes, and no stockings,
a heavy silver-headed cane in her hand, and an immense French *chapeau* on her head!

On Sunday, too, there is a display of *equipage*, not
seen every day. The chapel being near a half mile
from the village, some of the grandees ride to church:
—their carriages, to be sure, belong to " *the birth-day
of invention*"—especially the *state coach* of the late
king, which, I presume, was once a *tinker's waggon*.
Kaahumanu and *Taumuarii* always come in this;
the young queens, usually, in one more modern and
airy, of the kind called *Dearborn* in America. These
vehicles are always drawn by twelve or fifteen natives; their horses not having yet been broken to the
harness.

Whether the *nobility*, here, have been told that
those, *who wish to be considered most genteel*, in
America, do not go to church till after the services
have commenced; or whether, the newly introduced
duties of the toilette occasion the delay, I cannot
determine; but the most stately do not generally
arrive at the chapel till some time during the first
prayer, which consequently is disturbed by the rumbling of their *chariot* wheels, the hooting of the rabble
that hurry them along the plain, the bustle of alight-
ing, and the parade of entering. You could not

void smiling, were you to see, with what dignity some of these saunter up the aisle.

I have been led to these little notices, protracted much beyond my intention when I commenced this date, by the observations unavoidably, and almost unconsciously, made yesterday. I witnessed them all, in the detail in which they are given; and, afterwards, in *grand assemblage*, by a single *coup d'œil*, when the meeting was dismissed: with the addition, however, of the lofty umbrellas, and proud kahiles, on the favourable side; and of a party of naked horsemen on the other, who were flying in the distance, mounted without saddle or bridle, except a string of twisted grass, with looks more wild than their long hair, and ragged tapas, that were streaming in the wind.

One or two of the Missionaries attend family prayers, at the king's residence, every evening. Last night, at nine o'clock, I accompanied Mr. Ellis and Mr. Chamberlain to this service. Riho-Riho was just commencing supper, in a large ranai, or bower, by the side of his house. The table was well set with blue china and cut glass, for about twenty persons; and besides the lamps and spermaceti candles which were burning on it, was surrounded by a glare of torches of the tutui or oil nut, which, tastefully wrapped in green leaves, made a splendid appearance. The king was seated at the head, with one of his queens on his left, and a favourite chief on his right side. There were about half a dozen others at the table. He, immediately ordered room for us to be made on the left of the queen, and begged us to help ourselves to

o

whatever we chose of the variety of soups, meats, and vegetables before us, and to excuse his doing the honours of the table, being "*porori roa*, "very hungry," and having just filled his plate with rich turtle soup.

Some of the chiefs do not cook their food on the Sabbath; the king is aware of this, and himself some-times follows their example; but last night every thing was smoking fresh from the cookhouse; and, by way of apology, he remarked, that the hot supper was not prepared for himself, but, on *account of the "mai" the sick person*, (Kamehameru being indisposed,) but that every thing on the table *was killed the day before*.

Our own practice is to have our dinner, for the Sabbath, except the vegetables, cooked on Saturday. The preparation of food in the native manner, espe-cially the making of poe and baking of meats, requires the attention of several hours; and the Missionaries, in their instructions, have suggested to the chiefs and people, the propriety of preparing their food for the *la tabu*, on the preceding day. The remark of the king was made, from a knowledge of our opinion on the subject.

After taking a cup of tea, and waiting till his majesty had completed half a dozen courses, we retired from the table, at ten o'clock, to the *palace;* where the principal part of the chiefs were waiting for the ordinary worship.

Nine o'clock, P. M. This has proved a much more important date than I anticipated when I wrote in the morning. The Mission was informed yesterday, that the king's mother is going to Lahaina, on the island of Maui, to reside permanently there; and is extremely desirous that some of the Missionaries should accompany her. Mr. Bingham saw her last night on the subject. She said she must have a teacher, to speak the *good word, and pray to God with her;* that she would do every thing in her power to make those who might accompany her comfortable; and would delay her voyage, that there might be time for them to prepare to sail with her in the Cleopatra's barge.

A meeting of the Mission was, consequently, called this morning, when it was determined, that it was expedient to occupy a station at Lahaina immediately After agreeing that the choice of persons should be made by electing one by ballot, and allowing him to nominate his colleague, the votes were taken: I was elected, and immediately, named Mr. Richards for my associate: we, consequently are all in confusion, packing up our baggage for a permanent residence on Maui, instead of a visit to Hawaii, and a tour of the island. We are to embark on Wednesday.

CHAPTER VIII.

On board the Cleopatra's Barge, at sea, May 30*th*, 1823. On Wednesday the 28th, Mr. and Mrs. Richards, H—— and myself, B—— and C——, with William Kamahoula, and Mr. Loomis—who makes the voyage to see us established at our station—embarked with the queen Keopuolani for Maui.

Our designation was so unexpected, and departure so sudden, that we had scarce leisure to turn a thought on the separation about to take place from our fellow labourers, or to cast a glance of anticipation at the possible trials that might await us in a distant and solitary district. The topsails of the barge had long been unfurled before we had completed our preparations, and the last package was scarcely secured, before the farewell hymn and benedictions of our friends were sounding in our ears, and we were hurried to the open bosom of the Pacific.

Left to the deliberate contemplation of our situation, we almost trembled at the responsibility resting upon us, and at the arduous duties in prospect. Every thought was exquisitely awake to the life on which we had now actually entered. Months indeed had passed since we bad adieu to our country, home, and friends ; but, during a voyage of 18,000 miles, we had still been surrounded by those we loved; and, for the last few weeks, though on heathen shores, we had been calmly reposing in the bosom of a band of intelligent affectionate Christians, without a participation of their labours and their cares. Such, however, was no longer the case ; our eyes rested only on the uncivilized beings with whom we were to dwell, and our ears were saluted only by the sounds of an unknown and savage tongue. We were fully alive to the contrast; and, in the anticipation of those trials, by which we believe the work in which we are engaged must be accomplished, we could scarce refrain exclaiming, " *Farewell ease—farewell comfort —farewell every worldly joy.*"

But with these feelings there was no mingling of despondency. No, in the kind providence of God, every circumstance attending our situation was too auspicious to admit the indulgence of any unbelieving fear of the ultimate success of our enterprise.

We had been on board scarce an hour, before the polite and kind attention of those, under whose immediate and express patronage we had embarked, made us almost forget that we were not still in the bosom of beloved friends. Our hearts became more than ordinarily elated, in the belief that, " *unto us is this grace given, that we should preach among the gentiles the unsearchable riches of Christ ;*" and, while a splendid moon gave a softened beauty to the receding promontories of Oahu, and brought to light the distant shores of Morokai and Ranai, overtopped by the loftier heights of Maui, we found ourselves almost involuntarily chanting the favourite anthem—

"Wake, Isles of the South, your redemption draws near,
No longer repose in the borders of gloom, &c."

Previous to our embarkation, we had but little opportunity to judge, from personal intercourse, of the degree of civilization to which the chiefs have attained in minor points, and were somewhat surprised at the ceremonious attentions paid us. Immediately on going on board, we were informed that the after-cabin was appropriated exclusively to our use; though there were not less than two hundred persons on board, many of them high chiefs, with their particular friends; and we had hardly cleared the harbour, when the steward waited on us, to know what we would order for dinner, and at what hour it should be served.

Mr. Allen had sent us a fine ready-dressed kid, with some melons, for our passage; and Mrs. Bingham had kindly prepared coffee and other refreshments; but our table has been so regularly and comfortably spread, that our basket of cold provisions remains untouched. This attention is the more noticeable, because the trouble is entirely on our account, all the natives eating their favourite dishes on their mats on deck. Karaimoku, from courtesy, very politely took his seat with us the first time we sat down to meal, but excused himself from partaking of the dinner, by saying that he had eaten above.

There was something also in the attentions of the

king to his mother, when leaving Honoruru, that had a pleasing effect on our minds. This venerable old lady was the last person that came on board. After we had reached the quarter-deck of the barge, she appeared on the beach surrounded by an immense crowd, and supported by Riho-Riho in a tender and respectful manner. He would let no one assist her into the long boat but himself; and seemed to think of nothing but her ease and safety, till she was seated on her couch, beneath an awning over the main hatch. The king continued to manifest the utmost affection and respect for her till we got under way; and, apparently from the same filial feelings, accompanied us fifteen miles out to sea, and left the brig in a pilot-boat, in time barely to reach the harbour before dark.

We are now becalmed under the lee of Ranai, within less than a mile of an inaccessible precipice several hundred feet high, the base of which is lashed with heavy breakers. We had the hope of reaching Lahaina to-night, but now fear that we shall not before some time to-morrow.

Lahaina, Island of Maui, Saturday evening, May 31. After a very rough but splendid night, at sunrise this morning the wild mountains that overhang the district of Lahaina were in distinct view, and we advanced rapidly to the anchorage. The settlement is far more beautiful than any place we have yet seen on the islands. The whole district, stretching nearly three miles along the sea-side, is covered with luxuriant groves, not only of the cocoanut, (the only tree we have before seen, except on the tops of the mountains,) but also of

the bread-fruit and of the *kou ;* a species of *cordia,*
cordia sebestena, an ornamental tree, resembling, at a
distance, a large and flourishing, full, round-topped
apple tree. The banana plant, tapa, and sugar-cane, are
abundant, and extend almost to the beach, on which a
fine surf constantly rolls.

On coming to an anchor, Karaimoku expressed his
regret that there was no house at the disposal of himself
or the queen, suitable for our accommodation : and
wished us to procure a temporary residence with Mr.
Butler, an American established here, till houses could
be provided for us by Keopulani. Under the guidance
of Mr. Loomis, Mr. Richards and myself accordingly
landed for this purpose. We were soon met by Keoua,
the governor of Lahaina, to whom I delivered a *letter*
of introduction from his friend Laanui, at Oahu, and
proceeded in search of the plantation of Mr. Butler.

We found his enclosure pleasantly situated about a
quarter of a mile directly in rear of the landing place,
and were received by him in a kind and friendly manner. When acquainted with our object in coming to
Lahaina, he proffered every assistance in his power, and
tendered his best house for the reception of our families.
His civility greatly prepossessed us in his favour, and
made us almost forget that we were in the land of
strangers. He returned to the barge with us, to bring
the ladies on shore ; and early in the afternoon our
whole number were comfortably and quietly settled in
the midst of his luxuriant grounds.

The thick shade of the bread-fruit trees which surround his cottages—the rustling of the breeze through

the bananas and sugar-cane—the murmurs of the mountain streams encircling the yard—and the coolness and verdure of every spot around us— seemed, in contrast with our situation, during a six months' voyage, and four weeks' residence on the dreary plain of Honoruru, like the delights of an Eden; and caused our hearts to beat warmly with gratitude to the Almighty Being, who had brought us in safety to the scene of our future labours, and had at once provided us with so refreshing an asylum.

Before dark, the chiefs had all our effects landed, and secured in the storehouse of the governor, while our private baggage was brought to the house we occupy by the attendants of the queen. Nor did their attentions cease here. Early in the evening, a supply of ready-cooked provisions, with vegetables and fruits, abundantly sufficient for the Sabbath, were sent to us by different individuals. Mr. Butler hospitably prepared our first repast; and, though somewhat fatigued, we are now ready to retire to rest, prepared for the suitable observance of the holy day on which we are bordering. May it be the beginning of many blessed Sabbaths to the degraded inhabitants of Lahaina!

Sabbath, June 1. Early this morning a messenger came to inform us that Keopuolani, the princess, and chiefs, were waiting for us to come and worship with them. We accordingly hastened to the beach, to erect an altar to the true God, where heretofore idols only have been served. Our temple was the work of the hands of the Almighty. Its only pillars were those that support the foundations of the earth, and its canopy the broad arch

of heaven.   But we doubt whether a purer flame of devotion would have glowed in our bosoms, had we knelt
before the Lord on pavements of marble, or addressed
his throne from the midst of carving and gold.   About
three hundred and fifty persons had encircled the tent,
pitched for the temporary accommodation of the queen,
in a grove of *kou* trees, near a brick building,* the residence of the late king when he visited Maui.   We
have seldom witnessed a more orderly and attentive
audience.

A portion of scripture was read from the *Tahitian*
verson, by *Taua*, a Tahitian Christian, assistant Mission
ary to Mr. Ellis, who is attached to the retinue of the
queen, in the capacity of private instructor and chaplain ; after which other appropriate services were performed.   The chiefs desired to have the services repeated in the afternoon ; and the queen requested us
not only to worship God with her thus, on the Sabbath, but to attend prayers regularly, with herself and
daughter, every morning and every evening.

Monday, June 2.   Our schools have to-day been
commenced, one at the establishment of each of the
chiefs in company with the queen, and one also at the
house of Keoua the governor, making six in number :
that of Keopuolani, and Hoapiri her husband ; that of
the princess Nahienaena ; of the young queen Kekauonohi, a wife of Riho-Riho ; of Wahinepio, the sister of
Karaimoku, and Kehikiri her husband ; of Kaiko and
his wife Haaheo ; and of the governor.

Our pupils consist of the chiefs and a few of their

* Now used as a storehouse.

particular favourites. The rulers have, from the first
arrival of the Missionaries, opposed the instruction of
the common people in reading and writing, saying,
" If the *palapala, letters, is good*, we wish to possess it
first ourselves ; *if it is bad*, we do not intend our subjects to know the evil of it,"—and thus far a kind of tabu
has existed against any but religious teaching among
the commoners. And the whole number of islanders
who have learned, and are learning, to read and write,
does not amount to more than two or three hundred ;
about fifty of whom are now under our direction.

It may not be readily understood how we can teach
in a tongue of which we are almost entirely ignorant.
The rudiments of the language are so simple, that after
once learning the sounds of the letters and diphthongs,
there is no difficulty in pronouncing any word correctly,
or in mechanically reading any sentence. So that we
are fully competent to instruct in reading and spelling
the few sheets in print, and in writing.

Several are learning the English language ; but the
combination of its sounds are so foreign to the genius
of their own, and some of its letters so utterly beyond
their powers of enunciation, that, as Kaahumanu says,
they do indeed make " *crooked work of it.*"

Keopulani is indefatigable in her efforts to learn to
read in her own tongue. It is but a few months that
she has been interested in the object of the Mission ;
and being aged, she has great apprehensions that she
may not live till, as she herself expresses it, she " *has
learned enough of the good word* (of God) *and of the
right way to go to heaven.*" Her influence is so great,

that in this respect, and in every other, her example is
very important.   Her character has for some time
been free from all the reproaches of heathenism ; and
she appears sincerely desirous of fully imbibing the
spirit, as well as of observing the forms, of Christianity.
Karaimoku and Keoua dined with us to-day.   While at
the table, the prime minister informed us that Keopuolani had given us a plantation adjoining that of Mr.
Butler ; and directing the governor to put us in possession of it, by shewing the boundaries in the presence of
its tenants, according to the custom of the country : he
took his leave with a pleasant *aroha*, and the salutation
" *much happiness to you all on the island of Maui.*"

We have since ascertained, that the plantation is his
own ;   and that it is to his liberality, probably with
the knowledge of the queen, we are indebted for the
kindness.

By the word plantation, as used here, you are not, my
dear M——, to understand what its acceptation in
America would convey, an estate of 500 or 5000 acres,
but an extent of land, in general, much more contracted
than the pleasure-grounds around your own residence ;
consisting of a collection of taro beds, interspersed here
and there with a few rows of potatoes, a little sugar-
cane and some irregularly planted banana, and cocoa-
nut or bread fruit trees.

Such are the limits and appearance of the ground
given to us : the soil is, however, exceedingly rich, and
may be formed into a beautiful garden.

Tuesday, 3.   After evening prayers at the queen's,
we took leave of **Karaimoku** and his party, who shortly

after went on board the barge, to return to Honoruru.
Mr. Loomis also left us. The only object of Karaimoku in visiting Lahaina, was to escort Keopuolani,
who being the highest chief by blood in the nation,
receives every mark of honour and affection from the
government and people. At this interview, he appeared more kindly disposed than ever, repeatedly
taking us by both hands, a token of peculiar tenderness,
and pressing them to his bosom. He told us, that the
queen would continue to provide for us as she had
done. Our table has been bountifully furnished every
day from her stores. This morning she said to William, " Have they hog still ?" " Yes." " Any dog ?"
" *No eat dog*." " Any potatoes ?" " No." " Any
melons ?" " No." On which an order was immediately given, and two men despatched to us heavily
laden with potatoes and melons. Pigs, hogs, fowl, and
goats, have been sent constantly by one person or
another. No congregation in America could in this
respect have received a clergyman, coming to admi
nister the word of life to them, with greater hospitality,
or stronger expressions of good will.

Thursday, 5. Found leisure this morning to take
a cursory survey of the settlement in which I am now
a spiritual instructor. The first view of it from the sea
and anchorage, gives too favourable an impression of
its beauty ; and the appearance of great luxuriance
which it exhibits, does not expose the rude and imperfect
cultivation of the natives.

Lahaina is situated on the north-west end of Maui,
and lies between two points projecting slightly into the

ocean; one on the north, and the other on the south end, about two miles distant from each other. These, in their respective directions, terminate the view of the beach.

The width of the district from the sea towards the mountain, is from one half to three-quarters of a mile. The whole extent included within these boundaries is perfectly level, and thickly covered with trees and various vegetation. The taste, skill, and industry of an American gardener might convert it into an earthly paradise; but now it every where appears only like the neglected grounds of a deserted plantation. There is no uniformity or neatness to be seen, and almost every thing seems to be growing in the wildness of nature. The bread-fruit trees stand as thickly as those of an irregularly planted orchard, and beneath them are taro patches and fish-ponds, twenty or thirty yards square, filled with stagnant water, and interspersed with clumps of the tapa tree, groves of the banana, rows of the sugar-cane, and bunches of the potatoe and melon. All these flourish exuberantly from the richness of the soil alone, with but little attention or labour from the hand of man.

It scarce ever rains, not oftener than half a dozen times during the year; and the land is watered entirely by conducting the streams which rush from the mountains, by artificial courses, on every plantation. Each farmer has a right, established by custom, to the water every fifth day. The pathways, which are very narrow, are usually along the sides of these water trenches.

The number of inhabitants is about two thousand five hundred. Their houses are generally not more than eight or ten feet long, six or eight broad, and from four to six high: having one small hole for a door, which cannot be entered but by creeping, and is the only opening for the admission of light and air. They make little use of these dwellings, except to protect their food and clothing, and to sleep in during wet and cool weather; and most generally eat, sleep, and live in the open air, under the shade of a *kou*, or bread-fruit tree.

The land begins to rise rather abruptly about three fourths of a mile from the sea, and towers into lofty mountains, three rude elevations of which, immediately east of Lahaina, are judged to be four thousand five hundred, or five thousand feet, above the level of the ocean. From the first swell of the rising ground, almost to the summits of these mountains, there is nothing to be seen but the most dreary sterility and sunburnt vegetation, intersected by gloomy ravines and frightful precipices.

Every part of the island seen from Lahaina wears the same forbidding and desolate aspect, and after passing either point, the eye is met only by a barren sand-beach, occasionally interrupted by heaps of black lava, to which the wild dashings of a heavy surf add double gloom.

So far as our observation extends, this description is characteristic of the whole Islands. Instead of being the sunny and elysian fields which the imagination of many make them, they in fact are only vast heaps of rocks in the midst of this mighty ocean, with here and there, at long intervals, a rich and luxuriant valley and plain thronged with inhabitants. The outlines of the

whole group are wild and romantic, and the thick and
ever-verdant forests, which crown the heights of many
of the mountains, give them a refreshing appearance.
But to an eye accustomed to the varied beauties of an
American landscape, to its widely cultivated fields, its
stately groves, its spreading lawns, and broadly gleaming
rivers, its gardens and enclosures, its farm-houses, country seats, villages, domes, and spires, a more melancholy
place of exile could scarce be selected than the Sandwich Islands.

The islands of Ranai, Morokai, and Tahurawe, are in
full view from Lahaina ; the two former to the west and
north, and the last to the south ; and at the distance of
fifteen or twenty miles, are as dreary as the gloomiest
imagination could paint them. Not a sign of life, in
the animal or vegetable creation, can be discovered on
or about them ; and being constantly enveloped in lowering clouds, they are as emphatically the dark mountains of the natural, as they are figuratively those of the
intellectual and spiritual world. We here look in vain
for those beauties in nature, with which we once feasted
our admiration to enthusiasm ; for

> " Objects find we none,
> Except before us stretch'd the toiling main,
> And rocks and wilds in savage view behind."

The south point of Lahaina, however, presents one
subject of glorious meditation—the ruins of an *Hei-au*
or idolatrous temple. While wandering over this now
confused heap of stones, I involuntarily shuddered at
the thought that they had often been bathed in human
blood, a melancholy fact :—but, O how joyful, how in-

expressibly animating, the association inseparably connected with it.

> " The altar and idol, in dust overthrown,—
> The incense forbade, that was hallowed in blood;
> The priest of Melchisedec here shall atone,
> And the shrines of Lahaina be sacred to God."

Yes! we confidently believe, that the stifled shrieks of a devoted human victim will never again break on the midnight silence of these groves; and that the only sacrifice that will ever here be offered, will be that of " *a broken and a contrite heart*," which thou, O God, wilt not despise.

Saturday night, June 7. The first week of our residence at Lahaina is completed; and few Missionaries have ever been more highly favoured in forming a station, far from every abode of civilization and piety, than we have. The Lord hath dealt kindly with us, by disposing the hearts of the queen and chiefs to the most friendly and generous attentions.

Our table has been constantly and bountifully spread by our benefactress, who, clothed with regal power, in this respect literally fulfils the promise, " *Behold, I will lift up my hand to the gentiles, and set up my standard to the people, and kings shall be thy nursing fathers, and queens thy nursing mothers*." Preparations are already made for the speedy erection of our dwelling houses; and timber is collecting for a chapel and school-house, all by the liberality of the same interesting personage.

And where is the civilized heart, that will refuse its warm approbation, and zealous support, to the attempts

that are making, for the benefit of those who appear so
anxious to receive it.   Who, after once witnessing scenes
which have become familiar to us, will say, " *the heathen
cannot be enlightened ?*"   Who will assert that instruction to these is thrown away, when morning, noon, and
night, they may be found in groups of from ten to thirty
persons, spelling, and reading, and writing ; and, whether
in their houses or in the grove, whether strolling on the
beach, or, I might almost add, sporting in the surf,
making their books and slates their inseparable companions?

If, after the shortest and most imperfect tuition, many
are capable of composing neat and intelligent letters to
each other, now, almost daily passing from island to
island, and from district to district ; so far from judging
them not susceptible of attainments in the common
branches of education, we need not fear to encourage a
belief, that some may yet rejoice in the more abstruse
researches of philosophy and science.   They can be
civilized, they can be made to partake, with millions of
their fellow-beings, in all the advantages of letters and
of the arts.

Nor is there more doubt, that they may be converted to
Christianity. They eagerly seek our religious instructions
and prayers ; and morning and evening, with seriousness
and solemnity, surround the altar of the great I AM. The
approach of the Sabbath is anxiously awaited : and so
careful are they not to infringe its duties or defeat its
object, by unnecessary labours, that they prepare their
food before its commencement, with more punctilious
care than many in our own country, who are thought to

observe it with superstitious particularity. We do not
say this of the nation, for, alas ! gross darkness covers
the people, and thousands are every where perishing in
the depths of ignorance and sin; but of those only, who
have received the most constant and direct influence of
he Mission. If it can be said, however, of a few only,
(and in its full extent it can be,) who will not admit that
all are alike capable of receiving and obeying the precepts of the word of God ?

We thank God more warmly than ever, that of his
good pleasure he excited within our bosoms, the desire
*to forsake houses, and brethren, and sisters, and father,
and lands, for his sake, and for that of the Gospel;"*
and that we have the prospect of living and dying beneath the dark mountains of Maui. If ignorance of the
world and of our own hearts do not deceive us, we had
rather hear the warm and constant " *aroha*,"—" *aroha
nui*"—" *aroha nui roa*"—" *maitai, matai*," " Love to
you"—" great love to you"—" very great love to you"
—" good, good,"—of the crowds of these ignorant and
degraded immortals, with the cheering prospect of conferring on them blessings temporal and eternal, than to
receive the loud huzzas of an American or European
populace, shouting the plaudits of a hero or a monarch.

Wednesday, 18. A messenger from the queen came
to our cottage very early this morning, desiring Mr.
Richards and myself to go to the beach, to make a
definite selection of a situation for the Missionary establishment.   On going down, we found the timber on the
ground, and a large number of men, from a distant district, waiting for directions where to put it up. Keo-

puolani and the young princess both accompanied us to the site we had before partially chosen. It is a bank a few yards from the sea, elevated about six feet above the level of the water, and at present promises greater retirement than any spot in the section of the district in which the queen wishes us to reside. Its only advantage is a peculiarly fresh sea-breeze.

As soon as we expressed our preference for it, the men began digging holes for the corner posts, making each house twenty-three feet long, and fifteen feet wide, with a space of fifteen feet between them. The posts are about as thick as the arm of a man ; and after being fastened in the ground, are about five feet high. The whole number on each side of each of our houses, is seven. The tops are excavated, to admit a pole about an inch in diameter, which extends horizontally the whole length of the building, and to which the posts are all lashed with strings made from a small but strong vine.

The rafters are as numerous as the posts, and nearly as large, and are fastened to their tops with strings. The principal strength of this joint arises from an extension of the outside of the post, two or three inches above the larger and inner part, which is received into a corresponding notch made in the end of the rafters.

The upper ends of the rafters rest on and are lashed to a ridge pole, supported at each end by a long post reaching from the ground to the peak of the roof. Between the corners and these middle posts there are others parallel to them, diminishing in length according to the inclination of the roof. These complete the frame of the building. The next business is to prepare a foundation for the thatch. This is done by lashing small round sticks, at intervals of five or six inches, to the posts of the sides and ends, from the ground to the ridge pole; to these the thatch of grass is tied by strings made of the fibres of the cocoa-nut husk. In the best built houses, between the sticks and the grass there is an inner thatch, or lining, of the leaves of the sugar-cane or banana.

Our kind patroness remained on the ground till we ourselves left it for breakfast; and constantly addressed us, and spoke of us to the people, by the affectionate appellation of " sons."

The ship Dawn, of New York, touched here on the Sabbath, and sailed again for Oahu; the same day the Boston, Captain Joy, of Nantucket, arrived, and is still at anchor off Lahaina. After dining with us to-day, Captain Joy took Mr. Richards and myself to his ship. When returning, towards sunset, we observed an immense crowd of people in the grove, near the establishment of Keopuolani; and hundreds of others hastening from every direction, to the same spot. A *hura-hura* or *native dance* was performing in honour of the arrival of the queen and princess.

The dancers were two interesting girls, ten years of age. Their dresses were of beautiful yellow native cloth, arranged in thick folds and festoons from the waist to the knee; with wreaths of evergreen and wild flowers on their heads and necks,—ornaments of ivory on their wrists—and a kind of buskin round the ankles, formed of dog's teeth, loosely fastened to network of hemp, so as to rattle like the castanet in the motions of the dance. The musicians were six men, seated on the ground with large calabashes before them, which they beat with short sticks.   The sound of these, accompanied by that of their voices repeating the song, constituted the rude music.   The girls occasionally joined in the song ; and often were the only singers, continuing the subject in duet, and at times by a solo.   The motions of the dance were slow and graceful, and, in this instance, free from indelicacy of action ; and the song, or rather recitativo, accompanied by much gesticulation, was dignified and harmonious in its numbers.   The theme of the whole, was the character and praises of the queen and princess, who were compared to every thing sublime in nature ; and exalted as gods.

The chiefs, seated in front of the performers, were so intent on the exhibition, that we scarce expected to gain their attention.   Keopuolani, however, ordered the per-formance to cease the moment the sun began to set ; and, commanding the crowd to be seated and keep silence while she worshipped God, beckoned us to come to her sofa ; and we proceeded with the usual exercises.   The number of persons present was not less than two thou-sand.   To whom—and to many for the first time—the words of eternal life were proclaimed—and that Name made known, which is the only one, " *under heaven, given among men, whereby we must be saved.*"

June 19.   Hoapiri, the husband of Keopuolani, called at our cottage this afternoon, to request the ac-ceptance of *his name* for our son C——— : a mark of great friendship, and, in this case, of honour and condescension, according to the ideas of the islanders. An exchange of names between adults, is one of the strongest pledges of affection : and the conferring of his own name, by a high chief, whether on an individual in infancy, as in the present case, or in manhood, imparts a dignity here, not surpassed by that of " *the spur*" or " *garter*" in more polished monarchies. The *event* was formally announced to the chiefs and people at evening prayers, and a servant despatched with a very appropriate present for " the young Hoapiri"— *a large bucket full of arrowroot ;* an article spontaneous in its growth, prepared to some extent by the natives, and by them called *pia.*

June 20. In all external things here, there is a sameness, morning, noon, and evening—day and night— that, accompanied, as it necessarily is, by an utter want of society, would prove insupportable, I should think, to every civilized and intelligent resident, but a Missionary. True, the weather is perpetual June ; we have no rain, no storms, no lowering clouds, and all immediately around is perennial verdure ; but there is a death-like silence and want of animation in every thing ; *a stillness of desolation*, that drowns the spirits, and destroys the elasticity both of body and mind. There is nothing to be seen or heard of those things which enliven the most retired situations in our own country ; no chirping birds, no gamboling flocks, no lowing cattle. Even the few natives, who are at the same time at work on their small plantations, cause no interruption to the general silence : no sound of industry is created by the rude implements with which they cultivate the ground : and their labour is unaccompanied by any thing like " *the ploughboy's whistle,*" or " *the reaper's song :*"—in fine, little besides the shoutings of a midnight revel, intimates life, much less contentment and joy, among the dwellers of the land.

But our object, and our hopes, buoy us above the influence of this oppressive peculiarity, and impart a contentment and cheerfulness, which often rise to undissembled joy. In contrast with this our chosen lot, fancy sometimes sketches scenes which might have been our own—in which

" An elegant sufficiency—books—friendship—ease"—
are still combined with

" Useful life,
Progressive virtue, and approving heaven."

But I would not exchange my situation and prospects, with the temporal and eternal interests of this people, connected with them—slight as they may be—for all the earthly enjoyment the most fascinating of these could secure. Even while I cast a momentary glance at them, my better judgment tells me, and, I doubt not tells me true, that the enchantment by which they are surrounded, exists only in " *the visions of romantic youth ;*" and that any supposed addition to the happiness now in my possession, which the world could make, is but imaginary and deceitful. Little as I have ever experienced of the ills and disappointments of life, I know that were I to realize such scenes in their highest charms—of them I should be compelled at last to exclaim,

" Oh ! what, in truth, is mortal pleasure—but
The torrent's smoothness, ere it dash below !'

Monday June 23. The first humble temple for the worship of Him " *who dwelleth between the cherubims,*" ever founded beneath these dark mountains, has to-day been commenced. While we remarked the cheerfulness and animation, with which the numerous natives engaged in the work, performed their task—though it has cost them already many days of hard labour in the mountains, and will detain them still many more from their families and plantations—while we heard one and another, on every side, saying to us, as we passed, " *Ke hale a ke Akua,*" "*Ke pale pule,*" " *maitai,*" "*nui maitai.*" " The house of God," " The house of prayer ;" " good, very good;" our thoughts and our hopes hastened us through the spiritual darkness of the present time, to that period of light and gladness, " when the Lord's house shall be established on the tops of the mountains, and shall be exalted above the hills, and all nations shall flow unto it."

Evening. A sail was descried this afternoon, in the channel between Ranai and Morokai : soon afterwards, five guns fired in rapid succession, (the private signal of Riho-Riho,) announced the approach of his majesty. The brig came to an anchor just as we had finished evening worship with Keopuolani : and Mr. Richards and myself, accompanied Kekauonohi and Nahienaena to the beach, already thronged by the common people, to receive him. He landed in. a small boat with a single hief, and saluted us in a polite and friendly manner. After embracing his queen and the princess, he took one under each arm, and hastened up the beach. The parting of the mother and son, when we left Honoruru,

had interested us so much, that we felt desirous of witnessing their first interview after a month's separation.
The chiefs had assembled, and were formally seated on
their mats in a large circle, before the tent of Keopuolani, waiting the approach of their monarch. He
entered the circle opposite to his mother, and where
Wahine-pio, the sister of Karaimoku, and mother of his
youngest queen, was seated. Dropping on one knee, he
saluted her : on which she burst into tears ; and springing
from her mat, led him to that of his mother. He knelt
before her, gazed silently in her face for a moment,
then pressed her to his bosom, and placing a hand on
each cheek, kissed her twice in the most tender manner. The whole scene was quite affecting : I scarce
ever witnessed an exhibition of natural affection, where
the feelings were apparently more lively and sincere.
The king is a fine-looking man, and graceful in his
manners ; while gazing on him, the queen's heart seemed
to float in her eyes, and every feature *told a mother's joy.*

Tuesday 24.   On going to the beach as usual this
morning at sunrise, we found every indication of a scene
of revelry just ended.   Riho-Riho had taken possession
of his mother's establishment; and, instead of the
orderly and pleasant group which had uniformly before
been waiting our arrival, we saw the ground every where
strewn with the bodies of men and women, who evidently
had sunk unconsciously to sleep, amid the vapours of the
bottle.   Several empty liquor cases, of brandy, gin, and
rum, stood on a large mat in front of the tent in which
the king was sleeping ; and bottles, drained of their
contents, were dispersed widely around.

None of our former party, chiefs or people, were to be found. At eleven o'clock we repeated our visit: but all was riot and debauchery, and, not meeting with any of our pupils, we quickly turned from so melancholy a scene of licentiousness and intoxication.

At sunset we again went to the beach. The wild and heathenish sounds of the song and the dance were distinctly to be heard, long before we reached the place of our customary worship: and the tent of the king was still the centre of revelry.

On arriving near the crowd, Taua, the private chaplain of the queen, quickly approached us, saying, he had been sent to await our arrival, and to inform us, that Keopuolani would attend prayers at the residence of her daughter, to which she had removed. This was a pleasing message to us; and our satisfaction was greatly increased on entering the ranai of the princess, to find the whole of our pupils assembled—even Kekauonohi, the young queen.

Never can we forget the appearance of Keopuolani. The countenance and manner of no *pious Christian mother* could have manifested more real anguish of spirit, in witnessing the dissipation of a beloved son. As we approached, her eyes filled with tears, and, with a voice almost inarticulate from emotions ready to overpower her, she lifted her hand, and, pointing to the scene of intemperance and debauchery, exclaimed, " *Pupuka ! pupuka !*" " Shameful! oh shameful!" and throwing herself backward with a convulsive sob, hid her face and her tears in a roll of tapa, against which she was reclining.

Our hearts were deeply touched : and our spirits at once assumed an elasticity, that caused them to rise to a height proportionable to the depression under which they had laboured.   With an excitement of hope never known before, we commenced the evening sacrifice. Taua seemed to partake deeply in our feelings, and exercised a spirit of prayer that would have elevated hearts far more insensible than ours were at the time. While he affectionately presented the queen herself before the throne of God, and fervently besought the outpourings of the Holy Spirit upon her, we could scarce resist the belief, that the strong principles of moral rectitude, which she had uniformly manifested, and which were then so strikingly displayed, were but the dawnings of that light, which would securely guide her immortal spirit to the realms of everlasting day : and touched with sympathy, as for a fellow child of God, we were constrained to mingle our tears with those of the parent, while he proceeded most humbly and importunately to supplicate the forgiveness, reformation, and eternal redemption, of her son.   Before bidding her good night, she earnestly begged us to pray for the king ; and on our replying that she must also pray for him, she said she constantly did, but that they both needed our prayers.

We afterwards learned, that early in the morning, she had reproved Riho-Riho for his habits of dissipation ; warned him of the temporal and eternal consequences of them ; and, finding that he disregarded her advice, withdrew to the house of her daughter, where she was joined by the chiefs, except those he had brought with him.

Seeing how much his mother was devoted to her spelling book, and how deeply interested she was in all our instructions, the king, under the influence of his unhappy indulgences, said to her, " You study too much, it is not good ; you are old, and it is well for you to study a little only :" to which Keopuolani replied, " True, I am indeed an old woman ; soon I shall die : therefore, I must learn soon, or I shall die before I obtain the good thing that I desire." The king advised her to throw off all the restraints of our instructions, saying, " The Missionaries are not good. They do not permit us *to drink rum*, or to do any thing we formerly did. Their teachings are false and evil ; their prayers are not good ; let us return to our former customs ; let us now, as we formally did, drink a little rum together." The queen answered, " Why do you call my teachers evil ? They are good only, and great is my love for them. Good is their prayer, evil only has been ours ; all their ways are good, bad only are our own. Did you not in former times tell me that the teachers were good, and beg me to regard their instructions, and cast away the customs of our old religion ? So I have done ; and I know that I have done well. Are not the Missionaries the same, and their instructions the same . But now you disregard the new religion, and wish me to do so likewise ; but I will not. I will never forsake my teachers. I will obey their word. Come you therefore with me ; for never will I take *my dark heart again !*"

Two or three other chiefs, fond of dissipation, added their persuasions to that of the king, and said, " We have just discovered from the ' *poe haori* '—' company of

foreigners,' the thing that is right respecting the Missionaries. Part of their teachings are *true* and *good*.
It is well to attend to the *'palapala'*, reading and writing; but there is no good in the *'pule'*, religion, in the
prayers, and the preaching, and the Sabbaths. In India, we are told, they have the *palapala ;* and are so
rich, that all the people in England and America go
there for property; but they keep their stone and
wooden gods still. It will be well for us, then, to secure
the palapala, for it will make us rich; but let us cast off
the pule, it is of no use !"

From Taua, Keopuolani quickly ascertained the true
state of India, and replied : "The inhabitants of India
are still pagans. They are in the darkness of heart
which formerly was ours. If you wish, like them, to
keep your black hearts, and to be heathen, and to live
like the people of Satan, then live so, cast off the prayer
and the Sabbath ; and when you die, go and dwell with
Satan, in a world of misery : but leave me to myself,
and trouble me no longer !"

Thursday, 26. This morning Keopuolani sent word
to the king, that unless he reformed, " *he would die and
go to the fire ;*" which had such an effect, that he has
ceased to indulge to excess, and has commenced a course
of medicine—his usual practice, when his better thoughts
and resolutions gain a triumph over the power of temptation.

In passing his tent at eleven o'clock, H—— and
myself called for a moment. He was tossing on his
couch, groaning in all the horrors of a recovery from his
debauch, and scarce capable of saying, " *aroha*." Pau-

ahi, the only one of his queens who has accompanied him from Oahu, was seated, *à la turc*, on the ground with a large wooden tray in her lap. Upon this, a monstrous cuttle-fish, (*sepia octopus*, an animal of the *molusca-vermes* tribe,) had just been placed fresh from the sea, and in all its life and vigour. The queen had taken it up with both hands, and brought its body to her mouth : and by a single application of her teeth, the black juices and blood, with which it was filled, gushed over her face and neck, while the long sucking arms of the fish, in the convulsive paroxysm of the operation, were twisting and writhing about her head like the snaky hairs of a Medusa. Occupied as both hands and mouth were, she could only give us the salutation of a nod. It was the first time either of us had ever seen her majesty : and we soon took our departure, leaving her, as we found her, in the full enjoyment of the luxurious luncheon.

Friday, 27. The Cleopatra arrived this afternoon, with Tamehamaru and Kinau, and two or three hundred attendants, on board.

Monday, 30. Reached the beach this evening, just in time to witness an interesting sight, the presentation to the king of a tax levied on a district, on the windward side of the island. The procession consisted of one hundred and fifty persons, led by the headman or overseer of the district. They were all neatly dressed in new tapa, and walked in single file ; the first twenty men bearing each a baked pig or dog, ornamented with green leaves. These were followed by fifty others, bearing thirty immense calabashes of poe, twenty of which were suspended, each on a long pole, and carried by two men, and ten others on the shoulders of the same number of men. Then came females, to the number of seventy or eighty, each bearing on her shoulder a large package of tapa, or native cloth. The whole was deposited in front of the royal tent, and the company, with hundreds who followed them, seated themselves in a circle at a respectful distance, apparently with the expectation that the king would present himself.

In the course of half an hour he left his tent, and paced the large mat in front of it for fifteen or twenty minutes. He appeared with dignity, and we could not but remark the similarity of his air and whole appearance to that of persons of rank in our own country, whom we have seen exhibit themselves in the same manner, to gratify the curiosity of the populace. He took not the least notice of the throng, and conversed with us as if there had been no persons present but ourselves.

July 1. Witnessed another triumph of the respect and attachment which the chiefs feel for the *new system* over former habits of folly and dissipation. On going to prayers, found the whole court with an immense crowd of common people assembled at a dance. The collection was altogether the most numerous and noisy of any we had seen. The dancers were females, eighteen in number; the musicians, seven men. They continued to dance some minutes after we entered the circle, but when the usual period for prayers arrived, notwithstanding a manifest and most eager desire of the multitude for the continuance of the amusement, Tamehamaru beckoned to one of us to proceed to the ranai of the princess, and, taking the arm of the other, was herself the first to break up the circle, and put an end to the dance. She was immediately followed by all the principal personages, the three other queens, the king, princess, and chiefs, and by many of the natives. We seldom have so great attention as was given to the religious exercises that followed.

July 4. We were made happy by the arrival at Lahaina this morning, of our highly valued friend, Rev. Mr. Ellis. He came in a schooner with Kalakua, and is on his way to Hawaii. The other gentlemen of the deputation have gone direct from Oahu.

Having heard an infant near us cry much during the day, and, on making inquiry, learned that it was sick; after tea this evening, accompanied by the ladies, I went to see it.

The disease was one of the eye; the inside of the lids were protruded on the cheeks, and swollen to the bigness of pigeons' eggs, while they throbbed almost to bursting with inflammation. The balls of both eyes were entirely hid. This had been the condition of the child for seven days, without an application of any kind, or even the least covering to protect the irritated organ from the light and wind, or from the flies which constantly lit on the almost excoriated surface. The hut of the parents could only be entered by stooping on our hands and knees, and was too small to contain more than two of us at the same time. They had no light, nor an article of any kind necessary to be used in attending to the infant. Their all consisted of the tapas they wore, the mats they slept on, and the calabashes from which they eat and drank.

This is by no means a solitary case of suffering, that has come to our knowledge. Within three days, two other infants have been brought to our yard, in most distressing situations ; one, with a shocking wound on its arm from a cut by a broken bottle, and the other almost expiring with the croup. Both are already in a state of safety ; and probably have been rescued from death by the prompt exertions of B——, who took them immediately under her care. Indeed, we seldom walk out without meeting many, whose appearance of disease and misery is appalling, and some so remediless and disgusting, that we are compelled to close our eyes against a sight that fills us with horror. Cases of ophthalmia, scrofula, and elephantiasis, are very common.

Saturday, 5. The king and his queens, and many other chiefs, sailed for Morokai.

Monday, 7. All the public services of the Sabbath were performed by Mr. Ellis. His afternoon sermon led to a very serious and affecting conversation among the chiefs, on the subject of the eternal destiny of their ancestors and former heathen friends. The fate of the rebel chief, who fought and was slain, at the accession of the present king to the throne, in defence of idolatry and of the tabu system, was particularly adverted to. They questioned whether he could possibly be in a state of happiness, since he died in the cause of the false gods ; and also inquired whether the greater guilt of having worshipped idols was theirs, or that of their parents who had instructed them to do it. All agreed, however, in saying, that now they had received the true light, if they did not walk in it, their guilt would be much more aggravated than that of their forefathers, who had lived and died in heathen darkness.

On our way to attend public worship, we found several persons at work. Mr. Ellis inquired of one, " Whether Karaimoku had not given orders to the people, not to work on the Sabbath ?" He replied, " *He has, but I am working secretly, and Karaimoku will not find it out.*" " That may be," said Mr. Ellis, " but there is a greater than Karaimoku, the only living and true God, who always knows what you are doing; and he can punish you, though Karaimoku may not." " *Well,*" answered the man, " *he will not be angry with me for watering one bed more, and then I will stop.*" Another, who had ceased to work at a wooden bowl, after speaking to him in the morning, we found with it again as we were returning home in the evening. On speaking to him a second time, he said, " *He had been to hear us pray, and thought he might go to work again.*" We replied, No, and told him he must not work during the whole day. " *Not when the sun gets into the sea ?*" No, not till to-morrow;—on which he with much good nature said, " *Well, it is good—let it be so,*"—and put away his work.

Wednesday, 9. Mr. Ellis embarked this morning in the brig Ainoa, for Hawaii. I should have accompanied him, but for an indisposition with which I have been affected for some days, and which has disqualified me for undertaking the hardships of the tour.

Mission House at Lahaina, August 12.   I have been ill for a month past; but within the last week have so far recovered, as again to be engaged in the duties of the station.   On the 5th inst. Mr. Bingham arrived from Oahu; and on the 7th, our families removed from the plantation of Mr. Butler to the Mission Houses prepared for us by Keopuolani on the beach. Our whole accommodations, huts, furniture, and food, would compare, in rudeness and simplicity, with the meanest abode of cleanly and industrious poverty at home.   We have succeeded in procuring boards for two tables, have two whole chairs, and one with a broken back: the fourth moveable seat, making the whole number belonging to the establishment, is of our own workmanship, a three-legged stool, such as that on which

> " the immortal Alfred sat,
> And sway'd the sceptre of his infant realms."

To the same age belongs our little cabin of grass, with ground floor and unglazed windows; but the poor thatch, through which on every side we see " *the broad glare of day*," is better suited to this region of perpetual sunshine, than it would be to latitudes, where is nightly heard " the freezing blast," that " sweeps the bolted shutter."

I made these loop-holes by which you may peep in upon us, not in a spirit of complaint, for I rejoice to assure you, that days of happiness, bright as any I have ever yet known, have been spent by me on these distant shores; but that you may see, that ours is no princely establishment, in which we dwell in luxury, and lay up treasures for our children, from the charities of the church.

Tuesday, 19. Ship Mentor, Captain Newell, of Boston, from the north-west coast, touched on her way to Oahu. The Champion, Captain Preble, also of Boston, was at anchor here two or three weeks during my illness. From both we have received expressions of great kindness.

Thursday, 21. Descried a number of sail, in the early part of the day, approaching Lahaina from the leeward of Ranai; and judged them to be the *Tauai fleet*, bringing Kaahumanu and king Taumuarii, who were expected from Oahu. In the course of the afternoon three brigs and two schooners anchored in the roads. They were exceedingly crowded with people, so much so, as to have not only the decks, but the chains, bowsprit, and tops, filled; and to cause the natives, as they passed our yard, constantly to exclaim, ' *pau roa mai*" " every body has come." We soon ascertained that a large number of the chiefs, besides Kaahumanu and Taumuarii, have arrived; Karaimoku and suite, Naihi and Kapiolani, Laanui and Namahana, Auna the Tahitian chief, and his wife, &c. Auna and Laanui took tea with us; after which, accompanied by Mr. Bingham, we called on the rest. They were partaking of a profuse supper of baked meats, soups, fish, poe, ship bread, and tea; and, scattered along the beach in temporary accommodations, surrounded by hundreds of the splendid torches of the *tutui nut*, made quite an imposing appearance. Kamehamaru was seated at her writing-desk in the open air, preparing a

letter, by the light of the torches held by several servants, to be sent express to the king, now on the windward side of Maui, to inform him of the arrival of Kaahumanu and Karaimoku.   They were all in high spirits,
and seemed greatly to enjoy the meeting which had
taken place.   Prayers were made at their particular
request, with separate groups in three different places,
before we returned home.

The tutui tree, *aleurites triloba*, is very abundant on
the mountains.   Its leaves are large, of a very light
green, the under surface almost white ; and bearing
large bunches of white flowers, the contrast afforded by
it, with the dark green of other mountain growth, has
a very pretty effect, both when viewed near and at a
distance.   The nut of this tree was the principal substitute for candles among the islanders, before the introduction of oil by the whale ships.   It is nearly as
large as a Madeira nut, to which it bears some resemblance.   It is full of a rich oil ; and after being slightly
baked, is formed into torches by stringing thirty or forty
nuts together on a rush ; and enclosing four or five of
these strings m the leaves of the ti or hala.   After
being lighted, before one nut is consumed, the flame
communicates to the oil of that next below ; as the flame
expires, the shell of the exhausted nut is struck off, till
the whole is consumed.

Sabbath, 24.   Thinking it a favourable opportunity
for opening the chapel, while Mr. Bingham and so many
of the chiefs are with us, we had the house prepared
yesterday, and gave notice that the public services of
the Sabbath would be held in it.   Mr. Bingham accord-

ingly preached a dedicatory sermon ; text, " *This is none other but the house of God, and this is the gate of heaven.*" Seldom have we seen any house filled with a more crowded and attentive audience. The chiefs appeared greatly interested in the sermon and exercises. May it prove the birth-place of many souls ; and an entrance to heaven, through which multitudes shall be added to the ransomed of the Lord !

CHAPTER IX.

Mission House, Lahaina, Sept. 2, 1823.   The queen
Keopuolani has been unwell for some days.   It is a
custom among the chiefs to assemble at any place,
where one of their number of much importance is ill;
the least indisposition of a very high chief will thus call
the "*poe ke Arii*," or company of chiefs, together.
The illness of Keopuolani, though not supposed serious,
has occasioned despatches to be sent by several native
vessels, for the high chiefs on all the different islands.

Thursday, 4.   When we rose this morning, three
vessels, two schooners, and a brig, were approaching
Lahaina.   Just after breakfast, one of the schooners
came to anchor, and brought to us Mr. Ellis, on his
return from the tour of Hawaii.   The deputation have
had a most interesting, but fatiguing journey; and a
slight glance at the journal and drawings of Mr. Ellis,
makes me regret more than ever the necessity that denied me the pleasure of accompanying him.   The rest
of the gentlemen have gone directly to Honoruru in the

brig Becket. The other vessels were the Waverley and the Waterwitch, from Oahu, bringing the chiefs sent for by Keopuolani.

Shortly after these had landed, I went to the residence of the queen, and witnessed one of the most striking peculiarities in the customs of the islanders, that of *wailing.* There were not less than fifty chiefs around the couch of the queen, and twice that number of their attendants, all weeping aloud with an apparent sincerity and depth of feeling that could not be witnessed, considering the present occasion of it, without exciting sympathy in the spectator. The young Kahalaia, a nephew of the late king, was the only one of the number just arrived, who entered the house after I did. He is one of the most stern and forbidding of the chiefs, but the general inflexibility of his character seemed to give way at the scene; and after kneeling and saluting the sufferer respectfully and tenderly, he struggled for a moment with a convulsive emotion, and then " *lifted up his voice,*" and wept in a manner that would have touched any heart.

To us these wailings appear extremely barbarous, though I doubt not they are precisely the expressions of sorrow made by the most refined and polished of the ancients; and I never witness them without being reminded of the mournings of the people of Israel, as spoken of in the Scriptures. Shortly after I reached the house, Mr. Bingham and Mr. Ellis came in, when Karaimoku immediately commanded silence, and requested that prayers might be made. I was affected with the propriety of the proposal, and have scarce ever before felt more interest in a hymn and prayer with the natives, than in those which immediately followed.

While at dinner, Mr. Hunnewell, the first mate of the Thaddeus, when she brought out the pioneers of the Mission, and who has resided on the islands as a commercial agent ever since, came in quite ill; he is an amiable and respectable young man, and has become justly dear to the Mission, from his unwavering friendship in the midst of much opposition. We were happy to have it in our power to secure to him a quiet room and bed, which he so greatly needed.

Saturday, 6. The Waterwitch, commanded by Mr. Hunnewell, left us for Oahu, to bring up Boki, on account of the increased illness of the queen. For the same reason, the barge has sailed for Kairua, to bring governor Adams.

Monday, 8. The exercises in the chapel yesterday morning were performed by Auna, the Tahitian chief, an assistant Missionary to Mr. Ellis. He is a noble-looking man, a graceful speaker, and an enlightened and zealous Christian. In the afternoon I preached through Honorii, as interpreter. This morning the Ainoa, a native brig, arrived from Hawaii, bringing Mr. Harwood, a young American, who has resided some time with the Mission family at Honoruru, and who accompanied the deputation on their tour through Hawaii.

Tuesday night. We were so much exposed to depredations by theft, that the queen some time since appointed a trusty servant to take charge of our yard, as keeper and guard of the articles necessarily in daily use. This evening, while at tea, we were alarmed by the hasty entrance of this man, exclaiming, " *ua make roa Keopuolani*," " Keopuolani is dead :" after interrogating him, however, we found that she was only more ill, and would soon die. Mrs. Richards, H——, and myself, immediately hastened down, though dark and late. We found the house, which is very large, crowded with the chiefs, who had assembled from all their different abodes, and were seated in silence and sadness, as near the queen as they could press. Her couch was surrounded by Hoapiri her husband, the king and favourite queen, prince and princesses, king Taumuarii, Kaahumanu, and Karaimoku.

Many of these were bathed in tears. The queen seemed very feeble, and could scarce speak. She reached her hand to the ladies, however, whispering an affectionate " *aroha*," adding, " *maitai, maitai,*" " good, good," in expression of gratitude for their coming out at night to see her. But what most delighted us was, the low, but expressive sentences which immediately followed, while she continued still to press their hands, " *Make make au i ke Akua*," " I love God ;" and shortly again, " *Aroha ino iau i ke Akua*," " Great indeed is my love to God !" She was too feeble to say more, but seemed in a state of mind to give much stronger testimony to the excellency and power, even in death, of the religion we had brought to her.

The cause of the sudden gloom and alarm, was not any very material change in Keopuolani, but the opinion of Mr. Law, the king's surgeon, that she could not recover ; and the declaration that he could be of no further use to her. The king asked me whether it would not be well for him to despatch a vessel immediately to Oahu, for Dr. Blatchely, of the Mission, to which I answered in the affirmative, being myself unwilling that any means of saving so valuable a life should remain untried. A pilot boat sailed, in a few minutes, with Honorii, as the king's messenger, to bring Dr. Blatchely.

Wednesday morning, 10. At 12 o'clock last night I was awakened by the young Kahalaia, with a message from Karaimoku—that the queen was worse, and they wished me to come down. I found the whole company much agitated; and although Keopuolani had recovered from the spasm which caused them to send for me, I remained till daybreak with her. She had two or three attacks, which I thought she could not survive. She bears her sufferings with much fortitude and patience, however; scarce a sigh escaping her lips, while all around her are drowned in tears.

The chiefs are most assiduous and indefatigable in their attentions. None of them left her, or slept for a moment, during the night; even the little prince and princess never closed their eyes. The kindness and attention of Kamehamaru is particularly observable; she watches every look and motion, and anticipates every wish. I have scarce ever had my feelings of sympathy more deeply touched than on seeing her and the king, and Hoapiri, bending over the queen whenever she appeared to be in peculiar agony—their strong desire, yet inability, of rendering her any relief, was deeply expressed in their looks, and manifested itself in renewed bursts of tears.

It was a profitable night to my own mind—every thing was calculated to confirm me in the importance of being prepared to meet and struggle with the king of terrors. I thought of the sufferings the Son of God endured for the salvation of sinners ; and the lively view of them, connected with their necessity and their end, caused me to mingle my tears with those that were flowing from all around me : and my prayer was not only that this gentile, lately made acquainted with the knowledge of God, but that I also, nurtured and brought up in the admonition of the Lord, might be saved.

Thursday, 11. Yesterday and to-day the surf has been excessively heavy, and often by its beauty and sublimity has attracted our attention and admiration. But the dark wing of death has been over it, and its loveliness for a time is shrouded in gloom. At eleven o'clock this morning the long-boat of the brig Ainoa was overturned in attempting to land by the usual passage, and four white men narrowly escaped drowning, while a fifth sunk to rise no more alive. The report flying among the natives, *Ka haori make roa i ka nalue,* " The foreigner is dead in the surf," collected a number of foreigners on the beach, by whom exertions were made to restore him to life, but without success. The spirit had fled through the foaming surges to the world of retribution ! Mr. Butler humanely had the corpse removed to his enclosure ; from whence in the evening, attended by most of the foreigners then at Lahaina, we bore it to a more decent grave, than is the last abode of many an inhabitant of Christian lands, whose destiny it is to die among the heathen.

Friday 12. The pilot boat New York arrived at noon, with Dr. Blatchely and Mr. Richards; the surf is still very high and dangerous, but they landed safely about two o'clock. Dr. Blatchely thinks the queen will not recover.

Governor Adams not having arrived, two additional vessels have been despatched for him.

Monday 15. At midnight a messenger came for Dr. Blatchely to visit the queen. I accompanied him to see her. She was very ill, but the fear of God seemed to predominate over every other feeling. When a little wine and water and arrowroot were recommended to her, she desired that Auna, the Tahitian, might be called to speak " *the good word, and to make a prayer.*" After she had taken the refreshment, she appeared more easy, and Auna, in compliance with her request, at the suggestion of the king, proceeded to address Keopuolani and those present on the subject of religion. He continued his remarks for half an hour, and concluded with a most spiritual and fervent prayer. This converted pagan is a correct and stable Christian : he was long a deacon in a church in his native island; and, I have no doubt, has been instrumental, under the blessing of God, of enlightening the mind of this dying chief unto salvation, through faith in Jesus Christ.

It was a profitable hour to my own spirit, though I could understand but little of what was said. I knew the subject, however, and saw that every word, and every look, and every gesture, sprung from an eloquence of soul, that originated only in a lively sense of the reality and importance of the things of eternity.

Tuesday 16.   This has been an interesting and memorable day.   Last night the Paragon, Captain Coles, of Boston, from Oahu, anchored among the vessels now here.   Mr. Hays, captain's clerk, landed at eleven o'clock, and informed us that Mr. and Mrs. Ellis and Mr. Ruggles were on board.   They came on shore at eight o'clock this morning, and called immediately on the queen ; but finding her in a deep sleep, passed on to the Mission House.

The arrival of Mr. Ellis was most opportune.   The dying hour of our kind patroness and friend was evidently fast approaching ; and "hoping" as we do " in her death," we were anxious that some words might be drawn from her in conversation, that would prove an encouragement to our hearts, and a blessing to the immortals, who with the deepest interest hung round her dying couch.   After an hour, Mr. Ellis and myself again called to see her.   She was still asleep.   The king, Kaahumanu, and Karaimoku, immediately and urgently requested that she might be *baptized;* saying, that it was her earnest and special desire, and that she had only that morning begged " *to be washed with water, in the name of God."* The king told Mr. Ellis, they did not wish her to be baptized, because they thought she could not be saved without it ; but because she was a Christian, had the true faith in her heart, had given herself to Jesus Christ long before she was sick, and because all the people of God were baptized, and she had herself so earnestly requested it.   Mr. Ellis told them he would consult Mr. Richards and myself on the subject, and when she awoke, would converse with and baptize her.

The certainty of her death had spread universal alarm among the people. She was known to be the highest chief on the islands; and, according to former and immemorial customs, the death of such has ever been attended with all kinds of extravagance, violence, and abomination. On such an occasion, every restraint was cast off, and all were in the habit of following the impulse of any and every wild passion that might seize them. Rights of persons or of property were no longer regarded : and he who had the greatest muscular powers, committed whatever depredation he chose, and injured any one he thought proper. Even the chiefs lost their ordinary pre-eminence, and could exert no influence of restraint on the excesses of their subjects. It was the time of redressing private wrongs, by committing violence on the property and person of an enemy; and every thing that any one possessed was liable to be taken from him. Their grief was expressed by the most shocking personal outrages. Not only by tearing off their clothes entirely, but by knocking out their eyes and teeth with clubs and stones, and pulling out their hair, and by burning and cutting their flesh ; while drunkenness, riot, and every species of debauchery, continued to be indulged in, for days after the death of the deceased.

Reports of these usages, and intimations of the danger to which we should be exposed from them, were brought to us from every quarter, both by foreigners and natives. We felt very little apprehension, however; for we were confident, that ourselves and families would be inviolate, however great the excesses among the natives might be.

About four o'clock, while on the way with Mr. Ellis and Dr. Blatchely, a third time to the queen's residence, I met Mr. Jones the consul, who arrived this morning in the Paragon, with one or two other gentlemen, and returned with them to the Mission House. The conversation soon turned on the anticipated scenes of violence; the gentlemen seemed fully persuaded that there was great cause for apprehension, and were just offering their boats and ship, as a refuge for the ladies in case of extremity, when Richard Karaioula rushed in, in breathless terror, exclaiming, " *The queen is dead !*" We immediately snatched our hats, and were involuntarily hastening down the beach, when, observing the natives flying by hundreds in every direction, through fish-ponds and taro patches, over walls and fences, apparently in a state of half distraction, bearing with them calabashes, tapas, and whatever of their property they had caught up in their flight; while the whole heavens rung with lamentations and woe; I returned without delay to our enclosure, fearing an alarm to the females, who were alone.

In about fifteen minutes, Mr. Ruggles came up, confirming the statement of her death, and adding that great excesses had already commenced. In about fifteen minutes more, while the confusion and alarm seemed every where to increase, Mr. Ellis came running to the house, with the information that she was not dead—had only fainted—had revived again— and that the chiefs were importuning him, in the

s

strongest terms, to baptize her immediately. We all went down. The orders of the king and Karaimoku had restored quietnesss, to a degree; and we found our friend so far revived, as to breathe regularly, and yet not so much so, as to speak intelligibly. An interested and interesting group of foreigners, missionaries, and merchants, and chiefs, near relatives and friends, surrounded the dying pillow, and waited a few moments, hoping that the fluttering spirit might still be roused entirely from its lethargy, ere it quitted its earthly tenement for ever. But there being little prospect of this, Mr. Ellis proceeded at length to administer the sacred ordinance, which entitles all who receive it to the name of Christian. It was a solemn moment, and an awful place; and our prayer was, that it might be none other than "the house of God and the gate of heaven," to the immortal soul, hovering on the borders of eternity.

Thus the highest chief of the Sandwich Islands, after having given satisfactory evidence of a renewed heart, and of sincere love to Jesus Christ, was initiated into the visible church of God: and as we hope and believe, in the course of an hour after, joined the invisible church above, having triumphed over the power of death and the grave.

It is not without good, and abundant reason, that we entertain this belief. It is but a year since Keopuolani began to manifest much interest in the object of the Missionaries, or to pay much attention to their instructions: but since that time, the evidences that her heart was deeply touched by the power of grace,

have been decisive, and in many instances truly affecting. The rejection of every practice which she discovered to be inconsistent with the principles of Christianity, an irreproachable external deportment, a
cheerful and rigid compliance with every observance
of our religion, the habit of constant secret prayer, of
regular family worship with her household, and strong
attachment to the services of the day of God, her proclamations among the people against their former
vices, and her rebuke of sin when detected ; all confirmed us in a belief of the sincerity of her attachment to Christianity, expressed in her daily conversations.

For months, at least, the predominating thoughts
and feelings of her mind and heart appear to have
been those connected with the eternal destiny of the
soul. Long before coming to Lahaina, she said to
Taua, her private chaplain, when conversing with him
on the subject of religion : " Great is the fear of my
heart, that I shall never become one of the people of
Jesus Christ : I have followed the customs of my
country, and have been of the company of dark hearts ;
my thought is, that I shall soon die : and great is my
sorrow, that the teachers of the good way did not
come to us in the days of our childhood !" And,
afterwards—" I know their word to be true; good
indeed is the word of God; and now I have found a
Saviour and a good King, Jesus Christ, the Lord."

We have been informed by Taua, that since her
establishment at Lahaina, messengers have arrived for
him at mid-night, to come and pray for her. On

going to her residence, he has found her, with a few attendants, waiting his arrival: as he entered, she on one occasion said, " I am sorry to call you from your rest; but my thoughts are upon God, and I cannot sleep. I am old, soon I shall die, and great is my fear that I shall not know enough of the right way to go to heaven. Speak to me of the good word of God, that my dark mind may be enlightened." And he has thus spent hours, in conversing and praying with her and her immediate attendants, while all the rest of Lahaina has been wrapt in sleep.

After praying with her, at one time, she said, " Now tell me something of Jesus." In complying with this request, he made choice of the last scene in our Saviour's life, the trial before Pilate, the condemnation, and crucifixion. He spoke of the scourging and crowning with thorns, and of the leading away to execution ; but when he came to describe the nailing of Jesus by the hands and feet to the cross, she burst into tears, and exclaimed, " Oh ! stop; I can hear no more: I and all my people, like the murderers of Jesus, are wicked and cruel !"

As I approached the grove in which she resided, to attend the customary worship, one morning, she was seated on her sofa, with one of her hands pressed upon her bosom, apparently absorbed in deep and painful thought. On arriving near, I heard her voice in an under tone, and caught the words, " *Te ahi! Te ahi aore pio! Te ahi a a roa!*"—"Fire; inextinguishable fire; everlasting fire !"—to which were added the exclamations, " Oh the sorrows of the wicked! They will cry for water, O yes they will cry for water! but there will be none: no, none at all; not even a drop for the end of their tongues!" A train of thought, which, as I afterwards discovered, had been induced by meditations on the darkness of her own life, and fears of the just punishment of sin.

From the time her illness assumed an alarming aspect, she was unceasing, so far as her strength allowed, in her Christian counsels and exhortations to the chiefs, individually and collectively. When Karaimoku arrived from Oahu, she said to him, "Great is the love of my heart for the good word of God, by which my mind has been enlightened. The word of God is true; it is a good word, and Jehovah is a God of goodness. Great is my love for him; great is my love for Jesus Christ, his Son. I have no desire for the former gods of Hawaii: they are false. My desire is unto Jesus Christ: and I have given myself unto him. My thoughts are much upon my grandfather Taraiopu, my father Kauikeaouli, and my husband Tamehameha, they lived not to see these good times, and to hear of the salvation of Jesus Christ. They knew not Jehovah, the true God. They died trusting to the false gods. I exceedingly mourn and lament, that they saw not these good times of salvation! Do not you neglect to pray to God; cease not to regard the Sabbath; commit no sin; and love Jesus Christ,—that we two may meet in heaven."

Her conversations with other chiefs of rank were of a similar character. She addressed the king in the following manner: "I am now about to die; I shall soon leave my children and my people, and these lands; and I wish now to give you my last charge."— and after recommending to him a mild and kind government of his subjects, added:—"Protect the Missionaries, and treat them kindly. Walk in the straight path which they point out to you. Regard the Sabbath. Serve God, love Jesus Christ, and attend to all the good word; follow not the example of the evil, when your mother is gone, but follow that of the good, that we may meet in heaven."

She expressed great solicitude for the prince and princess; and repeatedly commended them to the care of the chiefs, especially in reference to their morals, and to the instructions of the Mission.

This morning, before she fell into the stupor, Auna and Taua approached her couch, and asked what her thoughts then were. She replied, "I remember the word of my teachers. I pray greatly to Jesus Christ to receive me. I am about to die; but it is not dark now, as it would have been, had I died in former days. Pray for me; let all the Missionaries pray for me. Great is my love to them, great is my love to you. My thought is, that I love Jesus Christ, and that he will receive me to his right hand. Great is my desire to be washed with water, in the name of God, before I die. I have given myself to Jesus Christ. I am his; and I wish to be like his people!"

Mr. Ruggles informed us, that when a son of Taumuarii died at Tauai, the Missionary houses were guarded by sixty armed men, till after the burial of

Roberts. del.

J.Hinchliff. sculp.

Lamentation on the Death of Queen Keopuolani.

Published by Fisher, Son & Cº Caxton. London. April. 1828.

the body; and suggested the propriety of requesting a guard on the present occasion. Mr. Ellis accordingly spoke to Karaimoku on the subject. He answered, that there was not the least necessity for it, that we need not entertain any apprehension whatever, that Keopuolani had long before forbidden every heathen practice at her death; and that the people had received the strictest orders against all their former customs, except *wailing*.

Wednesday, 17. At nine o'clock last night, we went to hold prayers with the mourners. Instead of the anticipated confusion and riot, we found all still and orderly along the beach; except here and there a group, and a very large assemblage near the residence of the queen, who lifted up their voices, and wept aloud. All that we saw excited our sympathy, rather than any horror or disgust. The nearest relations were still beside the corpse, and presented an affecting spectacle; especially the little prince and princess, who appeared entirely inconsolable. Hoapiri, with one of these in each arm, pressed me also to his bosom, exclaiming: " Keopuolani, our friend, is gone to heaven; and we, alas, are left alone."

Prayers were held with them this morning also; when the royal family, for the first time, made their appearance before the multitude collected round the house of death. They were greeted with the loudest expressions of grief; and, though unaccompanied with personal violence, the scene was really frightful. I could plainly see how the enthusiasm, to which the people wrought themselves, might be heightened to a frenzy, that would know no law. The king and Karaimoku were convulsed with weeping, but did not, like the rest of the family, *wail after the manner of the heathen.*

During the whole day, while preparations for the funeral were making, every thing exhibited signs of woe. The whole district sent forth one uninterrupted sound of lamentation : while large companies, from distant settlements, were covering the beach in sad procession, and rending the heavens with their cries. Minute guns have been fired since daybreak, and all the vessels at anchor, fifteen in number, have their yards canted, and wear their colours at half-mast.

Many things that I have witnessed, have again called to mind the ancient customs of the Jews in times of affliction, not only the *" lifting up of the voice,"* and weeping aloud, but *" the rending of the garment"*—*" the clothing in sackcloth,"* *" and sitting in dust and ashes :"* here all disfigure themselves by the coarsest, and most ragged and filthy attire, of old mats and tapa ; while, in many cases, their heads are covered with dust and sand.

On meeting any high chief, they prostrate themselves on the ground, and redouble every expression of grief. I never witnessed such a scene as took place on the arrival of governor Adams, this afternoon : especially when the high chiefs and mourners came from the house in which the corpse lay, to meet him. I was near the governor at the time, surrounded by not less than five thousand of the natives, who seemed to become absolutely frantic, and ready to fall into any act of desperation that might cross their minds. Their wailings were indescribable, to one not present; and the noise so overwhelming, that the minute guns could scarce be heard through the din.

The word which they pronounce in wailing is " *auwe*" — " *auwe*" — " alas! alas!"—prolonging the sound of the last syllable, sometimes, for many minutes, with a trembling and agitated shaking of the voice. The tones in which it is uttered by different persons, vary from the lowest to the highest key,— and from that which is most plaintive, to that which is most shrill. There being no uniformity in the time of beginning or ending the word, the confusion and discord thus created is terrific. The attitudes of figure are as various as the tones of voice. Some stand upright, casting their arms and faces towards heaven, with the eyes closed, and mouth widely distended. Others, instead of throwing their arms upwards, clasp their hands, and place them behind their heads. Some bend forward their faces almost to the ground, and, with their hands braced against their knees, or violently pressed into their sides, as if in excruciating internal agony;—others clench their hands into the hair on each side of their heads, as if to tear it out by the roots: and all seem to emulate one another, in attempts at the most hideous grimaces and painful distortions, while torrents of tears flow from their heads to their feet.

The governor and chiefs, after approaching within eight or ten yards of each other, stood at least fifteen minutes wailing in this manner with the multitude around them, before they embraced, and entered the house.

Thursday, 18.   Every thing being in readiness for the funeral of our departed friend, she was, at two o'clock to-day, deposited in a substantial mud-and-stone house, lately built by the princess.   This is the first Christian funeral of a high chief that has ever taken place in the islands; and will probably be a precedent for all future burials among the heads of the nation. How different the rites of her sepulture from those of her fathers!   They, since time unknown, have been dissected in secret by their nearest friends; their flesh has been burned, and cast into the sea, with many idolatrous observances; and their bones carefully preserved and worshipped, while she calmly awaits the resurrection in the decent habiliments of a Christian's tomb.   So anxious was Keopuolani on this subject, that, when in perfect health, she charged the king to allow of none of the former practices, at her death; stating, that *they* all belonged to the time " of dark hearts"—that she had lived to see the light—had cast off all their former customs—had surrendered herself to Jesus Christ—and wished her body to be given to his people—the Missionaries—to be buried according to their direction, and wherever they might think best.

In consequence of this charge, Mr. Ellis had the arrangement of the funeral, which was conducted with the greatest order and propriety.   The concourse of people was very great, amounting to many thousands; but there was no greater irregularity or disturbance than there would have been among the same number in a

Christian land, on a similar occasion. The bell rang at twelve o'clock for the commencement of the religious exercises, which were held in the grove of trees near the queen's residence, the chapel being too small even for the chiefs.—We all attended in mourning; and after a hymn, prayer, and sermon, by Mr. Ellis, the procession, led by the American consul, was formed. The Mission family walked next to the foreigners, who, to the number of thirty or forty, followed Mr. Jones. Next came the household attendants and favourite servants of Keo-'puolani, headed by her own steward and that of her daughter—then the corpse, covered with a rich pall, the bearers of which were the five queens of Riho-Riho, and the wife of Boki—a daughter of Hoapiri—each carrying a beautiful black *kahile*—then the nearest relatives and highest chiefs, and a procession of at least six or seven hundred persons, principally chiefs of various ranks, with their favourites and friends.

All in the procession were dressed in the European style, and generally in black, with appropriate badges of mourning. Among the attendants of the chiefs, there were a few scarlet and yellow feather mantles and capes; and a considerable company of females dressed as it were in uniform, having scarlet *paus* trimmed with black, and black shawls followed in the rear of the procession. The bell tolled, and minute guns continued to be fired, till the body was deposited in the place appointed for it. The relatives and high chiefs encamped immediately around the house, and are now busily engaged in erecting temporary booths; designing to live near the body for some time to come.

It is a great joy to us, to have the dust of one so justly dear committed thus decently and honourably to the tomb. Such a funeral—one that would have appeared respectable even in a Christian country—is a great triumph over the deep-rooted superstitions and abominations of this nation on such occasions; and deserves to be recorded as a remarkable epoch in this Mission. I am persuaded it has given a death-blow, among the chiefs, to their former burial rites and ceremonies. It is viewed in this light both by natives and foreigners, inimical to the influence of the Mission. Such have openly spoken of it as a *triumph*, which they would most gladly have defeated, and which has roused much of their hatred and abuse. Some of the chiefs most favourable to the innovation, have suffered much ridicule and sarcasm for abandoning the customs of their fathers, and adopting the ceremonies of foreign nations. One, who is of a character to exult in the riot and debauchery of former times, and who looks on the restraints of civilization and piety with a malicious jealousy, ever since the death of the queen has addressed a serious and dignified compeer, either in ignorant or wilful blasphemy, by the word "Jehovah." Such, however, is far from being the feeling of any one of much consequence or authority; and only to-day, after the crowd had dispersed, Karaimoku was heard to say, as he took his seat by the king—" What fools we have been, to burn our dead, and cast them into the sea; when we might thus have committed their bodies to the tomb, and have had the satisfaction of still dwelling near them.'

Sabbath, 21. Mr. and Mrs. Ellis, Mr. Ruggles, and Dr. Blatchely, with all the Tahitian and most of the Hawaiian church members, being at Lahaina, we felt desirous of improving their visit by the celebration of the Lord's Supper. Accordingly that ordinance was observed to-day; we were happy to have so large a number to join us in exhibiting, for the first time on the island of Maui, the symbols of that " broken body" and " shed blood," through which only there is remission of sin and acceptance with God. The house was crowded, many of the chiefs and natives being present, besides a considerable number of our own countrymen, who, though born and brought up " under the droppings of the sanctuary," still, during the solemn feast, stood afar off " *in the court of the gentiles*," thus confessing that they had no better " part nor lot in this matter" than the heathen by whom they were surrounded. If ever I have felt pain of heart since I came to these islands, it has been in seeing those who are comparatively " the children of light," sojourning of choice in Mesech, and dwelling at ease in these tents of Kedar, " having no hope, and without God in the world."

Wednesday, 24. The whole district, men, women, and children, to the number of some thousands, have been daily engaged this week in carrying stones from the old *heiau*, or idolatrous temple, on the south point, to the place where Keopuolani is buried, to build a wall and monument around the house in which she is deposited : headed and assisted by their chiefs, male and female, of every rank, they have engaged in the work with much spirit, and pass and repass our door in troops

T

of a hundred and more at a time, singing their rude songs with as much merriment, as with bitterness last week they seemed to wail.

In their feelings they are like children, subject to sudden and violent excitements, and easily diverted by an opposite cause to a corresponding extreme, whether of grief or joy. The nearest relatives of the queen, except her husband and the king, Kaahumanu, and Taumuarii, are engaged in this servile work, and themselves each erect her monument, with as much merriment as they would form a festal bower. They are all followed by their *kahiles ;* and I have smiled more than once to see a queen or royal princess carrying a large stone,* while a stout man, behind her, has borne nothing but a light feathered staff, to proclaim the dignity of his mistress.

Ten o'clock, P. M. Scarce ever were my feelings more deeply wounded, than they have been this evening. During the fortnight of Keopuolani's illness, the king was perfectly sober. His heart seemed touched by the exhortations of his mother, and open to the persuasions of the Missionaries, to forsake every evil habit, and seek the favour of God. His sensibilities were greatly excited by her baptism, death, and burial ; and he resolved to abandon the habit of intemperate drinking. Apprized of this, some of the foreigners, here at present, determined to achieve a triumph over the Mission, as they consider it, by the defeat of an object so desirable and so important.

* The high chiefs engage personally in work of this kind, to evince their respect for the deceased, and to encourage their people in the labour.

With this view, two or three successive dinner parties were made by them, one on the Sabbath, which Riho-Riho was importunately urged to attend; but anticipating the design, he perseveringly declined. Other attempts were made to draw him into their company, but all proved unsuccessful till this morning, when he was induced to visit one of the ships, under the pretence, on the part of his seducers, as we are informed, of shewing some remarkably beautiful specimens of goods. After being some time on board, refreshments of various kinds, and liquors, were served; but of the last, the king refused to partake. A bottle of choice cherry brandy was then produced, as a liqueur incapable of intoxicating, and which having never seen before, he was led to taste, and to taste again, till he requested a bottle of it to take on shore: a favour quickly granted. The result has been, that, as Mr. Ellis and myself went down the beach at sunset, we saw the king seated in front of his tent under the full excitement of liquor; Pauahi, in a disgusting state of drunkenness, by his side; a woman in a similar condition, and almost naked, dancing and singing before them; and twenty or thirty others, of both sexes, with cases of gin and rum at hand, beginning a dreadful revel.

As we approached the circle, Riho-Riho immediately said to us, in a kind, but self-condemning tone, " *Why do you come here ?*" To which Mr. Ellis replied, " We have come to express our sorrow for the sad condition you are in, and to reprove these, your guilty people, for encouraging you to destroy yourself, both body and soul :" upon which he dismissed us with the answer

" You are good men, you are my friends, but, *eia no ke wahi o Debelo* ! this is the place of the devil ! and it is well for you not to stay here !" The individual, who has been thus successful in his end, has since boasted, not only that he has made the king drunk, but that he *will keep him so,* if he is obliged to send a vessel to Oahu expressly for more cherry brandy for the purpose !

But the sorrow of the evening did not rest here. At the request of the chiefs, we have attended prayers with them, at the establishment of Kaahumanu, every evening about eight o'clock. On going down for this purpose to-night, we saw a considerable collection of persons gathered round Governor Adams, as he was seated in the open air, surrounded by servants with torches. The bright glare of these presented the party in strong light to us, while we ourselves were shrouded by it in double darkness. In front of the governor was one foreigner upon his knees, making a *mimic prayer,* in imitation of a Missionary ; while another was writing, in large letters on a slate, and presenting to him for perusal, some of the basest words in our language ! As may be supposed, the recognition of our presence threw the company into some confusion ; and one person hastily brushed his hand over the slate, but not till the indignant eye of Mr. Ellis fully told a knowledge of its disgusting contents !

Friday, 26. Since the exposures at night, which I underwent during the sickness of Keopuolani, I have been considerably indisposed. A change of air may be beneficial, and as there is much important and

interesting business before the Mission at Honoruru,
I have been persuaded to accompany Mr. Ruggles
and Mr. Hunnewell, this afternoon, to Oahu, in the
Waterwitch.

Tuesday, Oct. 28. I sailed for Oahu on the expected evening, now more than a month ago, and
after a passage of nine hours, was at the mouth of
the harbour of Honoruru, which we entered at sunrise.
No opportunity to return occurred till last Saturday,
when the young prince came up with about seventy of
of his attendants, in a small pilot boat. I never suffered more than on this passage of forty-eight hours,
being exposed during the night to very heavy rains,
and during the day to a burning sun, from which I
could find no retreat. I did not leave the deck for a
moment; for though a part of the small cabin and a
birth were assigned to me, and reserved for my use
during the whole time, the heat and crowd below
were so intolerable, that I preferred lying in the rain
and water on deck, to enduring them, even when the
showers were most heavy and sun most powerful.
At five o'clock last evening, the captain of a whale
ship, recruiting here, kindly took me in his boat, from
the schooner, before she had come to anchor, and
brought me to my rustic, but neat and happy cabin.

Nothing of particular moment occurred while I was
at Oahu. It is the season at which the whale ships
recruit at the islands, on their way from Japan to the
American coast, and I had the pleasure of seeing the
captains and officers of nearly thirty ships in that
business. The harbour looked quite like a busy port;

besides the whale ships, there were several merchant-men there, some discharging their cargoes, just arrived from Canton, others from the North-west Coast, and from the United States; some taking in sandal wood for China, while others, hove down, were stopping leaks, &c. two small vessels also were on the stocks, building, to sell to the government.

The distribution of the Missionaries to their several stations took place before I returned, and arrangements were happily made for occupying two new stations—Kairua and Waiakea—on the island of Hawaii.

Mr. and Mrs. Thurston sailed from Oahu the evening before I did, for Kairua: the brig in which they were, anchored here during the night; and we had the happiness of receiving and welcoming them at our establishment to breakfast this morning, after the *severe trial*, of a voyage of four days in a dirty crowded native vessel; *trial*, I say, for I have known none equal to that of the voyage I last made, since I have been a Missionary: a gale in the Gulf-stream, or passage round Cape Horn, in a decent vessel, in point of comfort and enjoyment, is not to be compared with it.

The most important event at Lahaina, during my absence, was the marriage of our friend Hoapiri, the husband of Keopuolani, to Kalakua, one of the *queens-dowager*, mother of Tamehamaru, the favourite wife of Riho-Riho. I received the information of it in a letter before I left Oahu, in which it is said, " Hoapiri was this day joined in *holy wedlock* to Kalakua; they were married in the chapel by Mr. Richards. A large audience attended: the ceremony was solemn, and would have honoured any land." This is a most happy innovation on the former habits of the people; it is the first Christian marriage ever known among the chiefs, and the second ever solemnized at the islands. Like the funeral of our late patroness, it will stand as a precedent, which I doubt not all friendly to the Mission will readily acknowledge, and be anxious to imitate.

Polygamy is an evil that will probably be among the last eradicated from the nation; but whatever has the least tendency towards its abolition, is desirable and gratifying. Had Hoapiri followed the ordinary custom on such occasions, immediately after the burial of Keopuolani, or even before, he would have taken one, two, or more wives, without any form or ceremony; and, in fact, she was scarce deposited in her tomb, before there were five candidates for his hand, from among the highest females in the nation, he being one of the most wealthy and respectable of the chiefs. But he at once declared, that he designed to follow the practice among Christians, of deferring his marriage for some time, and then taking one wife only, being married to her publicly in the house of God. This was also the wish of Karaimoku, which of course was earnestly recommended by the Mission, and has happily been accomplished. Both parties were fully instructed, by Mr. Richards, in the reciprocal obligations of the marriage contract, as understood and entered into by the members of Christian churches.

Thus, my dear M——, are we enabled to take courage in our labour of enlightening and christianizing this people ; hoping for a bright day of glory, and rejoicing even in this, " *the day of small things.*"

Six or eight ships have touched here for refreshments, and two yet remain. Many of the officers and men were kind in their attentions to the Mission family ; and some of them appeared to be of the number who love and serve God. It is a joy indeed, to meet, in this land of pollution and sin, those who exhibit the light, the purity, the blessedness of the Christian character. O that every wanderer " *o'er the mountain wave,*" and every " *dweller on the deep,*" might speedily become a light and a blessing to the dark places of the earth.

Monday, Nov. 30. Mr. and Mrs. Thurston remained with us one week, and then left us in fine spirits, to take their station, and unfurl the banner of the cross on the rocky shores of Hawaii. I admired the spirit with which Mrs. Thurston, after bidding us farewell, sprang into a rude canoe with her two children ; and I watched them with a glass with lively interest, as they were paddled through the breakers to the open sea. No preparation appearing to have been made on board the brig, to hoist her on deck in a chair, which is usually done ; she intrepidly mounted the ship's quarter by the manropes, and stood ready to wave us a distant farewell, before many others of the same refinement could have determined even to attempt ascending to the quarter-deck as she had done.

A few days afterwards, the brig Arab, Captain Meek,

of Boston, from Oahu, paid us a visit of a day, and then passed on to Kairua, where the king had gone in the Princess Mary, an English whale ship. The Arab returned in about a week, bringing Riho-Riho and his train, when it first began to be stated that he would speedily embark for Great Britain. In a few days a grand council of the chiefs was called at this place on .e subject; when we had the pleasure of again entertaining our beloved friends Messrs. Bingham and Ellis, who had been requested by the heads of government to attend the meeting, and who arrived in the whale ship L'Aigle.

It was soon determined, that the king should embark for England in the L'Aigle, Captain Starbuck. Kamehamaru, governor Boki, and Liliha his wife, Kapihe and Kekuanaoa, are to accompany him, with Manuia his steward, and a few male servants.

The whole body of chiefs, together with the king, was most earnest in their desires for Mr. Ellis and his family to accompany the party, offered a large sum for his passage—at one time, even made his going a *sine quâ non;* and determined, in case Captain Starbuck would not accommodate him, that the barge should be fitted up for the expedition. Mr. Ellis himself was desirous of going, principally on account of the very critical state of the health of Mrs. Ellis; but Captain Starbuck stating that he could not possibly take him, the king and chiefs were obliged to assent to his remaining. We all regretted this, for we wished the king to have the benefit, during his absence, of so wise and in every respect competent a counsellor; but most especially from a regard to the welfare and happiness of Mrs. Ellis and her family. We fear she cannot long survive, without some change of the kind; and wished her, after eight years of Missionary toil and suffering, to be restored to the bosom of her country and her friends; though the loss of Mr. Ellis's services at this time would be most sensibly felt by the Mission in all its branches.

The king embarked from this place on board the L'Aigle on the 18th instant: at the time, and for two days before, we were almost stunned with salutes from the squadron at anchor before our door. He left us with no inconsiderable display of the "*pomp and circumstance*" of royal embarkation: signals for sailing were made from the L'Aigle early in the day, in which she was followed by all the vessels, ten or a dozen in number—excepting the American brigs Arab and Owhyhee, and one or two small schooners—but all waited till the L'Aigle should lead the way, which was not till near sunset. As soon as she had well cleared her moorings, the whole squadron was in motion, and, with a fine breeze, "*filled away*" beautifully, amidst columns of smoke and fire, and a roar of cannon, that the waters and mountains of Maui probably never before heard.

We have just learned that the king left Oahu on Thursday last, the 27th. We are happy that he has actually undertaken the visit, and believe it cannot fail of benefiting himself and nation. We

think the party a good specimen of the chiefs ; Bokı
is an amiable man, though far inferior in talent and
character to his brother Karaimoku; and Kamehamaru, one of the most noble and interesting of the
nation.

CHAPTER X.

Mission House, Lahaina, Dec. 3, 1823. We have for some time past been favoured with the society of Dr. and Mrs. Blatchely. They occupy a new house in our enclosure ; and were exposed to a serious accident last night, by the momentary touch of a candle against the thatch of the house, in passing through the door. The flame spread rapidly ; but, by prompt exertions, was happily extinguished.

The greatest danger to which we feel ourselves exposed is from casualties of this kind. It seldom rains at Lahaina, and, in a short time after erecting a house, the grass thatch becomes perfect tinder; and, in case of fire, unless suppressed at the instant it commences, the loss of the building, and of every thing it contains, is inevitable. The rapidity of the flames scarcely admits the rescue of life, much less of property.

Native dwellings are objectionable in many respects. The wind, dust, and rain find ready access to ours in every part; and not only put us to great inconvenience, but often greatly endanger our health.   The leaves of the sugar-cane with which they are lined, and the grass and mats forming the floors, are secure and appropriate harbours for the mice, fleas, and cockroaches which infest this land, and by which we are greatly annoyed.   But, were the buildings ever so comfortable for the time being, their frailty would be an objection : the thatch must be frequently repaired, and the whole house entirely rebuilt every third or fourth year.

We are at a loss to determine what the materials of our permanent dwelling shall be.   If constructed of wood, every part must come from America, the islands affording no timber for house-building, that is accessible, or to be obtained for a reasonable price.   If of stone, the lime and lumber necessary to finish them must be procured in the same distant country ; for the expense of burning lime here, would be greater than the cost of it in America, and its freight to the islands.

Dec. 6.   Two days ago we had the happiness of receiving Mr. Ely and Mr. Whitney to our habitations. Mr. Ely returned to Oahu again to-day : and was accompanied by Dr. and Mrs. Blatchely.   They sailed in the Arab, Captain Meek, to whom we have been indebted for much politeness.

Dec. 15.   Immediately after the last date, I was seized with a violent illness, from which I am now but just recovering.   Mr. Richards also suffered an alarming attack ; and B——, was at the same time confined to her bed.   Our situation required the unremitted attentions, night and day, for near a week, both of Mr. Richards and H——, on whom the care of Mrs.

Richards' infant, as well as that of C——, necessarily devolved.   Mr. Richards was obliged to be physician as well as nurse ; and spent many anxious hours in searching medical authorities, while alarming symptoms called for immediate relief.

We have deeply felt the importance of an additional physician to the Missionary establishment at the islands. One physician cannot possibly meet the necessities of families so widely dispersed as we are.   The extreme stations are more than four hundred miles apart ; and in any case of emergency, it would be impracticable to secure at one of these, the services of a practitioner who might be at the other.

But the want of a physician is not at such times the only cause of anxiety and distress—is not all that makes the difference between a chamber of sickness in a heathen land, and in the habitations of our fathers. Our nearest friends, instead of hanging on our pillows with kind and assiduous attention, are obliged to exhaust themselves in the lowest drudgery, without an assistant to share even the hardest of their labour. No kind friend calls, to sympathize with us in our sufferings, or to relieve, during the watches of the night, those who are overcome by the fatigues of the day.   Our establishment affords few of the articles which at home are considered indispensable to the comfort of a sick room ; and, when the violence of disease is removed, we have no delicacy to tempt the fastidious appetite of an invalid, or cordial to revive the drooping spirits of the languid and the faint.

We mention these facts, not to complain of the privations of which we are sensible; for through the grace of God we do sincerely esteem them the "*light afflictions,*" that deserve not to be named, in comparison with the everlasting benefits we trust we are securing to the heathen; but only to exhibit to you the various and true shades of Missionary life.

Dec. 17. Mr. Whitney who returned to us on the 14th instant, from a visit to Mr. and Mrs. Thurston, sailed again this evening for Oahu.

Dec. 27. On the evening of the day on which Mr. Whitney arrived at Oahu from Taui, a trunk, containing his clothes and papers, was stolen from the hall of the Mission House. No knowledge of the thief was obtained, till within a day or two; though suspicion rested on the attendants of some of the chiefs, who were at the house in the dusk of the evening. This morning a messenger from Kaikioeva, the guardian of the prince, came before sunrise to inform me, that Mr. Whitney's trunk had been found in the possession of a follower of the young chief, and to request me to be present at the examination of it, previous to its being delivered to the care of the Mission. On my arrival at the establishment of the chief, the trunk was produced, and as much of its former contents as could be found, replaced. It was then formally given up, in the presence of a large assembly of the people, of the prince and his guardian, including all their personal attendants, male and female; while the culprit was, with judicial solemnity, publicly reproved by Kaikioeva, and punished by dismissal from the service of Kauikeaouli.

In the course of the investigation, it was ascertained that the *kahu*, nurse, or chief personal attendant, of the prince, was accessary to the theft. He was immediately called, and ordered to bring forward the personal effects of the chief, of which he had the care, for inspection, preparatory to his dismissal from his situation. In the course of the morning, the clothes, furniture, books, &c. in his possession were examined, and after an inventory of them had been taken, in the presence of all the high chiefs, they were delivered, as insignia of the office, to another petty chief; while the former kahu was disgraced by a public expulsion from the household of the lad.

We were much gratified with the manliness and resolution of the prince on this occasion. He is only nine years old, was strongly attached to his kahu, having been carried in his arms from his birth, and wept much when parting with him ; still he said *he must go*, or by and by it would be thought that he himself was *heva*, guilty, and that if he kept thieves in his train, it would be said he had ordered them to steal.

This is the most decisive measure ever taken by a chief, for the suppression of theft ; and will, doubtless, produce a happy effect. Formerly, the chiefs themselves were greatly addicted to this crime ; but, finding it disgraceful in the eyes of foreigners, left the commission of it to their attendants ; most of them, it is said, have, till lately, taken with them in all their visits, persons expressly for the purpose. Not long before our arrival, one of the Missionaries suffered so much from the depredations of a high female chief, in the habit of visiting his family, that he openly turned both her and her husband from his house.

The islanders are exceedingly expert in the achievement of theft. Not many weeks since, a chief of rank, with two or three servants, called for a few moments at our establishment. The attendants remained about the door, while their master entered the house. On a clothes line, in open view, three or four French silk handkerchiefs of very peculiar pattern and colours were hanging; although all the doors and windows were open, and some of the Mission family in sight the whole time, on the departure of the company, one of the handkerchiefs was missing. We could however scarce suspect them; for it seemed impossible that any one of their number, in the short time of the call, and under such circumstances of exposure, could be guilty; but not long afterwards an islander, who had been within a short time at the residence of the chief, on another island, seeing me with an article of the same kind, exclaimed in admiration of the colours, " O, that is a very handsome handkerchief—*just such a one as our chief wears*."

We are constantly losing, in this manner, articles of greater or less value; in two or three instances, clothes to a very considerable amount have been taken from trunks, the locks of which are broken while the persons have been sitting upon them, and apparently deeply interested in conversation with some of the family. In these instances, however, they were dressed in large kiheis, which gave concealment to their movements, and afforded a cover for the booty in their retreat.

The remedy of the evil is with the chiefs; if they

really discountenance this vice, which we believe many now do, and punish it, when detected, with promptness and determination, as in the present instance, stealing will soon be unpopular.

Sabbath, Jan. 4, 1824. The services of the chapel to-day have been distinguished by the baptism of the infant son of Mr. and Mrs. Richards, and by the administration of the Lord's supper. The day has been one of peace and blessedness; and the language of our hearts that of the Psalmist—" We will give thanks to thee, O Lord, among the heathen, and will sing praises unto thy holy name."

Jan. 7. Our customary visits to the chiefs this morning were more than usually pleasant. We found them at their several establishments intently occupied in their studies, and uncommonly solicitous for instruction. We were particularly gratified with the appearance of our friends, Kaikioeva, the guardian of the young prince, and his wife Kea-weamahi. The former was reclining on a neat Chinese sofa, earnestly engaged with the few pages yet printed in the native tongue ; and the latter seated at a very handsome cabinet with book-case top, writing a letter.

Besides these two pieces of furniture, which would be neat and ornamental in any common parlour, there was another sofa in the room, a very large mahogany dining table, two circular tables of the same material, with an elegant escritoir on each, a handsome card table and dressing case, and a large and expensive mirror. The whole house exhibited a degree of neatness, comfort, and convenience, not often found in the dwellings even of the highest chiefs, and excited a pleasing hope of seeing still greater improvements in the *externals* of social and domestic enjoyment.

They were both clothed in loose dresses made in the European fashion; and in their persons, more than in the furniture of their apartment, presented a strong contrast to the appearance they made but a year or two since, when seen only in unblushing nakedness; and when they knew no higher subjects of thought or occupation, than to " eat, drink, and be merry."

These two are among the most amiable of our friends. Their deportment is at all times modest, dignified, and interesting; and their whole character, so far as we can gain the knowledge of it, so consistent with Christian propriety and purity, that in our intercourse with them we almost forget that they have been heathen. They are assiduous in their attention to every means of instruction—are never absent from the services of the chapel—and not unfrequently are seen bathed in tears, under the preaching of the Gospel of Jesus Christ. May they be found among the first fruits of Hawaii !

Friday, Jan. 9. While at tea this evening we heard a herald passing through the district—the manner in which all the general orders of the king and chiefs are communicated to their vassals—making a proclamation to the people. On inquiring of the native boys in our yard, we learned that the object of it was to inform the people that the next day but one would be the Sabbath, and to command them to have all their food prepared on the morrow, and not to break the commandment of God, by working on the "*la tabu,*" sacred day. Heralds have very frequently been sent out on a Saturday even-

ing, to give intelligence of the approach of the Sabbath, and to command its observance; but this is the
first time we have heard it notified so seasonably, as to
take all excuse from those who disregard it.

Jan. 12. There is, perhaps, no one in the nation,
who has given more uninterrupted and decisive proofs
of a saving knowledge of the truth as it is in Jesus, than
Puaiti, a poor blind man. No one has manifested more
childlike simplicity and meekness of heart—no one
appeared more uniformly humble, devout, pure and
upright.

As a singer, he formerly occupied in the retinue of a
high chief, the place of " *the blind bard*;" in the baronial hall. When " the setters forth of strange gods,"
arrived, and began to preach in the language of the
country, he requested to be led to the chapel; and ever
after, with the return of the Sabbath, groped his way to
the house of God. He soon became deeply interested
in the glad tidings which proclaimed sight to the blind—
relinquished his situation as musician—and from the
most indefatigable inquiry and attention, quickly made
himself so familiarly acquainted with the outline of
Christian belief and practice, as to become an instructor
and chaplain to others. Only a few weeks before the
Thames reached the islands, Keoua, governor of Lahaina, then on a visit at Oahu, appointed him his private chaplain, and brought him to Maui with him in
that capacity. He was the first to welcome us on our
unexpected arrival here, as we stepped upon the beach;
and testified his joy by the most cordial shaking of our
hands, and bursting afresh every few minutes into the

exclamation—" *aroha roa no !*"—" *aroha ino roa !*"—
" great indeed—very great is my love."

He is always at the house of God, and there ever at
the preacher's feet. If he happens to be approaching
our habitations at the time of family worship, which has
been very frequently the case, the first note of praise or
word of prayer, that meets his ear, produces an immediate and most observable change in his whole aspect.
An expression of deep devotion at once overspreads his
sightless countenance, while he hastens to prostrate
himself in some corner in an attitude of reverence. Indeed so peculiar has the expression of his countenance
sometimes been, both in public and domestic worship—
especially when he has been joining in a hymn in his
own language to the praise of the only true God and
Saviour—an expression so indicative of peace and elevated enjoyment, that tears have involuntarily started
in our eyes at the persuasion that, ignorant and degraded
as he once had been, he was then offering the sacrifice
of a contrite heart, and was experiencing a rich fore-
taste of that joy, which in the world to come shall terminate in " *pleasures for evermore.*"

He is poor and despised in his person, small almost
to deformity, and in his countenance, from the loss of
his sight, far from prepossessing; still in our judgment
he bears on him " *the image and superscription*" of
Christ. If so, how striking an example of the truth of
the apostle's declaration : " God has chosen the foolish
things of the world, to confound the wise ; and the weak
things of the world, to confound the things which are
mighty ; and base things of the world, and things which

are despised hath God chosen, yea, things which are not, to bring to nought things that are; that no flesh should glory in his presence."

Evening. Scarce a day passes on which we are not most painfully reminded, that we dwell among the habitations of cruelty. We have been much grieved this evening, by seeing the attendants of the young prince stoning a lunatic on the beach. It is the customary way of treating such objects throughout the islands, and the manner in which they here usually terminate a wretched existence. Kaikioeva sent a messenger to reprove them, and bid them desist from their inhuman sport; not, however, till by the barbarous practice the poor creature was much bruised and lamed.

The afflicted and the deformed of every class are objects of ridicule and contempt, if not, as in this case, of persecution. The helpless and dependent, whether from age or sickness, are often cast from the habitations of their relatives and friends, to languish and to die, unattended and unpitied. An instance recently came to our knowledge, in which a poor wretch thus perished within sight of our dwelling, after having lain uncovered for days and nights in the open air, most of the time, pleading in vain to his family, still within the hearing of his voice, for a drink of water? And when he was dead, his body, instead of being buried, was merely drawn so far into the bushes, as to prevent the offence that would have arisen from the corpse, and left a prey to the dogs who prowl through the district in the night!

But the truth of the apostle's description of the heathen, that they are "*without natural affection, implacable, and unmerciful,*" is found most fully here, in the prevalence of the abhorrent and tremendous crime of infanticide. We have the clearest proof, that in those parts of the islands where the influence of the Mission has not yet extended, *two-thirds of the infants born, perish by the hands of their own parents, before attaining the first or second year of their age!*

The very periods, when the infant of a Christian mother, is to her the object of intense solicitude, and of the deepest anxiety, in times of sickness, suffering, and distress, times at which the affections of the parental bosom are brought into the most painful exercise, are those when the mother, here, feels that in her child she has a care and a trouble, which she will not endure : and instead of searching into the causes of its sorrow, or attempting to alleviate its pains, she stifles its cries for a moment with her hand, hurries it into a grave already prepared for it, and tramples to a level the earth under which *the offspring of her bosom is struggling in the agonies of death!*—As I see and hear, and learn all the abominations and cruelties of a heathen land, my soul often melts within me: and I cannot but think, how little a majority of the inhabitants of Christian countries are aware of the extent of their obligations to the Gospel, for many of the domestic and social blessings they prize most dearly. Happy indeed is the people whose God is the Lord!

The perpetration of this crime is by no means confined to cases of sickness, or of deformity, or of distress : not unfrequently, it is provoked by the simple necessity of half an hour's additional labour a day, for the support of the child, till it can seek its own living; and sometimes merely because its helplessness would interfere, for a period, with the freedom and pleasure of the mother! In view of a crime so relentless, as to sink the guilty perpetrators of it below the nature of the brutes, and which still forms but one of a fearful catalogue,—I am often led to exclaim— "Oh! can there be for such, a redeeming and enlightening power? Can these ever be transformed into beings of purity, of tenderness, and of love?" Lord, thou knowest! Thou didst say, "Let there be light; and there was light:" and Thou hast said, "As truly as I live, all the earth shall be filled with the glory of the Lord!" Thy power will yet make true thy word— *The isles have waited for thy law, and the abundance of the sea shall yet be converted unto Thee!*

Jan 16. Last night, there was a beautiful and almost total eclipse of the moon. We had just retired to rest, when an alarm was given by the natives in our neighbourhood. Loud and lamentable wailings were heard in various directions, while the half-suppressed and plaintive murmurings of those who, with hurried footsteps, passed to and fro, gave indications of something new and melancholy. Hearing a voice in our yard, I inquired the cause of the agitation; and was answered, that "*the people thought the king was dead, because the moon was dark.*" This was the first intimation we had of the eclipse; and on looking out, at once saw the sublime, but innocent, cause of the alarm.

Considerable numbers had gathered round our fence, and we heard nothing but the exclamations, " *mahina mai, mai nui*"—the moon is sick, very sick—" *mahina pupuka no !*"—an evil moon, evil indeed !—" *ua pau sa mahina i ke akua*"—the gods are eating up the moon, uttered in tones of deep anxiety and distress. All agreed in considering it an omen of great calamity to the nation. The king had died at sea, or would soon die ; or the prince, princess, one of the queens, or some member of the royal family, would soon die : for the moon had formerly appeared just so, before the death of several great chiefs !

A young Englishman, of considerable intelligence and nautical information, residing with Karaimoku, told us this morning, that he attempted to explain the cause of the phenomenon to the chiefs. They seemed rather sceptical, however, and, as an insurmountable objection to the truth of the rotary motion of the earth, pointed to the opposite island, and said, " *The world cannot turn round, for Ranai is always exactly there !*"

While we pitied their ignorance and superstition, we could not but be amused by many of their ideas and expressions on the subject. The more enlightened. both chiefs and people, have some correct impressions of the matter, and have made great sport of the credulity of others, calling them " *ka poe naau po*"— the dark-hearted party. The whole circumstance forcibly brought to mind, the appropriate and prophetic lines :—

> "They dread thy glittering tokens, Lord,
>   When signs in heaven appear,
>   But they shall learn thy holy word,
>   And *love*, as well as *fear*."

Monday, 19.   At three o'clock yesterday morning, we were roused from sleep by the voice of our friend Mr. Ellis.   On giving him admittance, we found him to be accompanied by Mr. Chamberlain, and quickly learned that they were only two of a party of thirteen from Honoruiu, on their way to Hawaii, in the schooner Waterwitch, Mr. Hunnewell, master, to occupy a new station at Waiakea, in the district of Hido.   Dr. and Mrs. Blatchely, and Mr. and Mrs. Ruggles and children, landed immediately after; but the rest, Mr. and Mrs. Goodrich, Mr. and Mrs. Ely and child, and Mr. Hunnewell, not till after daybreak.

The morning was one of the most delightful we have known, fresh and rich in all the splendid tints of sunrise.   Our admiration was especially excited by a full and distinct view of Hawaii, which we had never seen before since our arrival at Lahaina.   In general, the atmosphere is not sufficiently clear to enable us at a distance of eighty or a hundred miles, to trace even the faintest outline of land; but now, for an hour, while the sun was near the horizon, we saw the broad mountains, rising in purpled majesty from the deep, while the icy summit of Mounakea glittered like a cluster of brilliants in the sky.

This unusual addition to the beauty of our scenery, bringing five islands, besides Maui, into distinct view from our door, connected with the arrival of our friends, and more particularly with their immediate destination to that island, bearing the richest of conceivable blessings to regions, which for ages unknown nave been covered with the thick darkness of paganism, gave rise to emotions of a most pleasing and animating character.

The day, too, was uncommonly interesting. An immense concourse of people, at the native meetings, gave Mr. Ellis an opportunity to disseminate the word of life; and our own worship could not but be enlivened and warmed by the presence of so many of our fellow-labourers. " How good and how pleasant it is for brethren to dwell together in unity! It is like the dew of Hermon, and as the dew that descended upon the mountains of Zion: for there the Lord commandeth the blessing, even life for ever more."

At nine o'clock this morning they re-embarked to pursue their voyage, not without having partaken, as we trust, in the quickening influences with which the visit has been accompanied to our own spirits. Our prayers follow them. May they be permitted safely to arrive at their destination, and triumphantly to unfurl the banner of the cross !

Jan. 24. The surf, for some days past, has been uncommonly heavy, affording a fine opportunity to the Islanders for the enjoyment of their favourite sport of the surf-board. It is a daily amusement at all times; but the more terrific the surf, the more delightful the pastime to those skilful in the management of the board.

For this amusement, a plank of light wood, eight or ten feet long, two feet broad, and three or four inches thick in the middle, decreasing to a sharp edge at the sides and ends, which are rounded, and having the whole surface finely polished, is necessary; and forms an article of personal property, among all the chiefs-male and female, and among many of the common people.

With this plank under their arm, they leave the shore, and wade or swim into the surf. On meeting a roller, they dive under it with their board, to prevent being carried back by its power; and thus make their way beyond the reef, to the smooth surface of the sea,—at Lahaina, a quarter of a mile from the beach. They then wait the approach of a heavy wave, place themselves at full length flat upon the board, with the face downward, and the head and chest elevated above the forward end, headed for the shore. In this attitude, they take the breaker, mount upon its crest as it towers above the reef, and with the arms and feet skilfully keep their poise in the swell, so as not to be sufficiently forward to be overwhelmed by its combing, nor so far behind as to lose its impetus; and are thus hurried, with the velocity of a racer, on the rolling summit, their erected heads only appearing above the foam, till they are cast on the beach, or slip from the board, in time to escape striking upon the sand.

They then make their way out again, and return in the same manner. Hundreds at a time have been occupied in this way for hours together; while the waves are breaking on the reef, apparently twenty and thirty feet high. Riding upon the surf, in a canoe, in a similar manner, is also a common and favourite amusement.

Another pastime of the natives, where a spot of ground adapted to it can be found, is the *tropical counterpart* of *a winter sport* of boys in our own country, that of *sliding down-hill on a sled.*

The smooth sward of a suitable declivity is made to answer, in a good degree, the advantages of ice and snow, for this purpose ; and throwing themselves forcibly, at the proper place, in the manner of the boys in America, upon a long narrow sledge, having light and highly polished runners, with their breasts pressing on the forepart, they often succeed in making a descent of one or two hundred yards at a single slide.

Jan. 31. For the last fortnight there has been an unusual and increasing demand for books in the native language. We distributed fifty this morning, before breakfast; and since then, three times that number have been called for. But our stock is entirely exhausted, and we have been compelled to send away hundreds of persons, with the promise of a supply as soon as a new edition shall be printed. Some new excitement in favour of the *palapala,* appears to have been produced on the minds of the chiefs and their attendants; and though we are ignorant of any particular reason for it, we trust the first cause is, the power of Him, in whose hands are the hearts of all men.

Feb. 2. Immediately after breakfast we made our customary visit to the chiefs, and found them, with one exception, busily engaged in their studies. The queens

x 2

and princess were writing at their desks, and their favourites and attendants, seated on the mats around them, were equally engaged with their slates and spelling books. The chiefs have lately, for the first time, manifested a special desire to have their immediate followers instructed. Indeed, till within a few weeks, they have themselves claimed the exclusive benefit of our instructions. But now they expressly declare their intentions to have all their subjects enlightened by the *palapala*, and have accordingly made application for books to distribute among them.

In consequence of this spirit, we have to-day been permitted to establish a large and regular school among their domestics and dependents. We have always had several scholars at the establishments of different chiefs, amounting in the whole perhaps to fifty individuals, under regular tuition; and Mrs. Richards, H——, and B——, besides instructing the boys in our families in their own language, have daily taught a few persons in English at our houses. But we have never till to-day had a regular systematic school, except with the chiefs, and the special favourites in their respective trains. The school formed, was entirely from the household of the young prince; and was held in a neat and spacious house prepared by him for the purpose. The names of twenty-five boys and young men were entered as scholars. The young chief himself presided as head of the school, under our superintendence.

Feb. 6. Yesterday afternoon our whole family walked half a mile south of the Mission House, to visit our friends Kaikioeva and Keaweamahi, who have taken

possession of a new establishment in that part of the
settlement; and to call on Auwae, a chief lately arrived
at Lahaina from the windward part of the island. The
inland walk to their plantations is the most pleasant in
the district, passing, shortly after leaving the beach,
through a large and beautiful grove of the cocoa-nut,
and then through a succession of plantations, so thickly
covered with bread-fruit trees, interspersed with a great
variety of luxuriant vegetables, as to appear a continued
and well-planted garden.

We have seen nothing, in the domestic improvement
of the natives, that has pleased us so much as in this
visit. Both chiefs have many acres enclosed, which is
not common: Kaikioeva's, by a high mud wall; and
Auwae's, by a neat and substantial fence of sticks. The
entrance to each is by a painted cottage gate. Their
houses are larger and better built than those of most of
the chiefs; indeed, we have seen none, but that of the
king at Honoruru, that can compare with them, either
in the excellence of the materials, or in the neatness of
the construction. We were also particularly pleased
with the accommodations for their servants and people.
These, instead of having a part of the chief's house,
which is not uncommon, or of having rude and dirty
booths immediately about the doors, still more frequently the case, have neat but small houses, not more
than six feet by four on the ground, and about four feet
high, built regularly along the walls and fences. There
are not less than a dozen such in Auwae's yard, which
peeping from under the thick foliage of the kou trees in
the enclosure, add greatly to the beauty of the scene.

Keaweamahi is equally engaged in making improvements in her department; and we found her with an interesting group of female attendants, busily occupied in preparing a superb satin counterpane for the frame, which an American carpenter, in the employment of her husband, had made for her. Being, however, entirely ignorant of the manner in which it should be done, she was well pleased to have the ladies give her a half hour's assistance.

This evening Auwae and wife returned our call. They came in while we were at the tea-table, but could not be prevailed on to join us. We could not but be amused at the evident reason—the poverty of our board in their eyes. A plate of toast, with a little force-meat, were the only articles besides the tea-service on the table, which, for half a dozen persons, when compared with the variety and quantity of food placed *four times a day* before the family of a chief, appeared to them a most scanty repast. They said but little while they remained, but in exclamations of sympathy at what they conceived to be our unavoidable hunger: " *Aroha ino ia oukou*,"—" great is our compassion for you,"—burst repeatedly from their lips; and they hastened their return, to send us some fish and potatoes immediately.

Feb. 7. The favourable auspices in reference to the schools, mentioned at the commencement of the week have since greatly increased; and we have the happiness of stating, that, in addition to the school of the young prince, each of the chiefs now has one similar, under his special superintendence. The number of schools thus formed is ten, including in the whole nearly one hundred and fifty scholars. Applications have been made for the institution of several more, and we soon expect to have at least five hundred persons under regular tuition in this district.

The brig Neo came to an anchor this morning from Hawaii. The commander brought a present of oranges and a letter to H—— from our friend Kapiolani, the wife of Naihi. She earnestly entreats that books and slates may be sent to her people at Kearakekua, of which Naihi is hereditary chief, where she has lately returned, after an absence of two or three years at Oahu. Having herself been greatly benefited and enlightened by the instructions of the Missionaries, she says she has great sorrow in her heart for the ignorance of her people at Hawaii; for they are—" *Nui roa naau po*"—" very dark-minded."

Feb. 9. Mr. and Mrs. Richards, in company with Karaimoku, sailed in the brig Ainoa this evening, for a short visit to Oahu.

Feb. 11. A delightful evening; one of the very few that are here marked with the higher splendours of *sunset.* The west is filled with rich and brilliant tints, the reflections of which give a softened beauty to the rugged heights of Ranai and Morokai, while they cover the bolder mountains of Maui with purple, and line the crimson clouds, that overhang them, with the deepest shades of amber and gold. Every object was so uncommonly lovely, that on my way to evening prayers, I involuntarily stopt, to give utterance to the emotions of admiration I felt at the beauty and serenity of land, and ocean, and sky.

The natives themselves seemed to partake in the quietude and peacefulness of the scene, and instead of finding them, as is usually the case at this time of the day, sporting in the surf or singing and dancing on the beach, they were seated in numerous groups, studying, conversing, or musing in silence.   Two schools within a short distance of each other, each containing twenty or thirty scholars, were reciting to native teachers, while their respective chiefs, seated in large chairs, were presiding over the exercises.   The monotonous sound of another, within the fort, was distinctly heard ; while the distant hum of a fourth came across the water of a large fishpond, immediately in the rear of it.   With such objects and sounds in full view and hearing, the transition of thought from the natural to the moral state of things, was easy, and almost unavoidable ; and I never recollect having felt more calm and sober joy in the contemplation of my character as a Missionary to the heathen, than at that moment. In anticipation of what, we hope, the intellectual and spiritual condition of this people, at no very distant period, will be, I could scarce avoid exclaiming, " Lo ! the winter is past; the rain is over and gone : the flowers appear on the earth ; the time of the singing of birds is come !"

Sabbath, Feb. 22.   The most interesting circumstance of the day, is an application for baptism from Kaikioeva and wife, from another chief and wife, Toteta, a Tahitian in the family of our patron Hoapiri, and from our friend the blind man, or Bartimeus, as he is sometimes called by us. This is the more notable, from the fact, that there is, and has been, no external circumstance that could operate as an undue excitement to any thing of the kind. Every thing in the characters of these persons, as far as we can ascertain, sanctions the hope, that, through the knowledge of the truth as it is in Jesus, they have been turned from darkness to light, and from the power of Satan unto God ; and are proper subjects for the administration of the ordinance, the benefits of which they are desirous of receiving.

Such hopes, and such causes for high expectation, from this people, give sweetness to the Missionary life. The number of those, of whose saving conversion from sin to holiness we entertain even the faintest hope, is small indeed ; but in the midst of a generation " filled with all wickedness," though few, they are conspicuous and lovely. It is a glorious consolation to us in these " ends of the earth," to know, that, had we not forsaken things most dear, to bear the lamp of eternal truth in this darkness, these very individuals, now so indescribably interesting, would still have been groping in the thickest shades of spiritual death, and stumbling on the dark mountains of sin. What cannot the word of God perform on them in whom it " *worketh effectually !*" How changed are these ! Unto them the Gospel has been preached, and by it they have been transformed into new creatures ; have become gentle, temperate, industrious, modest, chaste, sober, devout—yes, even devout and holy. Such, at least, in our eyes they appear, and such we fully believe them to be.

Feb. 28. In returning from a walk before breakfast this morning, I witnessed, for the first time, a rite of sorcery. My attention was attracted by a collection of persons near the path along which I was passing. On approaching them, I saw in the midst a small mat covered with several thicknesses of tapa or native cloth, on the top of which were placed two very large trees, of a plant called by the natives *api arum costatum*. These seemed to have been prepared for the occasion with much care, each being nicely divided through the stem, half the length of the leaf, and one placed exactly over the other. They were firmly held by a man kneeling at one end of the mat, while the sorcerer kneeling at the other, and holding two of the divided stems in each hand, muttered his prayers over them. A few of the persons present, besides those immediately engaged in the ceremonies, were solemnly and intently occupied in the subject before them ; but the greater number seemed disposed to make sport of it, and turned to me with the exclamations, " *ino, pupuka, debelo*"— wicked, foolish, devilish."

On inquiring what was meant by it, they answered, that some one had stolen the tobacco-pipe of the man holding the leaves, and that the sorcerer was discovering the thief, and *praying him to death*. When reproved for their superstition and wickedness, they became evidently confused, and some unlucky movement of the leaves being made, the principal performer said the effect was destroyed, and ceased praying, apparently in a fit of vexation.

There is no superstition perhaps more general and deep-rooted in the minds of this people, than the belief that certain persons have the power, by prayers and incantations, to destroy the lives of others; and many, doubtless, have become victims to their credence in this device of darkness. A person who has fallen under the displeasure of one of these " *kanaka anana*," or sorcerers, is told that his power is exercised over him, and that he will die. He himself believes in the efficacy of that power—thinks perhaps that he has known many instances of it. Anxiety is awakened; his mind becomes filled with pictures of death; he cannot sleep; his spirits sink; his appetite fails; and the effects of his imaginary fears become the real causes of the evil he deprecates. Finding his health and strength affected by these natural but unperceived causes, he considers his fate inevitable; refuses all nourishment, as unnecessary and unavailing; pines, languishes, and dies beneath the influences of his own ignorance and superstition. The less enlightened of the people think no one dies natural death, and resolve every instance of mortality into the effects of this *pule anana,* prayer of sorcery, some other incantation of a similar kind, or into the equally insidious influence of secret poison.

Of the power of this superstition we had a proof in a native of our own household. A thief was put to flight from our yard one day while we were at dinner; this lad joined in the chase, and seized the culprit, but lost his hold by the tearing of his kihei, or outer garment. The thief was greatly exasperated; and immediately engaged a *sorcerer* to pray the boy to death.

Information of this reached the lad in the course of the afternoon; and we soon perceived him to be troubled by the intelligence, though he attempted with us to ridicule the superstition.

The next morning he did not make his appearance with the other boys: and upon inquiry from them, they said he was sick. We asked the nature of his sickness; to which they replied—" *mai no i ka pule anana paha*" —that he " was sick from the prayer of sorcery perhaps." We found him lying in one corner of his house, pale with fear, and trembling like an aspen leaf, and discovered that he had not slept during the night: we were satisfied that the whole arose from terror; and compelled him, notwithstanding his declarations that he was too sick, to come from his retreat—diverted his mind—set him at work—and before noon he was as full of life and spirits as ever—laughed at his fears, and began to defy the power of the *pule anana !*

The whole race are subject, from ignorance and superstition, to a bondage of terror. Not only do the eclipse and the earthquake—the burstings of a thunderbolt, and the eruptions of a volcano—fill them with apprehension and dismay; but to them, the darkness of the night is the covert of demons going about, " seeking whom they may devour;" and the least unusual sound that breaks upon its silence, is interpreted into the prowlings of spirits ready to destroy.

As the wind has sighed through the tops of the cocoanut tree in the silence of the night, or the sounds of the surf, breaking on the reef, have bellowed along the shore, I have seen fears gathering on the faces of the natives of our household, while with troubled and inquisitive look, and half-suppressed breath, they have exclaimed,

" *He akua !—He akua aore maitai !*"—" A god—an evil god !"—and the simple and plaintive notes of an Eolian harp, fixed in a window of the Mission House at Oahu, had such an effect on the mind of an islander belonging to the establishment—although the cause of the sounds had been explained to him—that it was necessary to remove the instrument, because he could not sleep !

CHAPTER XI.

RECOLLECTIONS OF HOME.

Mission House, Lahaina, March 1, 1824. There has not been a period my dear M——, since H—— and myself left America, when the privilege of writing to those we love—of making known to them the particulars of our situation, and of imparting the thoughts and feelings of our hearts—has appeared more precious than the present, when entirely alone on one of the *specks* of *desolation* that constitute this solitary group. The want of all society, except that of our own little family, predisposes in an unusual degree to frequent recollections of *home*: and we have never perhaps thought more, spoken more, and felt more, concerning yourself and family, and the many other objects of our warm remembrance, than at the passing time.

The weather too, to-day, is of a character to recall to our minds scenes in which we have often had a part, when a gloomy sky and driving storm have shut us within the walls of our houses; and by interrupting the ordinary engagements without-doors, have made us, in an especial manner, dependent on the family circle and fireside, for our pleasure and amusement.   Indeed, the present aspect of every thing without, is one principal reason why I have taken up my pen; it is so totally different from all we have witnessed, except in one or two instances, since we arrived at the Islands, that it is more worthy of notice than any thing that is just now taking place.

Instead of my own language, however, I will make use of a few lines from a " *Sea Sketch*," which occurs to my mind. They are highly descriptive of the actual state of things around us, and will convey, I think, a correct and lively image of the scene,—

> ——" Dark and portentous clouds o'erhang the sea,
> While here and there upon the surgy tide,
> With bellied sails, the vessels—dim descried—
> Against the opposing blast toil heavily;
> On sullen wing, the sea-gull wheels away
> To loftiest rock, beyond the utmost swell
> Of billow, lashing high its dizzy spray;
> The wild waves curl their bleak and foamy heads—
> Tumultuous murmurs through the ocean caves
> Ring dismal: while the gloomy tempest spreads
> Athwart the joyless deep; the showers down pour,
> Toss the rough main, and drench the sandy shore."

We have before us the reality of every image here presented; and none in more conspicuous and beautiful exhibition, than " the vessel" on the " surgy tide," with " bellied sails," against the " opposing blast."— The young prince is slightly indisposed, and, notwithstanding the violence of the storm, a schooner has been despatched for the chiefs at Oahu, and is plunging her way through the channel under a press of sail that buries her almost in every wave she meets.

Monday, March 8.   Mr. and Mrs. Richards returned
from Oahu, in the Haaheo o Hawaii, on Saturday morning.   Mr. and Mrs. Bishop came with them.   They have
been passing the winter at Tauai, with Mr. Whitney;
and sailed this morning for Hawaii, as permanent associates of Mr. and Mrs. Thurston at Kairua, the principal
town of the island, and the residence of the governor.
Karaimoku and Kaahumanu, who are the regents of the
Islands, in the absence of the king, despatched the barge
to the windward, expressly for the purpose of returning
Mr. and Mrs. Richards to Lahaina, and of carrying Mr.
and Mrs. Bishop to their station at Hawaii.   A mark
of kindness sufficiently indicative of their good will to
the Mission.

Until the present time, the hymns used in the native
worship have been in manuscript.   An edition is now
printed, and Mr. Richards has brought a quantity for
distribution at Lahaina.   The knowledge of their arrival
has spread rapidly through the settlement, and our
houses are thronged with eager applicants for them.
The richest treasure could scarce be received with greater
enthusiasm than these, " *himeni paiia*," — stamped
hymns, as they are called.

March 13.   Late at night.   The tempestuous character of this month is as marked here, as in most other
parts of the world, notwithstanding the general and almost uninterrupted serenity of the rest of the year.   I
am now writing in the midst of one of the most violent
storms I ever witnessed.   For the first time since our
residence on the Islands, the " *artillery of heaven*" is
playing so near our dwellings, as to turn the admiration

we have felt in its more distant peals, into momentary
terror.   An incessant glare of lightning breaks through
the chinks of our door and windows, and the various
loop-holes of our house, while the wind and rain rush
upon us from every part of the roof and sides, and
threaten our hut with instant destruction.   The water,
to the depth of a foot, is running in a rapid current
through B——'s room, forming a small wing to ours,
and Mr. Richard's house is entirely overflowed.

The raging of the tempest as it rushes from the
ocean, the tumult of the waters, the thundering of the
surf on the reef, and its heavy lashings along the shore,
the wrenching, bending, and cracking of our huts, as
the gale sweeps over and around them, make a total of
circumstances, that would present rather a gloomy
picture to our friends, who have known the desolating
storm only by the sound as it " *howl'd o'er their steady
battlements.*"   We are seeking a partial refuge from the
rain under our umbrellas ; and H—— has been sitting
for hours with C—— in her arms—watching the motion
of the rafters in the contentions of the wind—ready to
make an escape with him from the ruins of our cabin.

March 18.   Our friend Hoapiri, in a call after dinner
to-day, told us that some of his men who had just come
from the mountains, reported a ship in the Morokai
channel.   Feeling disposed for a ramble, I took the
glass, and proceeded up the mountain two or three miles,
to ascertain in what direction the vessel, said to be in
sight, was proceeding.   I soon descried the sail, and
perceived it to be the native brig Waverley.   Finding
myself in the vicinity of a couple of lofty mounds, that

form a prominent feature in the scenery to the north of Lahaina, I extended my walk to them.

They form the opposite sides of an ancient crater, still bearing strong marks of the action of fire, though the bottom is covered with grass. On the top of the highest elevation, there is an irregular enclosure, with a number of large conical heaps of stone at the corners and along the sides. From its situation and general appearance, I judged it to be the ruins of an *heiau ;* in which impression I was soon afterwards confirmed by the melancholy evidence of several skulls, and various bones of the human body, but partially buried beneath the fragments of lava with which the area was covered.

In returning, after descending a precipice of fifty or sixty feet, I followed the windings of a deep and romantic glen—scarce a hundred yards wide—filled with taro, sugar-cane, and bananas ; and through which the largest mountain stream, that waters the plantations of Lahaina, makes its rapid course. Both sides were overhung by monstrous ledges of black rock ; in many clefts of which, whole families were living without any defence from the weather, by night or by day, but such as nature had provided.

Before I reached home, the Waverley had come to an anchor. Shortly after, Captain Smith and Mr. Dana, of Honoruru—who have chartered the brig for a voyage to the Society Islands and New Zealand, called on us ; and, much to our joy, put into our hands a large packet of letters and papers from America. They were brought by the Parthian, Captain Rogers, of Boston, arrived within a few days at Oahu. You may judge of the interest with which they were received, from the fact that the tea table, at which we were just taking our seats when the gentleman entered, was standing *in statu quo* till after ten o'clock.

Disease and death, it appears, are still carrying on their work of destruction among those we have known; and dispensations, which with the most touching eloquence say to the lover of the world, " *Turn ye, turn ye at my reproof*," and to the child of God, " *This is not thy rest*," have filled the halls of some with sadness, and hung the habitations of others with the tapestry of woe. If we needed any thing to reconcile us to the sacrifices we have made from a sense of duty, we could find sources abundant, in some of the intelligence brought us by this arrival, in most striking and melancholy lessons on the folly and danger of any course of conduct that centres in the pleasures, the riches, the honours, or any of the perishable gifts of the world.

We are still blessed with health, strength, spirits, and the happiness that springs from a prospect of continued life and usefulness; while some, who thought and spoke of us a little better than idiots, for removing far from all possibility of an advancement in life, and throwing ourselves away in an enterprise so wild and visionary, as they considered that in which we are engaged, have already been suddenly arrested in their aspiring career; and, while " *seeking great things for themselves*," have been cut down like a summer flower, and now lie withering in the grave. Their visions of worldly honour and of earthly joy are fled for ever; and an eternity, which recognizes nothing as praiseworthy or honourable in itself, that the world calls good or great, is their all. Such instances, though melancholy in the extreme to the mind that is accustomed to follow the naked spirit to the bar of God, still are salutary in their admonitions. They teach us the end of *" the pride of life,"* and shew what vanities wealth and honour are, when compared with the salvation of our own souls, or the spiritual benefit of our fellow immortals : and in view or them, we cannot but thank God that grace was ever given to us, if such is the happy fact, to withdraw the supreme affections of our hearts from the things that are *" seen and temporal,"* and to elevate and fix them on those which are *" unseen and eternal."*

Sabbath 21.   The audience at the native service this morning was unusually large, attentive, and solemn. The sermon was on the judgment, and many seemed deeply affected by it ; especially our friend Keaweamahi, the wife of Kaikioeva. She shed tears frequently during the preaching, and when we closed the worship by singing a version of the hymn, " Lo ! he comes with clouds descending," burst into an uncontrolled fit of weeping. Auna, the Tahitian chief, led the exercises of the afternoon, before embarking on board the Waverley to return to the Society Islands, on account of the health of his wife.   He is a noble example of the power of the Gospel on the heart and character of a pagan.   His wife is a very handsome woman ; and in her general appearance and manners remarkably like one of the most polished females I ever saw.

Friday 26.   This morning a squadron of native vessels passed, with the body of Governor Cox, who died

this week at Oahu, bound to Kairua, where the corpse
is to be deposited. All the principal chiefs who have
been residing here, excepting Wahine Pio, at present
governess of Lahaina, went some time since to attend
him in his illness; and have now gone to Kairua to the
funeral.*

Thursday, April 8. The John Palmer, Captain
Clarke, an English whale ship; the Hydaspes, Captain

* Governor Cox was the son of *Keecaumoku,* the warlike and
ambitious chief of Kairua, and the northern part of Hawaii,
who was commander-in-chief of Tamehameha's forces, in all his
war campaigns; and was succeeded by Karaimoku, as prime
minister in the government of the Islands. He appears to have
been a man of adventurous, daring, and sanguinary character;
was a principal agent in elevating Tamehameha to the throne of
Hawaii; and in the battle of Keei, the assassination of Keona,
and the subjugation of the other islands, he bore a conspicuous
part. His family comprises by far the most powerful portion of
the aristocracy of the Islands. He left four children, viz.
Kaahumanu, the queen-dowager of Tamehameha, (in whom at
present, with Boki, is vested the regency of Hawaii,) Piia, and
another of Tamehameha's queens. Kuakine, the present chief
of Hawaii, and Governor Cox who bore his father's name, and
was called by the people *Keecaumoku,* literally the Island-climb-
ing Swimmer,—from *Ke,* the ; *a,* swimmer, or to swim ; *ee,* to
climb, as upon a rock, or up a ship's side ; and *moku,* an island.
Under Keopuolani, Keecaumoku was governor of Maui ; in
person and in disposition, he resembled Kaahumanu more than
any other member of the family ; and, prior to the frequent attacks of disease that he experienced during the last years of his
life, appears to have possessed in some degree the enterprise
which marked his father's character. He was among the first
to sanction the residence of the Missionaries from America, and
uniformly befriended them. On our arrival in 1822, we found

Paddack; the Cyrus, Captain Folger; the Martha,
Captain Pease; the John Adams, Captain Joy; and the
Hesper, Captain Chase; all American, have left us to-
day, after a visit of a fortnight. We have received
many expressions of kindness and friendship from
them: and saw them take their departure with regret.

Wednesday 14. Laanui, who is particularly desirous
of conforming to the customs of civilized and Christian

the steward of his household was a native of the Society Islands,
a brother to the wife of one of our native teachers. This procured us an introduction. He was the first to desire instruction,
to establish a school for the instruction of his people, and establish family worship in his house. The illness that immediately
preceded his dissolution was painful, and somewhat protracted;
at first some of the chiefs imagined he was suffering from sorcery, but afterwards imbibed more rational ideas. I visited him
daily during his illness, and hope and fear alternately occupied
my mind respecting him. I sometimes found him engaged in
ejaculatory prayer, "Lord, thou knowest my deeds from my
youth up—Thou knowest my sins—Lord, forgive them—Save
me by Jesus Christ the only Saviour," were some of the expressions I once heard him use. He wished to be baptized when
near his end; this, however, we thought proper to decline, lest
he or the natives should think there was any *saving* efficacy
connected with such Christian rite, in regard to the soul's
acceptance with God, irrespective of that moral purity, or
cleansing and sanctifying, of which it is the appointed emblem.
He died on the 22nd of March, while I was engaged in the act
of prayer by his bedside, and we hope his spirit entered the
abodes of rest and happiness.—W. E.

Matheson in his "Narrative of a Visit to Brazil, Chile, Peru,
and the Sandwich Islands, in the Years 1821 and 1822," gives
the following account of a visit to his establishment.

August 5.—This morning I went to Coxe, intending to pur-

society called on us this morning. He arrived only a
day or two since from Kairua, where he has been to
attend the funeral of Governor Cox; and expects to
sail for Oahu this evening. When taking his leave, he
laughingly said, that it was not his farewell call—that
towards night, when he was near sailing, he would come
again to say *aroha*, and to *wail :* referring to a custom
of the natives of weeping aloud when they meet and

chase some goats. I expected to find him as usual, either sleeping or smoking, or drinking, or busy trafficking like myself.
The door of his hut was half open, and I was about to enter un-
ceremoniously, when a scene too striking ever to be forgotten,
and which would require the hand of a master painter to do it
justice, suddenly arrested my whole attention.

About a dozen natives of both sexes were seated in a circle,
on the matted floor of the apartment, and in the midst of them
sat John Honoree, the Hawaiian catechist. All eyes were bent
upon him ; and the variously expressive features of each individual marked the degree of interest excited by what was passing in his mind. So absorbed, indeed, were they in their reflections, that my abrupt appearance at the door created for
some time neither interruption nor remark. The speaker held
in his hand the Gospel of St. John, as published at Otaheite,
and was endeavouring, by signs and familiar illustrations, to
render its contents easy of comprehension. His simple yet
energetic manner added weight to his opinions, and proved that
he spoke, from personal conviction, the sincere and unpremedi-
tated language of the heart.

The Chief himself stood in the back-ground, a little apart
from the rest, leaning upon the shoulder of an attendant. A
gleam of light suddenly fell upon his countenance, and disclosed
features, on which wonder, anxiety, and seriousness, were im-
printed in the strongest characters. He wore no other dress
than the *maro* round the waist ; but his tall athletic form, and

part. It was, however, only in pleasantry—for he has long ceased to wail on any occasion.

In continuation of the conversation he remarked, that the Hawaaiians thought us a very cold-hearted people, because we only shook hands, and nodded our heads at each other, when we met or separated. Whereas their love was so great, that they always touched noses and wailed. Namahana his wife, one of the queens of Tamehameha, he said, wailed still, but he himself had not, since the teachers came. " *I knocked out my teeth too,*" he added, putting a finger in the place where two of his front teeth were missing, " *when Tameha-meha died, so great was my love for him.* I then thought it was very good ; but when the light came, I

bust seen bending over the other's shoulders, and dignified demeanour, marked at one glance his rank and superiority over all around. One hand was raised instinctively to his head in a pensive attitude. His knitted brows bespoke intense thought ; and his piercing black eyes were fixed upon the speaker with an inquiring, penetrating look, as much as to say, " Can what you tell us be really true ?" I gazed for some minutes with mute astonishment, turning my regards from one to the other, and dreading to intrude upon the privacy of persons whose time was so usefully employed. At last the Chief turned round, and motioned with his hand in a dignified manner, for me to withdraw. I did so ; but carried away in my heart the remembrance of a scene to which the place, the people, and the occasion, united in attaching a peculiar interest.

I learnt afterwards that Coxe had promised to build a schoolhouse, and present it to the Missionaries for their use : a donation, which, considering his acknowledged love of money, affords no mean proof that his inquiries into the truth of the new religion had not been altogether fruitless.

found it to be very bad: and there was *great sorrow among the rest of my teeth* for the *two that were gone* but I could not make new teeth." " *Naau po, nui roa elieli*"—" dark was my heart—very, very black !"

Thursday 15. Keaweamahi, who is making a dress of fawn-coloured satin, under the superintendence of H——, and at present spends greater part of the day with us, asked this morning with great simplicity, " from what part of America *sailors* came—whether they *did not worship idols—and had never heard of God ?*" The question does not speak much for the character of some of our countrymen, even in the estimation of the heathen ; and made us sigh to think of the depravity of example, that could call forth the query from this interesting pagan.

Thursday 22. Captain Wilds of Boston, lately arrived at Oahu in the Parthian, came to Lahaina yesterday. It has been requested that I should join Mr. Ellis at Oahu, while Mr. Bingham and family make a proposed visit to Taui : and Captain Wilds having very politely offered a passage to myself and family, we shall probably go to Honoruru on Saturday.

Mission House at Honoruru, Island of Oahu, Monday, 26. H——, myself, C——, and B——, embarked with Captain Wilds on Saturday afternoon, and landed at this place yesterday morning, just after breakfast. All our friends are in health except Mrs. Ellis, who has long been suffering under severe and protracted disease.

Tuesday, April 27. The day being unusually fine, Mr. Bingham proposed after breakfast this morning, that I should acompany him to the *pari*, or precipice, of

Kolau, about seven miles in the interior. Nothing short of the testimony of my own eyes, could have made met believe that there was so much of the " *sublime and beautiful*" in the vicinity of Honoruru. It seemed like enchantment, to find myself transported in the short space of an hour, from the dusty plain, stagnant pools, dreary beach, and various desolations of the seaside, to the freshness and verdure, luxuriance and bloom, of a woodland region, where the eye rested only on objects of grandeur and beauty, and the ear caught no sounds, amid the solitude of the forest, but the chirping of birds, the murmurs of the mountain-stream, or the dashing of the distant cascade.

The path we took led up the valley immediately in the rear of the village. As this gradually contracted from a width of three to that of one mile, the scenery became more and more picturesque and delightful, till at a distance of five miles from Honoruru, it far surpasses any thing I have ever witnessed. The mountains are so lofty and so graceful in their outlines—so rich and beautiful in their foliage—so diversified by dark grottos, projecting cliffs, and spouting waterfalls, while all below presents an exuberance of vegetation almost incredible—that I cannot but think it among the finest of the exhibitions of nature, in a state of undisturbed simplicity and wildness. Such was the character of the scenery for the two last miles of the walk, while our path led successively through glade, copse, and dell, and was frequently for long distances together, entirely embowered by the interlacing branches of the spreading hau-tree—a species of *hibiscus.*

After ascending from one of these dark passages, Mr. Bingham suddenly cautioned me against the violence of the wind we should soon meet; at the same time the rushing of heavy blasts was heard, intimating, like the roarings of a cataract or the mutterings of a volcano, an approach to one of the most sublime phenomena of nature; and on abruptly turning the angle of a projecting rock—with an admiration approaching to terror, I found myself balancing, in strongly conflicting currents of air, on the brink of a precipice little less than a thousand feet in perpendicular descent, without the parapet of a single stone to guard against the fatal consequences of a false step.   Immediately before me at the foot of this tremendous offset, in most perfect bird's-eye view, lay a widely extended, cultivated, and thickly inhabited country, against whose distant shores the peaceful billows of the Pacific were rolling in ever varying and snowy brightness, while farther still, the blue waters of the ocean rose in gradual ascent, till, apparently midway between heaven and earth they met the sky, in a haziness that rendered either distinguishable from the other, only by the regularity of a scarcely discernible horizon.

To the right and to the left, within a stone's throw of the rock on which I stood, two richly covered pyramidal peaks rose many thousand feet above my head; while beyond them, on either side, summit after summit of mountains, whose broad bases were planted in the valley below, appeared in long perspective, till, with a semicircular sweep, both chains terminated in the sea by bold and romantic headlands, rendered more picturesque by a partial continuation of detached cliffs and islets.   In full view behind was the beautiful valley through which we had ascended, gradually sinking, from the very spot on which we stood, to the now miniature town and port of Honoruru, beyond which again rose " *the illimitable sea.*"

The sublimity of the whole was not a little increased by the almost overwhelming sounds of the trade wind, as it swept along the mountains, which resisted its progress to this narrow pass, and through which it rushed with irresistible velocity and power, bearing in its broad current and whirling eddies, leaves, sand, and even pebbles.   Such was the effect of this, that though every thing far and near, gleamed in the brightness of a cloudless sky and noonday sun, I could scarce resist the impression that we were standing amid the ragings of a tempest—an illusion not diminished by the harsh screams of the sea-gull and cry of the tropic bird—as they passed us on rapid wing to the lofty peaks above, or hastened again to sail in the calmer regions beneath our feet.

None but an atheist could have kept his thoughts from rising to that Being of majesty and of power, who " founded the earth, and hung it upon nothing,"—" who formed the mountains and created the winds,"—" who shut up the sea, and said, Hitherto shalt thou come, but no farther; and here shall thy proud waves be staid." And in the lively contemplation of the marvellous wisdom and omnipotence that overlooks and upholds the mighty wonders of the universe, we could not but feel the force of the humbling interrogative, " O LORD, what is man, that THOU art mindful of him; or the son of man, that THOU visitest him?"

After gazing on the various objects of grandeur and beauty by which we were surrounded, till our eyes were fatigued, we made a short descent by a narrow footpath, by which clinging from rock to rock, and from cliff to cliff, you may reach the plain below. Having gratified our curiosity in this manner, by what I considered a dangerous experiment, we returned to the summit; and in the cleft of a rock, where we were shielded from the wind, partook of the refreshments we had brought with us.

Before commencing our return to the village, I tried my pencil on the scene, but the merest outline is all I can ever make of the sketch; to give any thing like the distance and the depth necessary to produce the required effect, would demand more than a master's skill.

The battle that decided the fate of Oahu, in the conquests of Tamehameha, and by victory in which he became sole monarch of the group, was fought in the valley leading from Honoruru to this pass. The king of Oahu, after a desperate conflict, fell bravely at the head of his army. Upon which a complete rout ensued. One party of more than three hundred warriors, fled towards this precipice, and were pursued so closely, and with such relentless purpose, as to have been plunged, without an exception, from the tremendous offset to the depths below!

Saturday, May 1. At two o'clock this afternoon, I accompanied our highly valued friends, Mr. and Mrs.

Bingham, with their children, to the beach, where they embarked on board the whale ship Washington, Captain Gardiner, for Taui.

Monday, 3. By preaching to the English congregation yesterday morning, I commenced the discharge of the regular duties which will devolve on me during my residence here. These duties will be, an English sermon on the morning of every Sabbath ; a sermon in the native language at Waititi, in the afternoon of the same day ; another at the same place every Wednesday afternoon ; the instruction of twenty or thirty native teachers, in reading, writing, and singing, three afternoons in the week ; and an attendance with Mr. Ellis every Monday evening, at a meeting for religious conversation with chiefs and people.

The meeting of this kind to-night was opened by a very spirited address, to about a hundred persons present, from the powerful chief Kaahumanu : she was followed in much the same manner by Karaimoku ; after which, the whole company entered into a free and promiscuous inquiry on the subjects of three regular sermons, that had been preached in the chapel since the preceding Monday. It was encouraging and delightful, to see the deep and tender interest with which so large a company, from the very highest to the most obscure of this people, entered on the discussion, and listened to enlargements upon the things of eternity. To be the guides of such, from the darkness and death of paganism, to the light and glory of the religion of the Cross, is indeed a happy privilege. The Missionary has privations, cares, and sorrows, that no one can know but by experience, and such as often prostrate him in the very dust; but when successful, he has also a consolation and a joy, and if perseveringly humble, faithful, and devoted, will doubtless meet a reward, which might make even an angel covet his office.

To see, as I have but lately seen, an interesting, intelligent, and youthful chief, who but a year ago was a drunken and debauched idolater, but who now gives good evidence of an entire change of character and of heart, come, and, with an expression of the highest benignity and tenderness, exclaim, " *aroha, aroha nui, aroha nui roa !*" love to you, great, very great love to you ; while starting tears, and a faltering voice, interrupted farther utterance; and to have the full conviction, that this declaration of his affection arose simply from an overpowering sense of gratitude to the man, who had made him acquainted with the words, and brought him to the light, of eternal life, would be sufficient to make the coldest Christian that ever felt an emotion of genuine piety, the supporter and advocate of Missions, and the warm and zealous friend of the heathen.

Monday, May 10. Being all in good health and spirits, we succeeded this morning, soon after breakfast, in forming a party to visit a principal natural curiosity of this island ; a lake or pond, in which large quantities of salt are continually forming. The distance to it in a direct line from Honoruru is four miles : but the path we took made the walk about six, before we reached the bank of the lake. Our whole number consisted of nine : H—— and myself, C—— and B—— ;

Mr. Chamberlain and Mr. Harwood; Robert Haia, an islander educated at Cornwall; and two natives, to carry provisions for the day.

We had scarcely passed a hundred rods from the village, before we found something new to admire in the vineyard of Mr. Marini. After crossing a small stream, which bounds it on one side, our path led us the whole length of another. It is well planted and cultivated, and yields grapes sufficient to make considerable quantities of wine. Along the fences in some parts, are bushes of the damask rose in full bloom, which appeared to fine advantage, in contrast with the pale yellow blossom of the cotton tree, with which they are interspersed. The vineyard is also skirted with pineapples, in different stages of maturity, from the first swollen pulp to the ripe fruit. Shortly afterwards we crossed what is called the river: the congregated body of fresh water, which makes its way after passing through the various plantations of the valley to the sea. A short distance before it enters the harbour, it is several rods wide, and a number of feet deep; but where we passed it was divided into two streams, and, as we stept from stone to stone entirely over it, deserves there, at most, only the name of brook. Such are most of the rivers on the Sandwich Islands. On leaving this stream, our path led to the west; and for the first mile lay through an uninterrupted succession of taro plantations.

After passing the taro ground, we entered on a barren and dreary plain, with scarce a sign of vegetation. This, at the end of two miles terminated abruptly by an

almost perpendicular descent of near a hundred feet
into a small but beautifully verdant valley, filled with
several large groves of cocoa-nut trees, and refreshed by
two or three cool and babbling streams. On the smooth
sward, finely carpeting the grove through which our
path led, we partook of some refreshment, and rested
during the heat of mid-day. The scenery from this
place to the lake, was altogether more interesting than
any we had before met. The deep and winding dell
through which we pursued our course, was cool and
pleasant from the noisy brook that swept under its precipitous banks, and imparted luxuriance to the vegetation with which it was covered. Enormous and mis-
shapen cliffs of dark rock appeared every where around
us, and on our left, for the greater part of the distance,
an unbroken ledge, more than a hundred feet high,
overhung our heads. The ascent from this ravine was
very steep, and on reaching the top we found ourselves
at a sufficient elevation to command a view of the
greater part of the leeward side of the island, including the port and town of Honoruru; and, immediately before us, the object of our search—the *Salt
Lake.*

It is between two and three miles in circumference,
having a few feet of water only in its greatest depth ;
and from the entire incrustation of its bottom and
shores with salt, at the distance at which we first saw it,
appeared precisely like a frozen pond in the spring,
with the water standing on the snow and ice, before it
has become completely broken up. After descending
from the hill, we followed the southern shore of the lake

for some distance, and collected many beautiful specimens of the salt, as it had formed on twigs, grass, and
pebbles, over which the water had flowed. The im-
pregnation of the water is exceedingly strong, and the
crystallization so rapid, that from this natural work
alone, immense quantities of salt might be exported,
It has no outlet, and is supplied with water by a very
small stream from the rocks on the western side.

Besides the supply of salt from this pond, and others
of a similar kind, the natives manufacture large quantities from sea water by evaporation. There are in
many places along the shore, a succession of artificial
vats of clay for this purpose, into which the salt water
is let at high tide, and converted into salt by the power
of the sun.

On our return we met Karaimoku and his retinue in
the valley of Cocoa-nuts. He had just landed from his
barge, having come by water, and expects to remain
some days in the vicinity of the lake, to superintend
the preparation of four hundred barrels of salt, for a
Russian brig now in port. Three dollars are to be given
for each barrel. He seemed much pleased, though
surprised to meet us, especially H——, on so long a
walk ; and very politely offered us refreshments of
wine, &c. We accepted a melon and a few cocoa-nuts,
the water of which is a favourite beverage, when warm
and fatigued.

Before we reached the taro ground in the valley of
Honoruru, the wind had risen, and showers of rain occasionally reached us from the mountains, which were
buried in clouds, and we were glad to take the shortest

path to the village. In doing this, however, we came near to increasing our fatigue and exposure, for the path led to the deepest and widest part of the river; on reaching which, no one could be prevailed on, though the opposite bank was covered with natives, and their canoes were stowed all along the shore, to ferry us over without a payment in dollars. It was in vain we told them " of silver and gold have we none;" and after waiting some minutes to see if our evident fatigue and anxiety to cross would not touch the sympathy of some one, we were about taking the only alternative of walking a mile round, when the wife of a young chief, who was one of H——'s pupils in English at Lahaina, happened to come to the bank, and immediately ordered a canoe to bring us over.

Wednesday, May 26. Have just returned from witnessing a solemn scene in the dying moments of the kind and amiable chief, the warm friend and patron of our Mission, *King Taumuarii!* He expired this morning at nine o'clock, after an illness of a fortnight. He was not thought in a dangerous state till within the last day or two. On Monday morning he made his will, and yesterday at twelve o'clock became insensible. I visited him almost daily during his sickness, and only on Saturday evening made one of a sad group of friends who followed him, as he was borne on a sofa through a loudly wailing multitude, from a small frame house, in which he was taken ill, to a larger and new one, which had just been completed for Kaahumanu: but even then, I had little thought that he would so soon be in the world of spirits.

2 A

Mr. Ellis and myself were sent for early this morning, to attend him in his dying moments. Mr. Ellis remained about an hour; and as Taumuarii seemed to have revived a little after offering prayer, he returned to the Mission House. A few moments only, after he left the room, the king without a struggle breathed his last: and I had the melancholy satisfaction of smoothing his features, after the hand of death had passed across them.

The moment it was evident that he was in the very last agony, Kaahumanu ordered the door fastened and the window curtains dropt, and began preparing the corpse for exhibition to the people, who had assembled in multitudes about the house. A Chinese lounge, or settee, was spread with a rich mantle of green silk velvet, lined with pink satin; on this the corpse was laid, the lower extremities being wrapped in loose and heavy folds of yellow satin; while the chest and head were without covering, except a wreath of feathers placed round the head,* so as to pass over and conceal the eyes. The splendid war-cloak of the king, composed of red, yellow, and black feathers, was spread over the arm of the settee at his head, and a large cape of the same material and colours, occupied a corresponding place at his feet. The crowd without had in the mean time received some intimation of the event; and redoubling their lamentations, were rushing from all directions towards the windows and the doors, so that it

* This was an important matter, connected not only with the adjustment of the body immediately after death, but a necessary act in order to the departed spirit's entering Meru, or joining the society of happy spirits in the other world.

was difficult to keep them closed; as soon therefore as the body was thus laid out, the curtains of the windows in the room were again drawn up, and an indescribable scene of wailing ensued.

The death of scarce any other chief could affect us so deeply and sincerely. My first interview with Taumuarii, the day we arrived at Oahu, inspired me with a feeling of respect that I have scarcely known for another native, except our patroness at Lahaina, He always appeared more civilized, more dignified, more like a Christian, than any of his fellows; and I can, with the strictest veracity, say of him that which I can hardly do of any other in the nation, that I have never heard from him a word, nor witnessed in him a look or action, unbecoming a prince, or, what is far more important, inconsistent with the character of a professedly pious man. His high features, and slightly stooping shoulders, gave him a patrician and venerable look. His manners were easy and gentleman-like, and as a " *royal captive*," to those acquainted with his public and private history, he was truly an interesting object. A shade of melancholy was always traceable in his countenance, and when visiting him, I have often been reminded, by his case, of the early history of the amiable Prince James the First, of Scotland.

The introduction of the religion of salvation in this perishing land, has not been, as we trust, without everlasting benefit to him. He professed to have the hope of eternal life through the redemption of Christ, and his last days were marked with a peace which we believe to have been that of the righteous man. Mr. Ellis

was greatly gratified with his conversations during hi
illness, till he became insensible. His body is to be
carried to Lahaina, to be deposited, at his special request, in the same sepulchre with Keopulani.

Thursday, 27. Spent this morning with Kaahumanu and the nearest relatives of the deceased, and at
their request took a sketch of him, as he lay in the full
dress of a British hussar. Mr. Ellis succeeded at the
same time in getting an excellent profile likeness from
the corpse.

Friday, 28. At nine o'clock this morning all the
members of the Mission family now at Honoruru, went
to the royal residence, to attend religious services before
the embarkation of the funeral party. There was a very
large assembly of chiefs, foreigners, and common people
At ten o'clock, the coffin, covered with black silk velvet,
and enveloped in a rich pall of the same material, was
carried into the open air in front of the house, in the
middle of the circling crowd. The chiefs dressed in full
mourning surrounded the coffin — Kaahumanu and
Keariiahonui, taking their seats near the head. The
Mission family and the foreign residents occupied the
verandah, into which the doors and windows of the
second story open; while Mr. Ellis and myself stood in
the front door below. After a hymn and prayer, Mr.
Ellis preached from the words, " Be ye also ready."
The services were closed by singing a native version of
Pope's " *Dying Christian*." The corpse was immediately carried on board a pilot boat, followed by the
nearest friends and Mr. Ellis, who accompanies them to
Maui. They chose the pilot boat as the best sailer.

Several schooners and brigs filled with people, followed during the morning. Every thing was conducted with the propriety and order of a Christian burial, and testified to the benefits derived from moral and religious instruction. *

Since I have been at this place, I have often made a

* The illness of Taumuarii, was but short. During its continuance I visited him daily, and engaged some hours of most delightful conversation with him. He was not, even when in perfect health, so loquacious as the generality of the Hawaiians are ; and although he was abundantly supplied with every article that could conduce to his comfort, there was not only an habitual dejection on his countenance, but, unless on topics unusually interesting, an apparent aversion to conversation. When he spoke, his words were few, but weighty and judicious. I have every reason to believe he was, in the strictest acceptation of the term, a true Christian ; every evidence afforded distinct apprehensions of Divine truth, with lively and permanent susceptibility of its influence and, a uniform, upright, honourable, and irreproachable life was furnished by him after he became acquainted with the Gospel. The last evening of his life, he observed, with visible satisfaction of mind, that he was resting on Christ, that he thought only and constantly of him, and that he believed he was not by him forgotten. His last hours were remarkably tranquil. I accompanied the chiefs with the corpse to Maui on the 28th ; and on the 30th, which was the sabbath, his interment took place at Lahaina, in a style somewhat similar, though less imposing, than that in which Keopuolani's remains had been conveyed to the tomb. Taumuarii and Keopuolani agreed, prior to her decease, that directions should be given, to have their bodies deposited side by side together in the grave, that they might rise together in the morning of the resurrection. This was complied with, and the body of Taumuarii was placed by the side of his late departed friend. W. E.

retired walk on the side of Punch Bowl, or Fort Hill, a place of study, in the cool of the morning and evening. As I was walking backward and forward there this afternoon with a paper in my hand, a small party of the natives approached, and charged me with being a *wicked man for praying their chiefs to death*, that Taumuarii was dead by my prayers, that I was killing Karaimoku, and soon there would not be a chief left on Oahu. I explained to them their mistake, as to the object of my frequenting that spot, and the inability of any one, by prayer or incantation, to take away the life of another; but they said my words were "*falsehood only;*" and an old woman hurried off to a quarry, where a number of men were digging stone for a large house Karaimoku is building, and bade them go and kill me at once, or Karaimoku would be a dead man. They only laughed at her, however, and Karaimoku himself, who was near on his way to see me, joined heartily with them. It seems the place I had thus occupied, was the site of an old idolatrous temple, and of course intimately associated, in the minds of the less enlightened of the people, with the superstitions of the tabu system.

Sabbath evening, 30, *nine o'clock.* About an hour since, we were alarmed by the ringing of the chapel bell, and, on reaching the door, discovered the south end of the building in one entire blaze. Being entirely of grass, in five minutes the whole was on fire, but not till, by the prompt exertions of a few foreigners and natives, every article of any value, such as the Bible, lamps, pulpit (which was moveable,) window and door frames, and seats, were removed. The loss is trifling, as to real value; the house was very old and shabby, and to be used at all much longer, would have required rebuilding. The chiefs have determined to build a stone chapel, as soon as Karaimoku's house is finished, but to have a house of the kind destroyed by an incendiary, is painful. Suspicion, as to the perpetrator of the deed, has fallen on a drunken man, who was reproved for improper behaviour during the service this afternoon, and who was heard to threaten to burn the " hale pule,'' house of prayer. Others say it has been destroyed by way of retaliation for the death of Taumuarii, who they think was the victim of our prayers. Whichever may have been the cause, it originated only with the father of evil. We could not see it sink into ruins without an emotion of sadness, especially as it fell by the hands of baseness. Many of the natives wept aloud, I doubt not, with most unfeigned sorrow, and the air was filled with the exclamations, " *Aroha ino! aroha ka hale pule—ka hale O ke Akua! auwe! auwe!*"—great is my sorrow, great my love for the house of prayer, for the house of God! alas! alas!—uttered in most piteous tones. The class of native teachers, who are at present under my instruction, were most of them quickly on the ground, and carried all the articles rescued from the fire, within the walls of the Mission yard; they manifested much indignation at the wickedness of the " *kanaka naau po*"—dark-hearted fellow—who had done the deed.

Monday, 31. Namahana, her husband Laanui, and several of the chiefs, were at the Mission House before sunrise this morning, to sympathize with us for the loss of the chapel. They design punishing the culprit, if he can be discovered, and have already given orders for the erection of a new and larger house of worship, without any suggestion of the propriety or necessity of it, from us.

Monday, June 7. After the monthly prayer meeting with the natives, H——— called with me this afternoon to see a young American sailor who is very ill, and who I have visited regularly for some time past. He is one of the many infatuated beings, who desert their ships, to wander among the licentious inhabitants of the island, without a home, and with scarce a subsistence. He suffers exceedingly, and is entirely destitute of every comfort: his bed is a dirty mat spread on the ground, with a piece of native cloth for a covering, and a block of wood for a pillow. We do all in our power to prevent his suffering for want of medicine, food, and necessary attentions; but we have become so familiar with sights of misery, which we cannot even attempt to alleviate, that we are often compelled to turn from them with a sigh, and banish them as quickly as possible from our recollection. We dwell in a land of disease and death, and, in many respects, of inconceivable corruption and horror. This lad, like many others who live at ease in sin, while their health and strength are continued, now, that he is in a situation of agony and of danger, is overwhelmed with guilt and shame, and with trembling and tears supplicates the counsel and the prayers, which in other circumstances he would have disregarded, and perhaps scorned.

Such are to be pitied, to be instructed, and to be

tenderly and fervently prayed for; but I doubt whether
any one can discharge the duty without the lively fear,
that if it is to them the hour of death, it is eternally too
late for their salvation; and if they recover, that their
fears and their penitence will be only as the morning
cloud and early dew.

Tuesday, 8. It is quite sickly among the natives at
present. Two chief women died on Sunday; one here,
and one at Waititi; and from the daily wailing heard
in various directions, it is probable there are many deaths
among the common people. Before breakfast this morning, Namahana and Laanui, with their retinue, called
for me to accompany them to the funeral of the chief
at Waititi.

After a cup of coffee we set off, and even the object of
our excursion, and the deep mourning dresses of most
of the party, did not suppress a smile, provoked by the
appearance we made, when brought in the scope of a
single coup d'œil. The queen, seated on a mat, completely filled the body of the small waggon in which she
rode. She was drawn by a pony, which, in size and
weight, could stand no comparison with her majesty;
while Robert Haia, perched on the foreboard, immediately over the little horse, acted as charioteer. Laanui,
who is a tall stout young man, bestrode a nag, equally
sorry and diminutive in his appearance as the one in
harness, but far more restless and stubborn in his movements, without saddle or bridle, except one of twisted
grass; his feet, while not engaged in beating the ribs of
his beast, dangling just above the surface of the ground.
He was richly and fashionably dressed; but for the

benefit of the air, in the labour of his arms, legs, and
feet, necessary in the management of his horse, or, from
a fear of injuring it by a fall, he committed an elegant
cap of velvet and gold to an attendant, and rode bare-
headed.   Three or four of the native teachers, in good
American clothes, but most wretchedly mounted, kept
him company; while a large number of servants, covered
only by a few dirty strips of native cloth, scampered
along, some behind and some before, on horses as
shabby and uncivilized as their riders.

My charger was the Mission horse; a raw-boned, high-
hipped, long, lean old animal, quite characteristic of
the whole establishment.   You can readily imagine, that
this escort of horsemen to the royal equipage—some of
the horses kicking and running, while the ragged tapas
and long hair of the riders were streaming in the air,
others balking and backing, and others again standing
in stubborn fixedness in spite of whipping and goading,
—made no common spectacle; especially, when viewed in
connection with a large train of attendants, in every
colour and variety of drapery, bearing Chinese umbrellas of yellow and crimson damask, different coloured
kahiles, calabashes of refreshments, tobacco-pipes, and
spittoons; some running and hooting after the carriage
of their mistress, and others standing in silent admiration of the skill of the horsemen and the various tem-
pers of the beasts.

On reaching the settlement, the coffin was still un-
finished; and I improved the necessary delay in visiting
a large *heiau*, which had often attracted my attention,
situated about a mile above the bay and groves of

Waititi, immediately under the promontory of Diamond Hill. It seems well situated for the cruel and sanguinary immolations of the heathen, standing far from every habitation, and being surrounded by a wide extent of dark lava, partially decomposed and slightly covered with an impoverished and sunburnt vegetation. It is the largest and most perfect ruin of the idolatry of the Islands I have yet seen; and was the most distinguished temple in Oahu. By a rough measurement, I made its length forty, and its breadth twenty yards. The walls of dark stone are perfectly regular and well built, about six feet high, three feet wide at the foundation, and two feet at the top. It is enclosed only on three sides, the oblong area, formed by the walls being open on the west; from this side there is a descent by three regular terraces or very broad steps, the highest having five small *kou* trees, planted upon it at regular distances from one another.

A native, of whom I had inquired on the beach the direct path to the heiau, and who had obligingly offered his services as a guide, gave me an explanation of some of the rites of the former system, interspersing his statement every few moments, with an emphatic—" *aore maitai !*" " *naau po !*"—" no good !"—" dark hearted !"

Pieces of cocoa-nut shells, and fragments of human bones, both the remains of offerings to false gods, or rather to demons, were discoverable in different parts of the area, and forcibly hurried the mind back to the times of superstitious horror now gone, as we firmly believe, from this interesting people, for ever. It was at this place that ten men were doomed to be sacrificed about twenty years since, for the recovery of our late patroness Keopuolani, then dangerously ill, in the neighbouring groves of Waititi. It was her happy destiny, before her death, to see a bright and glorious day dawn on the gloom that overshadowed her birth, and rested on her riper years; and eventually, herself to become the blessed recipient, as we trust, of all the riches of eternal grace.

As far as my knowledge of the language would permit, I endeavoured to direct the attention of my companion to the glories of this latter day, to the only acceptable sacrifice, the Lamb made ready from the foundation of the world, and to convince him of the necessity of a life of holiness, and of loving and worshipping the only true God.

The terraces of the heiau command a beautiful prospect of the bay and plantations of Waititi, of the plain and village of Honoruru, rendered more picturesque by the lofty embankments of Fort Hill on one side, and the tall masts of the shipping on the other, and still farther in the back ground, of the dark eminences in the vicinity of the Salt Lake, and the picturesque chain of mountains that forms the northwestern boundary of the island. The view to the east is of a perfectly different character, presenting nothing but the precipitous projections and shelvings of the indescribably rude promontory of Diamond Hill. This, on the side next the heiau, is entirely inaccessible, and though it is without a single germ of vegetation in its whole extent from top to bottom, a space of many hundred feet, is still one of the most imposing and beautiful features in the scenery of Oahu.

Shortly after I reached Waititi again, the funeral service, consisting of a hymn, prayer, and address, was performed in a beautiful grove of cocoa-nut trees. Many hundred natives were present, and after giving a respectful attention to the services, followed the corpse to the grave in a regular procession.

Saturday, 12. Our friends, Mr. Elwell and Mr. Hunnewell, having trained their horses to the harness, politely called for H—— and the children to take an evening airing in one of the coaches recently brought from America. The plain affords a beautiful drive, but we little thought, on our first arrival, so soon to see it enlivened and ornamented by so neat and genteel an equipage.

Tuesday, 15. The morning promising a pleasant day, it was determined at breakfast, that we should visit the mountains; once more to enjoy the retirement and sweetness of woodland scenery. Our party consisted of H——, C—— and B——; young Mr. Halsey, of New York; Robert Haia, and myself, with Henry, a young English sailor, living in the Mission family, and two or three native boys, to carry refreshments.

We left home at half past nine o'clock. For the first mile, in crossing the plain to the north, and passing under and around the western side of Fort Hill, we met nothing but the objects of our daily observation. At about that distance from the village, we crossed a stone wall, which secures the plantations of the valley from the depredations of the herds and flocks feeding on the plain, which is a common; and, for another mile, made our way through a succession of taro plantations, by a path so narrow as to require a cautious step to avoid falling, either on one side or the other, into the water and mire in which that vegetable grows.

The first entire novelties we met, were a couple of tamarind trees, the property of Mr. Marini. The tamarind is among the most beautiful of the larger productions of tropical climates. The trees were covered with blossoms of a light yellow, tinged and sprinkled with red, and with fruit in every stage of growth, from the bud to that which was perfectly ripe.

As we proceeded up the valley, the ground became more uneven and picturesque, and the variety and luxuriance of vegetation rapidly increased. At the distance of two miles from the village, the hills near us began to be clothed with shrubbery and trees, and the air became sensibly more cool and sweet: a note from a bird also occasionally reached the ear, while the babblings of the water-courses, leading from one taro bed to another, and from one side of the valley to the other, were exchanged for the heavy rumbling of the mountain torrent. After an hour's walk, the valley had diminished from a half to a quarter of a mile in width, and instead of the gentle swellings of the hills at its entrance, our path was overhung by mountains, almost perpendicular, and covered with a variety of the richest and most beautiful foliage, interspersed with bold ledges or single projections of

rock dripping with moisture, and gracefully mantled
by vines and creepers, growing in all the brightness
and luxuriance of perennial verdure.

At half past eleven o'clock, we reached the head
of the glen, a place where it branches into two narrow
ravines, one on each side of a mountain jutting from
the east. We here found a delightful resting spot,
in a clump of lime trees planted by Mr. Marini. They
are eight in number, and stand in a recess of rocks in
such a manner, as to form a large and beautiful
arbour, impenetrable to the sun, and filled with the
fragrance of the blossoms and fruit of the trees.

We remained two hours at this spot, during which
I secured the outlines of two or three of the most
striking scenes around us, a sketch of our bower
among the rest. I will send one of these, to illus-
trate this part of my journal.

After a cup of coffee, we prepared to ascend the
mountain immediately on the east, by far the most
arduous part of our excursion, our path being an
uninterrupted but winding ascent, of the steepness of
an ordinary staircase, for near two miles, through the
thickets and cliffs, which had been so much the objects
of our admiration. About three o'clock we reached
the summit, and found ourselves more than a thousand feet perpendicularly above the place of our
refreshment, and not less than three thousand above
the level of the sea, surrounded by scenery as
enchanting as it was novel and picturesque. Not an
object, simply natural, was wanting for the perfection
of woodland beauty in the spot where we stood; while

near, and apparently on a level with us, almost on every side, were the narrow ridges and pyramidal peaks, which but the hour before we had seen intercepting the clouds, that were hurried along by an impetuous trade wind. The valley, too, through which we had passed, lay like a map at our feet, the ocean looked like a blue wall built around us, to the skies, while the old fortified crater near Honoruru, was scarce distinguishable from the level of the plain; and Diamond Hill, an object approaching to sublimity in almost every extensive view we had before enjoyed on this island, though still conspicuous and beautifully unique, was so diminished and softened by height and distance, as to appear only like the dark ruins of some stately castle jutting into the sea.

The whole forcibly reminded me of the descriptive correctness and spirit of an effusion of one of our American bards; and had the author himself been of our party, I believe he would have forgotten the ramble and the objects which first elicited it, and with me have exclaimed—

Oahu!—In thy mountain scenery yet,
　All we admire of nature in her wild
And frolic hour of infancy is met,
　And never has a summer morning smil'd
Upon a lovelier scene, than the full eye
Of the enthusiast revels on—where high
Amidst thy forest solitudes, he climbs
　O'er crags, that proudly tower above the deep,
And knows that sense of danger which sublimes
　The breathless moment—when his daring step
Is on the verge of the cliff, and he can hear
The low dash of the wave with startled ear;—

In such an hour he turns—and on his view
  Ocean—-and earth— and heaven burst before him.
Clouds slumbering at his feet, and the clear blue
  Of summer's sky, in beauty bending o'er him.

From this place we turned our steps homeward, by
a path leading directly along the top of the mountain,
as it stretched towards the sea, and gradually softened
down to the level of the plain at a distance of three
or four miles. In several places, there was barely
room for us to pass, one by one, on the very ridge of
the mountain, while on either side there was an almost
perpendicular descent of many hundred feet. We
were surrounded by a variety of beautiful shrubs and
flowers of most exuberant growth. The brake was of
astonishing size, I never saw any in America more
than two or three feet high, but here its long leaves
nodded gracefully over our heads, and in many places
arched and overshadowed our path. It was near six
o'clock when we reached home; but we felt much
less fatigue than we could have expected, and were
more delighted by the excursion than we had even
hoped to be.

The only trees and plants known to us, which we
saw, and, which I have not yet mentioned, were the
koa, *acacia*, a large and beautiful tree of dark, hard
wood, of which the canoes of the natives are formed;
the Ohia, *eugenia malaccensis*, bearing a beautifully
tufted crimson flower, and a fruit called by foreigners,
the native apple, from its resemblance to our fruit of
that name, juicy and refreshing, but rather insipid to
the taste: and the castor tree, *palma christi*. Of

fruits, besides the tamarind, Malacca apple, and prickly pear, *cactus ficus indicus,* which grows to a large size here, we met with the banana, plantain, lime, lemon, pine-apple, and musk and water melons : and saw of vegetables, potatoes, principally, the sweet, though some few common American or Irish, yam, taro, pumpkin, cabbage, Indian corn, onion, bean, cucumber : and pepper, ginger, mustard, and tobacco.

The bread-fruit is one of the finest of our vegetables. A full-grown tree is about the size of an ordinary hickory in America, or an ash in England. The fruit, when flourishing, is larger than a pine-apple, and more circular in its shape ; when perfectly ripe, its colour becomes yellowish, and its taste sweet, but not plea-sant. We eat it before it is ripe, when it is a light green colour. The outer coat, or peel, is thin but hard, though not shining like the rind of a melon, and is entirely covered with slightly marked, and small pentagonal sections. It is cooked, by throwing it directly from the tree, upon a bed of coals, or into the blaze of a fire. The outer coat immediately becomes charred, while the inner parts only roast like a potatoe. When cooked through, the rind is easily removed, leaving a beautiful, light-coloured, smoking loaf. Its general consistence is that of a fine Irish potatoe ; but more spungy, and, towards the centre, quite porous. In taste it is very like the hard-boiled yolk of an egg.

Tuesday, 22. The ship Sultan, Captain Clark, of Boston, last from the North-west Coast of America, came to an anchor in the roads this morning. Shortly after, I received a note from the consul, requesting me to attend the funeral of a passenger, who had died on board, the day she made the Islands. His name is Prescott, first officer of brig Frederick, of Boston, which has been sold on the Spanish coast, and her captain and crew brought to the Islands by the Sultan. There was a very respectable attendance ; the procession moving from the consulate, where the religious services were performed. It will be a consolation to the friends of him thus called into the world of spirits, far from the tender sympathies of home, to know that he has found a resting place, though in a heathen land, near a Christian chapel, and not in the dreary caverns of the deep.

June 23. Were you sitting with us this evening, my dear M——, you would scarce believe yourself in the torrid zone, and that too in midsummer. The wind howls around us as boisterously, if not as coldly, as it does through the colonnades of your own mansion, when a northern storm sweeps down the lake on a winter's night and we have been obliged to close all our doors and windows, and resort to woollen garmens, to keep us comfortable. The whole day has been blustering, gloomy, and wet, similar to the weather of March in America, and such as in this climate, especially at Lahaina, is seldom known. There is a heavy swell of the ocean from the south, and the high surf occasioned by it, though near a mile distant, has been the object of constant attraction from its varying beauty and tumult. The interest of the scene in this direction, is much increased by the appearance of the Sultan, still outside of the reef. She labours at her anchor in the violence of the gale, with a stateliness of motion becoming the proud name she bears.

There has been so much of a tempest at sea, that Governor Adams, who sailed for the windward on Saturday, returned this morning with the loss of a topmast and yards.

Thursday 15. Mr. and Mrs. Ellis having become partially established in a new stone cottage, gave a special invitation to the Mission family to spend the day with them. We were happy indeed to see our valued friends so comfortably accommodated—after having been subjected for eighteen months to great inconvenience, from the want of a suitable residence— rendered doubly desirable by the extreme ill health of Mrs. Ellis.

Seated at table with none but dear companions and confidential friends near us, we could almost fancy ourselves again at a family party at home; and in the illusion, for a moment find a melancholy pleasure. After the cloth was removed, we passed the afternoon in listening with lively interest to the journal of the deputation which explored the island of Hawaii last summer, and which Mr. Ellis is preparing for the public. We also again examined the drawings which are to accompany the work, copies of which I have taken to accompany the manuscript for the American Board. The originals will go to the London Missionary Society.

After tea we held the customary weekly prayer meeting of the Mission family: when Mr. Ellis gave a warm and affecting address from the words, " Bless the Lord, O my soul; and all that is within me, bless his holy

name"—" Bless the Lord, O my soul, and forget not all
his benefits"—in which he recounted the various deal-
ings of Providence towards himself and family, since his
arrival in the Islands, and testified to the unfailing
goodness, mercy, and faithfulness of God.   Many circumstances conduced to make the hour deeply interesting; we felt the high and holy ties by which we were
united to each other ; and could any one have looked
in upon us, while the lively sympathies of our hearts
entered into all the feelings of our associates, though
strangers till we met on pagan ground, he might with
truth have exclaimed, " Behold how these Christians
love one another !"

> " Lone exiles, on these northern isles,
>   Placed far amid the melancholy main."

It is a happiness inconceivable to any one not of our
number, or in a similar situation, to meet here those we
can tenderly love; and to find in them the refinement,
the intelligence, and the piety, which in any place give
the highest zest to the enjoyments of social life.

CHAPTER XII.

KARAIMOKU'S NEW PALACE.

Mission House at Honoruru, Friday 16. Dined
to day at the residence of Captain Ebbetts, of New York,
in company with Mr. Crocker, American consul; Mr.
Small, a Scotch gentleman, recently from South America;
Mr. Bruce and Mr. Halsey, of New York; Mr. and
Mrs. Ellis; and Mr. and Mrs. Loomis, and H——, of
the Mission.

Tuesday 20. This evening, at 8 o'clock, Karaimoku
sent to request us to attend prayers with himself and
household at his new house, in which he sleeps for the
first time to-night. We passed a happy hour with him,
and consider the circumstance a strong evidence of the
interest he takes, and the importance he attaches, to the
exercises of family worship.

This building will bear the name of *palace*. It is of
stone, plastered and whitened, two and a half stories
high, sixty-four feet in front, and forty in depth; and
externally, except in the roof, is not unlike Mr.
J. Fennimore Cooper's house, at Fennimore. The second
story, the front doors and windows of which open on a

Ellis del.

J. Hinchliff. sculp.

Palace of Karaimoku. — Native Chapel. — Cottage of Mr Ellis.

Published by Fisher. Son & Co. Caxton. London. April 1828.

covered piazza or verandah, is that in which the regent will live. It consists of one very large apartment in front, upwards of fifty feet long, and proportionably wide, designed for a saloon, in which to entertain strangers—commanding, from its elevation, a fine view of the island and the ocean—and a small neat room at one end for a cabinet, to be furnished with an escritoir, &c. The rest of the floor is divided into sleeping rooms, for himself, and one or two confidential attendants.

The expense of the building, exclusive of the stone, is estimated at six thousand dollars. It stands in an enclosure of several acres, which is to be planted, and kept in a state of cultivation: and the whole establishment will give quite a new aspect to Honoruru, from whatever point it is viewed.

Kaahumanu has also had a new house built during the year; it is of wood, and was prepared in all its parts for erection, before it was brought from America. It is well papered and painted, and, in its dimensions and general appearance, similar to some of our best wooden houses at Cooper's-town. These two buildings, with the *consulate*, which is also a two-story frame house, a smaller one belonging to Kaahumanu, and the two Mission houses, give quite an European aspect to the town; and while they render it more picturesque, by the contrast with the native huts, afford evidence of the civilization to which the nation is approaching.

21. This morning the ship Jupiter, Captain Leslie of New York, anchored in the roads: and in the evening, most of our friends in the village, to the

number of fifteen, including Captain Leslie, took tea
with us.

Monday, Aug. 9.   Yesterday morning, at day-break,
B—— tapped at our door, to announce the arrival of
the long anxiously expected Tamaahmaah of New York.
Captain Meek politely sent up one letter before breakfast, and a packet of twenty-five or thirty, in time to
be read in the evening.

Tuesday night, Aug. 10.   We had just completed
every preparation this afternoon, for our return to Maui
to-morrow, in the Tamaahmaah, and were making a
farewell visit to our friends Mr. and Mrs. Ellis, when
the pilot-boat New York was seen approaching the harbour from Taui.   She had scarce come to an anchor
outside the reef, when, instead of welcoming Karaimoku
and Mr. and Mrs. Bingham, as we had expected, the
whole town, as well as our families, was thrown into
agitation, by the cry of " *ua Taua !—ua Taua !*"—" it
is War !—it is War !"—the intelligence of a rebellion and
battle at that island, and of the necessary desertion of
the station at Waimea by Mr. Bingham and Mr. Whitney, for the safety of themselves and families, having
been brought by the schooner.

G. P. Tamoree is at the head of the insurgents; they
attacked the fort at day-break on Sabbath morning, it
was with difficulty saved ; and not till ten of the assail-
ants and six of the government party were killed.   Karaimoku, immediately after the repulse of the rebel party,
a part of whose plan was to cut him off at the same
time they seized the fort, sent for the Missionaries, to
return thanks to God with him, for his deliverance ; to

inform them that the pilot-boat would sail immediately to Oahu for assistance; and to urge their departure with their families by the opportunity, assuring them that he would protect them with his life so long as he lived, but intimating a fear that, from the weakness of the party with him, they might all perish.

Our friends have suffered much from the horrors of the scene they witnessed at the storming of the fort, and on their visit to it after the battle, while it was yet filled with the bodies of the slain, and echoing with the groans of the wounded and dying; much from anxiety for the safety of Karaimoku; and much from fatigue and privation, having embarked without taking any refreshment, or preparing any thing for the voyage, which has been forty-eight hours long. They were all completely drenched with the surf, in getting off in a canoe to the schooner, and had not the means of changing the clothes, even of the two infants with them.

The evening has been one of intense interest, while we have listened to the narrative of our friends; and rendered our devout thanksgiving, that they have been brought safely to our arms from amid " *the ragings of the people,*" and the scenes of death.

One of the rebel chiefs, a fine looking young man, was made captive when his party were repulsed. He requested to be shot; but was bound hand and foot, according to a custom of the country, and carried on board the pilot-boat. Mr. Bingham saw him in the evening after they had put to sea, seated against the timbers of the vessel in her main hold. In the morning, the prisoner was gone; and on inquiry, the captain

2 c

without speaking, but by very significant pantomime, made known his fate; he had been thrown overboard in the dead of the night, with his cords upon him, when midway between Taui and Oahu! This is the manner in which, since the abolition of the tabu, those guilty of high offences against the government, have generally been despatched. In the period of idolatry, they were devoted in sacrifice to the gods.

A thousand men are already ordered to be prepared to embark, at sunrise to-morrow morning, for the relief of Karaimoku; and scarce any thing is heard, but the rolling of the drum and the discharging of muskets, by way of trying their fitness for use. Chiefs and people have entered fully into the spirit of the occasion, no one is to be seen without some of the *insignia belli*, caps, feathers, cartridge boxes, swords or muskets, while every step and every look is *en militaire*.

Mission House, Lahaina, Aug. 16.   Through the politeness of Captains Meek and Ebbetts, we were returned to the embraces of our associates, and to our home, on the 14th instant, after a pleasant passage of twenty-four hours from Oahu, in the beautiful brig Tamaahmaah.   This vessel, and two or three belonging to the government, have just sailed with all the leading chieftains, and three or four hundred of their vassals, for the seat of warfare; scarce any but chief females are left behind.

Saturday, 11.   On the 7th instant, all the chief women, except the governess Wahine Pio, the queen Kekauonohi, and the princess, left Lahaina for Kairua, on a visit to Governor Adams.   The news of the war a

Taui, and the absence of the most powerful rulers, have excited in the farmers and common people throughout the district, a more general spirit of drunkenness than at any time since our arrival among them. For the last few days, by far the greater portion of the whole population have been in a state of intoxication; and given up night and day to gambling, riot, and fighting, and every species of revelry. Almost the whole of our scholars have been sent to Taui, or taken off to Hawaii; so that, just at present, we are in rather discouraging circumstances.

Drunkenness is one of the most common vices of the people. Intoxicating liquors are imported in large quantities; but the principal means of indulgence among the inhabitants in general, is a species of rum, the production of rude distilleries of their own; and a fermented liquor of inebriating quality, which they manufacture from the sugar-cane, the sweet potatoe, and the baked root of the *dracæna*, an article exceedingly saccharine, and capable of being formed into a very strong beer. For the art of distillation, and for that of brewing also, the Islanders were early indebted, I believe, to the skill and vicious thirst of two or three citizens of *Port Jackson*, who found it convenient to exchange the place of their exile; and secured a passage from Botany Bay to Hawaii.

It is scarce possible for the inhabitants of a civilized country to imagine the scenes presented at one of these periods of general inebriation, when men, women, and children are every where met, under all the wild excitement of liquor; especially when to this state is added the singing, dancing, shouting, and fighting of heathenism.

At the present time, a favourite sport, moku-moku, or boxing, has been revived. It is a national game, regulated by established principles; to secure an adherence to which, managers and umpires are appointed, who preside over it, and determine points of dispute. The champions usually belong to different chiefs; and enter the ring inspirited by a *pride of clanship*, as well as by the ambition of personal distinction. When one has been prostrated, so as to yield the contest, the victor paces the circle with an air of defiance, challenging any other to a trial of strength and skill; and thus, in the course of half an hour, a dozen may successively lose an ultimate triumph, by being themselves knocked down by some combatant of greater tact, or muscular power, who at last clears the arena.

A well directed *blood-starting* or *levelling blow*, is followed by unbounded applause from the surrounding multitude, testified in the most appropriate manner, by *yells* and shouts of barbarity, that make the whole welkin ring; while the tossing of thousands of arms into the air, jumping, dancing, and clapping of hands, prolong the expression of delight.

These boxing matches often lead to wagers among the spectators, and not unfrequently end in violence and death. At almost every shout from the ring, the natives of our household exclaim, " *Taha ! taha ! mamuri make !*"—Ah! ah! by and by murder !—and inform us, that many are killed in the moku-moku; and that only a few years ago, forty men were murdered at one time, on the very spot now occupied by the exhibition.

The games which are the principal means of gambling,

and at which the natives spend much of their time, are chiefly, *the uru maita, the pahe, the konane,* and *the buhenehene.* The two first are similar to each other in their principles. *The uru maita* consists of the bowling, by two individuals or parties, of a circular, flat, and highly polished stone, two or three inches in diameter, and an inch thick, swelling with a slight convexity from the edges to the centre. The art consists in sending the stone, so as to pass between two short sticks driven in the ground near to each other, at the greatest distance; or in the driving of one party by the other, by bowling the stone farthest.

In *the pahe,* short blunted darts, of very hard and highly polished wood, from two to four feet long, are used in a similar manner, instead of the stone. The *konane,* is a kind of drafts, played with small black and white stones, on a board marked with a great number of squares. It appears to be an intricate and tedious game. The *buhenehene,* is on the principle of the childish amusement of *hiding the slipper;* and the art, on the one side, consists in hiding a stone so adroitly, in the full gaze of all present, under one of five loose bundles of native cloth, placed on the ground, between the parties for this purpose, as to lead to a mistake in the guess of the seeker for it; and on the other side, of so close a watch of all the muscular motions of the arm, chest, and shoulder, in the individual secreting the stone, as to lead to a discovery of the withdrawing of the hand from it, and thus to a knowledge of the tapa under which it lies. The two last games are played principally by the chiefs, and in them, the single wagers of Riho-

Riho have sometimes risen to forty, eighty, and even four hundred dollars. The common people not unfrequently become so much excited at games of the *uru maita* and *pahe*, that the greater number of thousands collected around, will be themselves betting on the different parties; though in doing it, hundreds stake the very last article they possess in the world, even to the maro or pau they are wearing at the time.

Wednesday, 16. The state of things referred to, in the preceding paragraphs, continued to become more and more dreadful, till the governess herself, who has never been very friendly to our object, felt it necessary to interpose with the arm of her power. On Saturday afternoon, when the boxing-matches threatened every moment to lead to scenes of unrestrained violence and murder, and stones and clubs began already to thicken in the air, she ordered an armed band from the fort to disperse the people by musket and bayonet; and, immediately afterwards, heralds were sent through the district to proclaim a law against all farther drinking of rum or beer, against all boxing and fighting, and against every breach of the Sabbath, on penalty of the displeasure of the government, and a fine of a hundred dollars for each offence. Since which, the whole settlement has been in perfect order and quietude.

Monday, 20. For some time past the chiefs have expressed their determination to have instruction in reading and writing extended to the whole population; and have only been waiting for books, and an increase in the number of suitably qualified native teachers, to put the resolution, as far as practicable, into effect. A knowledge of this having reached some of the maka ainana, or farmers of Lahaina, who did not enter into the recent dissipation, including the tenants of our own plantation, application was made by them to us for books and slates, and an instructor ; and the first school, consisting of about thirty individuals, ever formed among that class of the people, has, within a few days, been established in our enclosure, under the superintendence of B——, who is quite familiar with the native tongue.

This event we regard as very important : believing that the introduction of books and slates among the common people, will prove, as it did among the chiefs, the most effectual means of withdrawing them from their idle and vicious habits ; and of bringing them more readily under the influence of our teachings in morality and religion.

Thursday 23. The leading female chiefs returned on Saturday from Hawaii, and sailed again this morning for Taui, to visit Karaimoku, who has been successful in putting down the insurrection ; and has called a council of the chiefs, to sanction his arrangements for the future government of that island. George Tamoree, who has escaped death, will be brought to Honoruru, and kept as a prisoner at large. The principles of Christianity have been most happily exhibited by Karaimoku and his chiefs in the prosecution of the war : it has been conducted with as little as possible of the former sanguinary spirit of their conflicts. The rebel party proved small in number and weak in power, all avowedly pagans, with George, a professed sceptic, at their head.*

* Although George Tamoree, or *Humehuma*, as he was deno-

The whole result of this commotion promises to be propitious instead of adverse to the cause of Christianity. The chiefs have felt their dependence on the Mission for right counsel in a time of anxiety and

minated by the people, headed the rebels, the war did not probably originate with him. A day or two before his death Taumuarii his late father made his will I was present on the occasion, and heard him distinctly and explicitly state, in the presence of the assembled chief, his desire that, at his decease, the ships he possessed, the fort, and arms, and ammunition, together with the islands of Taui and Mihau, should be given to Karaimoku for the king Riho-Riho, then absent in En land. When Karaimoku, with about forty followers, went down to fix the future government of the Islands, many of the chiefs brought him presents, thereby paying him homage as their chief. Among others, George was proceeding down the river from his district, with a canoe laden with provision and fruits for Karaimoku, who by Taumuarii had been appointed his guardian. *Tiaimakaui*, who was the most active promoter of the war, with several other warrior chiefs, met him, stopped his canoe, and said, "You shall not pay him homage, neither will we; come with us, you shall be our king; the Islands are yours, as they were your fathers; you shall be king, and we are the *nae koa* warriors. Much will fight for you." George carried not his present, united with them, formed a party, and took a principal share in the attack and subsequent war. Tiaimakaui, after committing an act of most barbarous and treacherous murder in the onset, was afterwards slain, and his body treated with great indignity.

Among the friends of Karaimoku, who were slain in the attack on the fort, there was a fine tall intelligent young Englishman, whose name was Trowbridge. He had left the ship in which he reached the Islands, and commanded one of the vessels belonging to Karaimoku, by whom he was highly respected.—W. E.

emergency ; have experienced the happy consequences of our instructions in meliorating the horrors of warfare ; and have, apparently, fixed their confidence and affection upon us with fresh warmth and firmness.

Before leaving Lahaina, Kaahumanu gave orders to the head-men of all the districts of Maui, to have the following laws proclaimed by herald to all the people. First, " *There shall be no murder*"—referring especially to the crime of infanticide. Second, " *There shall be no drunkenness, no boxing, no fighting.*" Third, " *There shall be no theft.*" Fourth, " *All the people must regard the Sabbath.*" Fifth, " *When schools are established, all the people must learn.*"

Jan. 1, 1825. My first note at this date, my dear M——, must in part, at least, be retrospective. Since October, I have kept brief notes only of passing occurrences ; owing principally to an unexpected visit at Oahu, to the full occupation of my time with other duties while there, and to the accumulation of business during my absence, which required immediate attention on my return. We have also been much engaged, during the last month, in making preparations to go to that island, by the first favourable opportunity, to spend the winter. The duties of the station at Honoruru, since the embarkation of Mr. Ellis for England, including at present the formation of one or two new books, and the superintendence of the press, are such as to make it desirable that Mr. Bingham should have an assistant preacher, at least for a few months ; and several circumstances combine to make it most proper, that myself and family should be the persons to remove there.

My passage to Oahu was in the whale ship Enterprise, Captain Weeks, a gentleman among the most es-
teemed of the friends we have met in the Pacific : and
in whose officers and ship we have taken a lively
interest.   Nothing of particular importance occurred
while I was at Oahu ; and after a visit of three weeks, I
returned in one of the native pilot-boats.

The blessings of a new year meet us in circumstances
of more than ordinary quiet and regularity, and the
order of our little cabin is more systematic than it has
been since our establishment on the islands.

The sketch of a day at present will give you the
regular engagements of a month ; and in its peaceful
progress, I can assure you, we find no inconsiderable
degree of contentment and happiness.   We generally
rise with the sun, and spend the first hour in religious
and devotional reading ; breakfast at eight o'clock, a
frugal meal, as we are entirely without butter, sugar,
and coffee ; and immediately after have family worship.
The hours from nine to twelve, Mr. Richards and myself devote to the study of the native language, and to
the preparation of exercises for some one of the native
religious meetings.   At ten o'clock in the morning, and
at five in the afternoon, Kekaunonohi, the youngest
queen of Riho-Riho, and one of her favourite female
friends, an interesting and intelligent girl of fifteen,
come with their retinue to study, under the direction of
H—— ; while the young princess and another scholar
visit Mrs. Richards for the like purpose, at the same
hours.

After dinner we devote an hour to miscellaneous

reading, of which the periodical publications sent from America, and our united libraries, form a tolerable collection. I then visit the schools, call on the chiefs, and afterwards walk to our garden, about a half mile from the beach, on the plantation given us by Karaimoku, on our first arrival at Lahaina. This I have succeeded in reducing to a regular form, have enclosed it by rows of bananas, planted the grape, pine-apple, orange, and tamarind, besides a variety of vegetables, and some choice shrubs and flowers; and in its cultivation and improvement have great amusement, and much promised future delight. In these walks I am often accompanied by H—— and C——, while B—— is engaged in a fine school kept by her every afternoon, in the chapel adjoining our yard.

As to our evenings, though it is now our winter, they are ushered in with little of that *luxury of comfort*, which the Christian poet must often have felt, before he could so sweetly have sung,

> Now stir the fire, and close the shutters fast,
> Let fall the curtains, wheel the sofa round,
> And, while the bubbling and loud hissing urn
> Throws up a steamy column, and the cups
> That cheer but not inebriate, wait on each,
> So let us welcome peaceful evening in:

Still evening is the pleasantest portion of the day. Our yard is no longer crowded by noisy natives, whose chiefs are lounging about our writing-desks and work-tables. C—— forgets his mischief and his play, in the sweetness of infantile sleep; all out of doors is silent, except the restless surf; and we are left without interruption, renewedly to apply ourselves to this unformed language, that we may be qualified for more extensive usefulness in the stations we occupy. At nine o'clock, we turn to the Bible, which we are studying with Scott and Henry's Commentaries, and, after an hour spent in reading, and in passing an examination on the portion which occupied our attention on the preceding night, we again have family worship, and retire to rest usually between ten and eleven o'clock.

Our regular public duties with the natives are, two sermons on the Sabbath; a weekly lecture every Wednesday; a meeting for conversation and prayer every Friday afternoon; and the monthly concert on the first Monday of every month. We have worship in English every Sabbath, but only read a sermon, unless there are ships at the anchorage. Such is the employment of our time in this heathen land, and such the routine of duty which our little cottage in a greater or less degree daily witnesses; and had we, in addition to our present sources of happiness, only a ready, were it but an occasional, access to the society of those friends, around whom, far as they are from us, our warm affections are daily hovering, I could most sincerely exclaim,

> " O blest seclusion from a jarring world,
> Which we, thus occupied, enjoy !—
> Had we the choice of sublunary good,
> What could we wish that we possess not here !"

Jan. 7. We cannot write even at this season, from these mild latitudes, of " *nipping frosts*" and " *drifting snow ;*" still, even here winter comes

> ———" to rule the varied year,
> Sullen and sad, with all her rising train
> Of vapours, clouds, and storms."

The climate of the Islands is far more cool than might be supposed, judging from the latitude in which they are situated. This is partly owing to the vast unbroken body of water by which they are surrounded, but principally and more immediately to the prevalence of the north-east trade wind, which, during the larger portion of the year, sweeps over and about them with great velocity, and, from the direction in which it comes, and the surface over which it passes, possesses no inconsiderable refrigerative power. In the trade-wind, the mercury in Fahrenheit's thermometer (in the shade) seldom rises higher than 80° and 82°, during the summer, and 72° and 74° during the winter.

From the very great height of the mountains, however, there are places and districts on the leeward or western sides of some of the islands, which are inaccessible to the regular wind, except when it becomes a gale, breaking over the lower hills, and rushing in strong eddies round the points and promontories, which at ordinary times form a barrier to it. Lahaina is situated on one of these spots, and probably is the hottest district in the group; the mercury usually rising as high in winter here, as it does in midsummer where the trades prevail; and in summer frequently to 88° and 89°.

During the summer months, or from March to October, when the trade-wind is most strong and most regular, Lahaina enjoys a pleasant, and often fresh seabreeze; but even then, there is not circulation enough to give it the ventilation received wherever the former wind reaches. In winter, when the trades are generally light, and often interrupted entirely by calms and south-

2 D

westerly winds, the sea-breeze also becomes light and
variable, and a much greater stagnation of air takes
place, rendered doubly impure by exhalations from the
taro beds and fish-ponds, which are numerous throughout the settlement. These circumstances cause the climate of Lahaina to be rather unfavourable to health.

As to *clouds* and *rain*, from March to October the
atmosphere throughout all the Islands is usually clear
and bright, similar to your finest June weather. On
the windward or eastern parts, however, there are almost
daily showers, and in the mountains not unfrequently
continued rains, from the lodgment of clouds against
their tops and sides. In most places on the leeward
sides there are also occasional showers; but at Lahaina
scarcely a cloud, except on the mountains, is during the
summer to be seen, and a drop of rain during those
months seldom falls. From September to April the
atmosphere is more or less hazy, obscure and cloudy,
with frequent light rains in some places, and in others
heavy storms of two or three days' continuance. We
have had three storms only, at Lahaina, since our residence here, and they have been in December, January,
and March.

Monday, Jan. 17. Yesterday morning the native
brig, Becket, arrived from Honoruru, and at twelve
o'clock, our friends Dr. and Mrs. Blatchely, and Mr.
Hoffman, mineralogist on board the Russian discovery
ship, Captain Kotzebue, now at Oahu, landed at the
Mission House. Mr. Hoffman is an interesting young
man, apparently not more than twenty-two or twenty-
four years old, of highly prepossessing appearance, and

agreeable manners. He makes his home with us while the brig remains; and we feel ourselves happy in entertaining a guest of so much intelligence and good breeding.

Wednesday, 19. At noon yesterday, we discovered the pilot-boat Astor, bounding before a fresh breeze, over the waters of the Morokai channel, and, in the course of an hour, welcomed Mr. Chamberlain to Lahaina. He is on his way to Hido, on the east of Hawaii, with supplies for Waiakea, and will spend a few days with us while the vessel is taking in a cargo of salt.

Mr. Chamberlain, in his station of Agent of the Mission, with the superintendence of secular concerns, is a most indefatigable labourer, the servant of us all, and literally " *a hewer of wood, and drawer of water.*" In entering the situation he now occupies, he relinquished a partnership in a mercantile establishment of Boston, successfully engaged in business, with the most flattering prospects of affluence, placed his capital in the stocks, devoting the interest to the Missionary cause, and, in contrast to his former situation, may now almost daily be seen at Honoruru, with a cheerful face and happy heart, driving a team of oxen, or drawing a porter's barrow, from the Mission House to the village; or in a coarse carman's frock, toiling among the barrels and boxes of his storehouse.

For the last two days Mr. Hoffman, attended by Mr. Richards, has been scouring the country, in search of specimens in mineralogy; and this afternoon I accompanied him in a walk to the foot of one of the mountains immediately to the east of our settlement, for the

same object, but without meeting any thing new or particularly interesting.   The mineralogical kingdom here
presents little variety in its exhibitions ; every thing is
almost exclusively volcanic, and in forms long familiar
to the scientific world.   The arrangement and combination of these forms, however, are frequently such as to
create admiration and astonishment; especially on
Hawaii, which in this respect, taken as a whole, including the sublime and fearful exhibitions of the great
crater of Kirauea, is among the greatest phenomena of
the Pacific.

The Becket sails for Kairua to-morrow, and carries
from us all our visitors, excepting Mr. Chamberlain.
While at my writing-desk this evening, Mr. Hoffman
left on a sheet of paper the name of his ship, and a list
of her officers, as a little memento of his visit.

This gave rise to some remarks on the character of
Captain Kotzebue ; among other things Mr. Hoffman
stated, that he was a great admirer of Washington.
During the morning, in looking over some papers preparatory to my visit to Honoruru, I had found in the
folds of one of my pocket-books, a sprig of evergreen
plucked from a tree on the humble tomb of our illus-
trious countryman, when I visited Mount Vernon, in
1821.   I immediately handed it to Mr. Hoffman,
saying, " If Captain Kotzebue admires Washington,
even this trifle will be thought acceptable by him ;" but
the moment he knew its origin, with enthusiastic ear-
nestness, though not without evident embarrassment at
the liberty taken of directing it from the person mentioned, he exclaimed, " *Non, non, Monsieur, non Kot*

zebue, moi-même, moi-même ;" " No, no, Sir, not Kotzebue, not Kotzebue ; myself ! myself !"—to which I most
readily assented ; and added as a testimony of my personal regard, what I had before designed for that purpose, a neat pocket edition of the Testament in French,
the language in which we had attempted to hold most
of our conversations.

CHAPTER XIII.

Mission House, Honoruru, Feb. 4, 1825. We are again, my dear M——, visitors at this station. We embarked on board the Becket on the evening of the 1st instant, and arrived here the next morning to a late breakfast. Although the night was very cool for this climate, the thermometer standing at 64° Fahrenheit, we all kept the deck, in preference to enduring the confined air of the cabin.

We are delightfully situated, for Missionaries I mean, with our invaluable friends Mr. and Mrs. Bingham, in the stone cottage built by Mr. Ellis. Oahu never before looked so beautiful; for the first time since we arrived at the Islands, the whole of the extensive plain, on which Honoruru and the Mission Houses are, is covered with verdure, and appears like one continued field of grain, in the early months of the spring; the grass being coarse, and of a light green colour. The greater purity of the air than that of Lahaina is also very perceptible, and makes us feel that Oahu, so far as we are capable of judging, is the *Montpellier* of the Sandwich Islands : owing to the prevalence of the trade-winds, which sweep over the mountains—not here, as on most of the other islands, so high as to form a barrier against them. Every part of the island is thus constantly ventilated, and preserved from any degree of the stagnation to which Lahaina is subject.

Our young friend Hoffman, a fellow passenger from Maui, was met on the wharf with warm embraces by his friends of the *Pretpriatie.* The handsome dresses and gentlemanly appearance of these voyagers of the enterprising Czar, give an additional aspect of civilization to Honoruru. Mr. Hoffman, with some of his friends, visits us every day. He takes tea with us this evening; after which we are to go to an observatory erected for astronomical purposes on shore, with the special design of viewing the planet Saturn through a fine telescope.

Monday 7. On Saturday, Mr. Bingham and myself took tea, and passed the evening on board the *Pretpriatie.* She is a well-built, substantial, and fine ship, of twenty-two guns, constructed under the direction of Captain Kotzebue, expressly for the voyage she is now performing. Her deck is remarkably handsome, and the accommodations of the officers and crew very convenient The Captain's cabin is large, airy, and well, but not handsomely, furnished—no carpets nor drapery. The chairs, sofa, tables, and sideboard, are of plain mahogany, with one or two large mirrors. The most ornamental article is a richly painted half-length portrait of Alexander of Russia ; to which may be added a smaller engraved likeness of the same noble character, ex-

quisitely finished, and said to be much more correct
than the former. It is the production of a French
artist, executed at the time the Emperor was in Paris.

The officers' cabin is separated from the captain's
by the companion-way, and is fitted so as to afford,
besides a comfortable dining and sitting room, a large
state room for each of the lieutenants, midshipmen, and
naturalists. Immediately forward of this, is the forecastle, where the crew, one hundred in number, are
neatly and conveniently accommodated. One end of
this apartment is used as a chapel, and furnished with
an altar, a shrine of the Virgin Mary, a tolerably executed Madonna, one or two crosses, and a painting of
our Saviour, surrounded by portraits of the Apostles, in
twelve compartments of the same frame.

Every Saturday evening there is a public service, and
we were gratified by the opportunity of witnessing the
ceremonies of the Greek church. On this occasion,
they consisted of the services of the rubric in Sclavonic,
prayers, lessons, chants, the offering of incense by the
priest, who officiated in an embroidered mantle of green,
crimson, and gold ; the kissing of the Bible and of a
cross, at the close of the service, held by the priest to
each individual, after the benediction. There was no
exhortation, nor any thing in the form of preaching.
During the ceremonies, which occupied more than an
hour, the crew stood six abreast, three on the starboard
and three on the larboard side, in regular lines from the
altar to the bows, observed the greatest order, and
seemed to listen with suitable solemnity to the worship.
The officers, among whom we took our places, formed

a group immediately behind the chaplain, and, by their apparent reverence and devotion, set a commendable example to the crew. Their full, deep-toned voices, and, in some instances, good taste in singing, added much to the effect of the chants and anthems, the choruses of which, in two or three instances, were very fine.

Though, in the whole, there was a striking want of that simplicity, which, we believe, characterized the primitive church of Christ, still we could but regard with tender interest and complacency, a scene in which so large, so youthful, and so noble a company, publicly and solemnly testified their remembrance and fear of God; rather than in uniting in the shameless exhibitions of wickedness, which too often, by day and by night, scandalize the Christian name, of ships at anchor at these islands.

Within the last two days, there have been arrivals both from the leeward and windward stations, and the very animating letters received by them from the Missionaries and chiefs, promise a more interesting state of things in the Mission, than we have yet known.

Saturday, 12. We were last evening called to part with our Russian friends of the *Pretpriatie*, which left the harbour early this morning, and now looks only like a lofty spire in the midst of the ocean, as she is gently securing an offing from the island before night. We have formed a pleasant acquaintance with several of her officers, though only one, besides Captain Kotzebue, speaks much English. But none has taken such hold on our hearts as the interesting and accomplished young Hoffman; he has been so constantly in our family, has so greatly commended himself to our love by his intelligence and good breeding, by the warmth and polish of his manners, by the tenderness of his heart, and by a thousand evidences of a virtuous and amiable spirit, that our parting embraces were more like those of long beloved and bosom friends, than of strangers whose acquaintance has been only of a day.

March 10. The ships Peru and Almira came into port this morning. They are directly from America, and have brought letters and papers from some of our friends, and considerable supplies for the Mission. But every other feeling is lost in the melancholy intelligence of the death of our friends Kamehamaru and Riho-Riho. The truth is a shock to us; so much so, that we frankly confess, our tears are mingled with those of the chiefs and people, who are almost overwhelmed by the bereavement. We feel that we have lost those in whom we had a very deep interest, if they did not possess our warm and tender love; and there were circumstances in their embarkation, the recollection of which will always cause us to sigh, that they were denied, against their own strong wish, and against the wish of the Mission and of the nation, the privilege of having a pious teacher, interpreter, and guardian with them.

We think it probable our friends in America will feel some solicitude, lest the death of the king should prove an occasion of insurrection and bloodshed in the islands; but of this we have scarce had a thought, much less an apprehension. So long as the Prince *Keauikeaouli* lives, the right of succession is indisputable. Riho-Riho, in his council with the chiefs, previous to his embarkation, formally and publicly appointed him successor, in case he should never return ; and from the time of his departure, the lad has been regarded, and officially addressed by the chiefs and people, as their king.   This has been more especially the case of late; so that the intelligence has produced little or no change in his standing in the government, and none in his title, except the assumption of the name of Tamehameha III., as the official signature of the successor of Riho-Riho.

In every respect, a kind Providence seems to have been preparing the way most happily for the arrival of the tidings; and the chiefs in power were never before in a state so favourable to political integrity and peace. Auspicious as the whole history of this Mission has been ever since its establishment, still the last three months must be regarded as the commencement of a new and more happy era in its progress, than had previously been known.

We have every reason to believe that the principles of eternal truth, with the sanctions from which they are inseparable, which for near five years have been enforced on the minds and the hearts of the leaders of this people, are beginning to have their destined and desired effect on their characters and lives; and that many of the most powerful of them, from the fear of God and a sincere love of his righteousness, are ceasing in heart to do evil, and learning to do well.

The young king, and every chief of any importance, have regular family worship with their respective households morning and evening, never take a meal without thanksgiving, observe the Sabbath with becoming propriety, attend all the religious instructions, and studiously avoid every kind of amusement and pastime, not consistent with strict sobriety and Christian decorum. Their whole minds and their whole time seem given to improvement ; and so far from becoming weary, they appear more and more desirous of making night and day profitable, by the acquisition of new light and a new knowledge of the word of God. Such is the state in which the melancholy tidings found them, and the effect is apparently such as might be expected ; it was a dreadful blow, but we have seen and heard none of the extravagant expressions of heathen grief. For the first day or two, their sorrow was evidently keen and deep, but it was quiet, humble, and Christian ; their tears fell silently and rapidly, but they manifested no disposition to indulge in the loud wailing by which they were once accustomed to vent their feelings.

Sabbath evening, April 17. Nearly two years have elapsed since we landed on these distant shores. In all my communications since, in recounting the dispensations of Providence to me and mine, I have been called to mention only " *blessings undisguised.*" We have endured many petty privations, felt some anxieties, known some sorrows, and shed some tears ; but they were all such as to be classed among the " *lighter afflictions :*" too trifling to be mentioned, in connection with the general prosperity and overbalancing happiness we have enjoyed. During the last few days, however, the hitherto unclouded sky has gathered blackness, till this morning our fears were made exquisitely awake to apprehensions of an overwhelming calamity. But the darkness of the day has in much mercy been scattered, and the rainbow of promise and of peace is depicted on the blackness of the averted storm. You, my dear M——, will not think the figure I have thus inadvertently introduced, too strong, when I tell you, that H—— has been restored to her husband and her children, after having seemingly trod on the borders of the grave.

She has been ill ever since the birth of a daughter on the 7th of March; and this morning was thought to be dying. The family were assembled, and prayer made to God for the light of his countenance, as she should pass through the dark valley; but in the course of an hour, a happy alteration in her state took place; every symptom became decidedly favourable, and she is now, for the first time in forty-eight hours, sleeping, with a prospect of refreshment.

Tuesday, 19. Since the Sabbath our alarm for the safety of our dear H——, has, at two or three times, been even greater than it then was; but we are again encouraged by hope. It will give you happiness to know that, when we were most fearful as to the event, we had the high consolation of seeing imparted to her, by her covenant God, not only a spirit of resignation and peace, but thoughts of brightness and of joy, from a good hope through grace, of entering on " *the rest that remaineth to his people.*" The atonement and intercession of Jesus Christ afforded her subjects of comforting and delightful meditation; and in trusting the safety of her soul on them, she could say, that she found the Son of man to be indeed unto her spirit, " *as a hiding place from the wind, and a covert from the tempest.*"

Wednesday, 20.   The brig Active, from London, arrived on Saturday evening, bringing Mr. Charlton, lady and sister, as future residents of Oahu : Mr. Charlton having been appointed, by the British government, Consul General for the Islands in the Pacific. They left the Blonde frigate, Lord Byron, at Valparaiso ; she was to sail in a few days after the Active, and is hourly expected with the survivors of the party ; again diminished by the death of Naihi Tutui, or Captain Jack. He died suddenly at Valparaiso, from an inflammation of the brain.

Friday, May 6.   Yesterday a pilot-boat came express from Maui with intelligence that the Blonde frigate had just anchored at Lahaina.*   This morning at

---

* The following account of the Blonde's arrival at Lahaina, given by Mr. Richards, was published in the Missionary Herald.

At five o'clock, the vessel was becalmed about six miles from shore. I soon perceived that a boat was lowered, and filled with men. The people being still quiet, and suspecting nothing, I walked along the beach to ascertain who was on board the boat; but had not reached the landing, when I heard a cry from a canoe that approached the shore, " It is Boki, it is Boki." Hoapiri beckoned me to follow him. As I walked along, the princess caught my arm, saying, "Stay by me." Hoapiri took his seat in a chair upon the beach. I stood at his left hand, with the princess leaning on my side. Thousands collected around, some of whom began to wail. As the company approached, a passage was opened for them into the centre of the circle. The wailing increased, though it was not considerable until the company arrived within about four yards, when Hoapiri rose from his chair, threw back his head, and with a *roar* which scarcely resembled the human voice, he spread out his arms to receive his daughter. In an instant, all the chiefs present, except the

sunrise she was to be seen off Diamond Hill, and between nine and ten o'clock rounded to, immediately
opposite the Mission House.   On dropping her anchor
she fired a salute, which was answered by each of the
forts ; that on the point within the harbour, and that
above us on Punch Bowl Hill.   Shortly after, Mr. Bing-

one which leaned on my side, and all the thousands around, set
up a screaming, which drowned the roaring of the ocean, and
thus summoned to the scene of grief those who till now had not
heard the alarm.   The princess, in utter neglect of all their ancient forms, sprang forward, and, with a delicacy that would
not have disgraced a Charlotte, threw herself into the arms of
Tuini ; and the latter dropped into the sand, while the tears of
the little girl were falling on her breast.   At this instant, Hoapiri fell on the ground, literally plunged his whole face in the
dirt at Boki's feet, and thus gave the signal to all the old vete-
rans of barbarism, who instantly followed his example, and for
several minutes scoured their sable faces in the sand.   Boki
and his company were far more calm than the rest, and could
scarcely be said to wail.   After a few minutes, I said to Nahienaena, it would be well to thank Jehovah for this meeting.
She immediately spoke to Boki and Tuini.   They appeared
pleased, and immediately reached me their hands.   Boki said,
" Where shall we pray ?"   This was the first word, that was
spoken by any of the company.   Hoping that it might stop the
confusion and noise which now prevailed, I proposed to remove
to a neighbouring yard.   They approved, and as we began to
move, the wailing in a good measure ceased.   Several minutes
elapsed before the mats were spread, during which time messages were despatched to the Blonde, which was now furling
her sails.   After prayer, I conversed a while with Boki and
Tuini.   She spoke in the strongest terms of the good things
they had seen, and the kindness with which they had been
treated.   They express great love to lord Byron, and say he has

ham, Mr. Loomis, Mr. Chamberlain, and myself, accompanied the chiefs to the point near the fort, to receive Boki and party on their landing from the Blonde.

A more touching scene I have scarce ever witnessed. The chiefs, all well dressed in full black, arranged themselves in front of Kaahumanu's frame-house, within a few yards of the water's edge. As the well-manned

been exceedingly kind to them. We were awakened at an early hour this morning, by the *roll-call* on board the frigate, which was anchored directly in front of our house, and nearer the shore than I have ever seen any other vessel. When I reflected on the benevolent errand on which she had come, it was a pleasant sight; and I listened with satisfaction to her band of music, which I could distinctly hear, and which lost none of its charms by being removed a little distance on the water; it was a pleasant morning. All was still and quiet on shore, and the countenances of all beamed with joy.—It would occupy quite too much room to tell all that Boki has already said o the people, respecting his interesting voyage. At nine o'clock, I called on him, found him and his wife, Hoapiri and Nahienaena, in a house by themselves, prepared to wait on lord Byron whenever he should arrive. A messenger soon reported his boat to be on its way. Boki went out, and conducted him to the house, in company with several of his officers. The easy and unaffected familiarity of Lord Byron, and the interest he manifested in the welfare of our mission, were gratifying beyond expression. I accepted his polite invitation to dine on board the Blonde, and spent several hours in answering his lordship's numerous inquiries respecting our Mission, the former state of the Islands, and their recent improvements. I have rarely spent a few hours more pleasantly in the society of any man. At five o'clock, the frigate weighed her anchor, and, with a pleasant breeze, loftily retired from our shores, and soon was only a speck in the distant horizon.

barges of the Blonde approached the low quay, Kaahumanu, her two sisters, and the young queens of Riho-
Riho, slowly advanced from the body of the chiefs,
towards the place of landing.   All was silent, except an
occasional burst of grief from some one of the multitude,
who were kept at a distance, and prevented thronging
the beach by a file of armed men.   But when Governor
Boki's barge came near enough for the parties to recognize each other, the queens "lifted up their voices" and
wept aloud, with that melancholy tone of sorrow which
we have all heard, at least in some few instances, from
a heart deeply touched with grief.   A small house immediately on the wharf intercepted the view of the barge
at the moment of landing, perhaps to the more powerful
effect of the attitude and expression of Boki and his
wife, as they burst on the sight from behind it, wringing
their hands in agony, and exhibiting the strongest marks
of an overwhelming emotion of mingled grief and joy.
The parties stood thus for some minutes, without approaching each other, while the whole air was filled with
lamentation, and the ground shaken with the thunder-
ings of the minute-guns, which reminded the nation of
the fate of their king and queen.   They then rushed
into each other's embrace, passing from the arms of one
to another in a continued paroxysm of weeping, for an
hour, while some of the more humble friends of those
who had returned, embraced and kissed their feet, and
bathed them with their tears.   Liliha, or, as now called,
Mrs. Boki, at last sunk to the ground from exhaustion,
and was under the necessity of being assisted into the
house.

I never was so deeply affected with a wailing scene, and few have ever taken place, I suspect, in which there was a more general excitement of " *the sorrows, joys, and sympathies*," which, wh n thus awakened, testify to the " *high capacities*" of man. After an hour or two, the whole company proceeded to the residence of Karaimoku, who was too unwell to go out ; and shortly afterwards to the chapel to attend prayers, and tender thanks to God for the interesting incident of the day, Before leaving the chapel, Governor Boki delivered a short but excellent address, recommending, as the result of his observation and experience abroad, a renewed and devoted attention to the *palapala* and the *pule— letters and religion.*

Saturday 7. Last evening the government gave information by letter to Lord Byron, that they would receive himself and officers this morning, at the residence of Karaimoku. Arrangements for the interview were accordingly made, and the occasion has been one of great interest. The landing of his lordship about twelve o'clock, was announced by a salute from the fort. The firing was the signal for attendance at court, and Mr. Bingham and myself proceeded to the place appointed. Mr. Pitt chose to receive the company in his grass-house, rather than in the fine stone building lately erected by him. That fixed on, however, is one of the largest and best built native houses on the island, and being new, was as pleasant, and perhaps more appropriate than the other would have been. The whole apartment was floored with new and handsome mats, and made a pleasant and spacious room of audience. There are four doors, one on each side, and one at each end; that at the south was appointed for the entrance on this occasion. Every thing was in readiness when we arrived. At the upper or north end of the house, on an elevation of platform of mats, the top one of which was of very fine texture, and beautifully spotted and striped with stained grass, stood a Chinese sofa, on which the young king and the princess his sister, who came from Lahaina in the Blonde, were seated, both in plain suits of black. Between them, and partly round the princess, lay a splendid garment of yellow feathers, edged with the vandyke pattern, points alternate black and red, and lined with crimson satin.

This article, nine yards long and one yard wide, was made at great expense of time and labour during the past year, and designed to be worn by the princess as a *pau*, or native female dress, at the reception of her brother Riho-Riho, on his expected return. It was the desire of the chiefs that she should wear it, with the wreaths for the head and neck, necessary to form the complete ancient costume of a princess at this interview; but as it was necessary, in order to this, that she should be naked to the waist, nothing could induce her to consent. To escape importunity, she fled to the Mission House early in the morning. She wept so as scarcely to be pacified by us, and returned to the chiefs only in time to take her seat, and have it thrown carelessly about her over her European dress, with one end cast across the arm of the sofa. To have seen her in so superb a native costume, would have no doubt been gratifying to the company; but we could but commend and admire the feeling, which led her to object, and to persist in her purpose. Behind the sofa, and partly inclining over it, were four of the largest *kahiles* of state, the national insignia of their royalty.

On each side of the sofa the chiefs were arranged according to their rank; forming two closely filled lines along each side of the house, entirely to the door of entrance; Kaahumanu and the rest of the queens-dowager occupying the places next to the princess. Mr. Pitt sat in a large crimson chair opposite these last, near the king, but out of, and before, the line of chiefs. On his right were two chairs of the same kind, for Lord Byron and Mr. Charlton, and on his left two others for Mr. Bingham and myself. On the opposite side, chairs were arranged for the officers of the suite. The prime minister's dress was of black silk ; the upper garment, on account of his age and indisposition, being a very full and loose gown. Shortly after we had taken our seats, the procession from the Blonde made its appearance ; Lord Byron in the full uniform of his rank, supported by Mr. Charlton in his consular costume, and by Governor Boki in a rich military suit. All the company, except the king, princess, and Mr. Pitt, upwards of a hundred in number, received him standing, and, being well dressed in full black, made a very respectable appearance.

His lordship was introduced first to Mr. Pitt, and immediately presented each of the gentlemen in his suite, about twenty in number, and then in the same manner to the king, princess, and the queens, and after

a general salutation to the rest of the chiefs, to Mr.
Bingham, and myself. Among the persons I now recol-
lect, were Lord Frederick Beauclerc ; the Hon. Mr.
Talbot, a son of the Earl of Shrewsbury; the Hon. Mr.
Keith, a son of Lord Keith; Mr. Gambier, a nephew of
Admiral Gambier; the Rev. Mr. Bloxam the chaplain,
and Mr. Andrew Bloxam, the mineralogist, nephews
of Sir Thomas Lawrence, the celebrated artist ; Mr.
Davis, the surgeon ; Mr. M'Rea, the botanist; Mr.
Malden the surveyor; Mr. Dampier the artist ; and Mr.
Wilson, the purser. As soon as they were thus introduced, Lord Byron, through Mr. Marini, as interpreter,
presented the salutations of the King of England, and
his sympathy at the fate of the King and Queen; and
then ordered a boat's crew in attendance, to bring forward the personal presents of his majesty to the heads
of the nation. They consisted of a complete suit of the
Windsor uniform, for the young king, with the splendid
decorations peculiar to the sovereign's dress. The
buttons are of solid gold, having the impression G. R.
in the old English character on them, and the lacings,
embroidering, and epaulettes, superb — chapeau and
sword to match. The coat, hat, and sword, were immediately tried upon his majesty, and being found to fit
most perfectly, Lord Byron, partly by way of pleasantry,
led him to Karaimoku and Kaahumanu, and presented
him as their king; and putting his hand on his head,
bade him to be a good boy, attend well to his studies,
and mind all his kind friends the Missionaries said
to him. For Karaimoku there was a first-rate gold
hunting watch, having the royal arms of Britain richly

engraved on one side of the case, and the regent's name
on the other. And for Kaahumanu, an elegantly finished
silver tea-pot, marked in the same manner as the watch,
with the royal arms and her name.

As soon as these articles had been delivered and examined, much to our gratification, Mr. Pitt, entirely of
his own will, without the slightest suggestion for us,
proposed that we should have prayers of thanksgiving :
to which Lord Byron and his company most readily
and cheerfully agreed ; and Mr. Bingham made an excellent prayer, the first part in English, and the latter
in the Hawaiian language : at the close, we were happy
to receive the congratulations of the party, not only on
the degree of civilization and refinement manifested on
this occasion, but also on the evidence of Christian belief and practice, which the request of Karaimoku, and
the appearance of the assembly in this act of worship,
exhibited. It is an example which I fear the most
Christian courts in Christendom would blush to imitate
on a similar occasion. After this, a side-table was
spread with biscuit and fresh butter, cocoa-nuts and melons, wine, brandy, and other liqueurs ; and the company left to choose the time of their departure. On
leaving the house, several of the gentlemen renewedly
expressed their astonishment at the respectability of the
levee, and congratulated us afresh, on the prospect
we had, as teachers and preachers, to so interesting a
people.

The trumpet of fame has made the title, genius, character, and even person of the late Lord Byron so familiar to you, that I am satisfied the little information I

may have it in my power to give, of the successor to
the hereditary honours of the family, will not be uninteresting. At present I can only say, that the impression made by a first interview, are most favourable to
him as a man and a gentleman. In his person he is
tall and slender, fine dark eyes and hair, with strongly
marked but open and interesting features, no particular
resemblance to his cousin, except in what is usually
called a family likeness, unless it may be in the nose,
which is of the same style, but not so finely formed as
that in engravings of the poet. His eye is inquisitive
and penetrating, and shews him to be a man of a decisive and energetic character. In manners he is plain,
frank, and cordial; and in conversation perfectly affable and familiar; no affectation of dignity, no hauteur,
nothing in looks or expression of countenance, indicative of a trait of character, which, ever since I saw the
likeness of the poet, I have best understood by the
term, " Byronic curve of the upper lip."

On hearing of the illness of H——, he requested Mr.
Davis, the surgeon, to visit her; with the apology to
Mr. Davis, that he knew he would be happy in giving
his advice to Mrs. S., and with the assurance to me,
that the most unlimited confidence might be placed in
the professional ability of Mr. Davis.

Wednesday, 11. Suitable arrangements having been
previously made for the landing of the bodies of the
king and queen, at eleven o'clock this morning, the
minute-guns of the frigate, with a procession of barges
moving from her, became signals to us to be in readiness on the point, to take the places assigned to us in

the procession which was to escort the remains of our
friends and pupils to a temporary mausoleum. All the
chiefs, except Mr. Pitt, who was too much indisposed
to have endured the fatigue, with every foreigner of respectability in the neighbourhood of Honoruru, were
on the ground some time before the barges reached the
shore. Mr. Charlton improved the period in forming
them in the order in which they were to walk. At
twelve o'clock, the procession began to move through a
double line of native soldiers, formed on each side of
the street, from the fort to the chapel, a distance of
near half a mile, in the following manner :—

First. Twenty men, in the native costume of black,
some with the addition of rich feather cloaks, each two
bearing an immense feathered staff of state, about
thirty feet long, and from one to two feet in diameter,
some of black, some of crimson, others of green, and
others again of yellow feathers.

Second. The marines of the Blonde, arms reversed.

Third. The band, playing a dead march.

Fourth. The gentlemen of the Mission, with the
surgeon and chaplain of the frigate ; Mr. Bingham,
Mr. Bloxam, and myself, walked together, the chaplain, in his full canonical robes ; Mr. Bingham and
myself in plain dresses, with white scarfs and hatbands.

Fifth. The Coffins. These are highly finished and
splendid ; being covered with rich crimson Genoa velvet, studded with gilt nails, and having the corners of
each compartment of the sides, ends, and tops, as well
as the massive handles, filled with devices of the che-

rubim. They were placed on two cars, with black canopies, and each drawn by forty of the inferior male chiefs: it is customary to have all services to a dead chief of high rank performed by chiefs only, in European dresses of deep mourning.

Sixth. The young king, in his Windsor uniform, with crape on his arm and sword-hilt; and the princess his sister, in full black: the former supported by Mr. Charlton, in his consular character and costume, and the latter by Lord Byron, in full naval uniform.

Seventh. The rest of the high chiefs, according to their rank and relationship to the deceased, two abreast, with an officer of the Blonde, in full dress, on each side.

Eighth. The inferior chief women, in European dresses of black.

Ninth. The foreigners, mercantile agents, residents, and sea-captains in port.

And lastly, about one hundred of the men of the Blonde, in a uniform dress of white jackets and trowsers, white hats, and shoes bound with black, and black handkerchiefs and hatbands: the whole making a most respectable, and, for the Sandwich Islands at least, a truly splendid appearance.

The great weight of the coffins, each body having three, one of lead, one of mahogany, and one of oak, rendered it almost impracticable to have them taken into the chapel, which had been hung in black for the occasion: on reaching the door, therefore, the procession, instead of entering the building, fell into a circle around the cars, and Mr. Bloxam read a part of the

burial service of the Episcopal Church, and Mr. Bingham made an address in the native language; after
which the procession again formed, and returned down
the street a few rods, to the gate leading to Karaimoku's residence, situated in a cultivated enclosure of
some eight or ten acres. Here, as it passed by a cir-
cuitous way, it shewed to the best advantage.

On reaching the door of the house, the feather-
bearers, marines, and band, opened to the right and
left, and Mr. Bloxam, Mr. Bingham, and myself, entered the habitation about to be converted into a tomb. I
scarce know when I have been more tenderly affected.
It was the audience room, in which but a day or two
before, Lord Byron and his suite had been presented;
but how greatly was its whole appearance altered! A
low and well-defined arch had been thrown over its
lofty roof, converting it into a long vaulted hall, every
part of which, even to the pillars running through the
middle, was entirely covered with black. Its only furniture was a large platform at one end, on which was
to be deposited all that remained of Kamehamaru and
Riho-Riho: and the only person in it was Karaimoku,
standing to receive the lifeless bodies of those he had
ever called and loved as his children. His dress was
the same as on Saturday; but his appearance even
more venerable and interesting. He received our salutations in agitated silence : the trembling hand, the
quivering lip, the hasty and disturbed pressure of his
handkerchief to his eyes and forehead, all expressing
deep emotion of heart. He permitted himself to be led
to a seat, while the coffins, each borne by twelve men

of the Blonde, were placed on the platform. Immediately after, the rest of the company entered, and formed numerous groups around the apartment, while, accompanied by the band drawn up on one side, we sung the native funeral anthem to the tune of *Pleyel's Hymn*, and Mr. Bingham made a short prayer in the same language. This scene was by far the most striking incident of the day. The sable drapery of the room, the full mourning suits of the majority, interspersed and relieved by the rich and glittering uniforms of the officers, the handsome half-mourning dresses and white plumes of Mrs. Charlton and sister, Madam Boki, and one of the young queens-dowager, who has lately become a bride, with a variety of other becoming and appropriate dresses, the melancholy tones of the instruments, and the solemn truths of the chant in the chamber of the dead, combined to make it a truly interesting and affecting moment.

Thus, under the mournful reverberations of the minute-guns, have been received, and peacefully deposited on their native shores, the king and queen of the Sandwich Islands, whose short reign has been marked by epochs no less momentous than the abolition of a cruel system of idolatry; the introduction of the elements of literature, and the arts and usages of civilized life; and, above all, the promulgation of the Gospel, with all the bright hopes and eternal retributions of Christianity! To these dark monarchs of this western archipelago, in the gloomy mansion of their repose, I gave one more tear; one more tear, in remembrance of the better characteristics, which, not unfrequently, shone through their follies and their sins; one more tear for the attachment I had felt, and the prayers I had offered, for them; one more tear for the early disappointment of the hopes I had entertained, that they would return to their rude subjects, from the bright regions of Christendom, only *" to point to heaven, and to lead the way."* I shudder to think, that, so imperfectly instructed, so partially reclaimed, and, as it is to be feared, so little prepared, they have been launched into eternity, and have stood before their God.

CHAPTER XIV.

———

KINDNESS OF LORD BYRON.

Thursday, 26. The physicians having recommended a change of air, as most likely to benefit H——'s health, Lord Byron has most kindly assigned us accommodations in the Blonde, for a trip to the harbour of Waiakea, at Hido, on Hawaii, where he is going for a month, to refit and explore the windward of that island, with the intention of returning to this port again. It is uncertain on what day she may sail, though probably in the course of a week.

The very favourable impression of the character of this nobleman, made at the first interview, has been greatly strengthened and deepened by after-intercourse. To the apparent quickness, vigour, and cultivation of intellect, which you would naturally expect to see in a Byron, he adds a kindness of heart, and benevolence of disposition, that would secure your respect and affection, with any name. Few men of his rank, and indeed any rank, would have completed the objects of his mission to the Islands in so condescending and unexceptionable a manner; and the influence he is exerting, is calculated to open more fully than ever to this people, a way for the introduction of all the illimitable blessings of civilization and Christianity.

It is with no inconsiderable pleasure that I anticipate, from the excursion to Hawaii, a prolonged intercourse with himself, and some of his immediate friends, with whom I have become more particularly acquainted.

Nothing I have yet known on Missionary ground, causes me so deeply to feel the sacrifice of our situation, as the occasional society of such men. The lowliness of our habitation, the plainness and poverty of our table, the known and unknown inconveniences and privations of our whole establishment—never rouse the recollections of mind and heart, excited by the intercourse of a week, a day, an hour, with the polished, the intelligent, the amiable, the virtuous; those who have heads to think, hearts to feel, characters to respect, and conversation and manners to win. When I meet and when I part with such, at this extremity of the globe, I feel that I am cut off from some of the choicest enjoyments of life.

On board H. B. M. Ship Blonde, June 5, 1825. At eleven o'clock yesterday morning, a messenger from Lord Byron came to inform us that he was in readiness, on the point, to take us on board the frigate in his boat. H—— was carried down in an arm-chair, and his lordship's gig being in waiting, we were immediately rowed off to the vessel, a distance of two miles, in the open roads: the possibility that H—— might not live to return to Oahu, made the separation from her children a severe trial. We left them, however, with the persuasion, that they will receive every kind and affectionate attention from our faithful friend B——, and from the ladies of the station.

The anchor was not taken up till four o'clock, until which time, H—— remained on a sofa in Lord Byron's cabin : but beginning to be slightly affected by the motion of the ship after she was under sail, before we sat down to dinner, she was removed to her own cabin, adjoining the dining room. The captain and all the gentlemen of the ship are exceedingly polite and attentive; and our whole situation is made, by them, as pleasant as possible. We shall feel ourselves under very lasting obligations to Lord Byron, every development of whose character increases our respect, gratitude, and love. He is at all times affable and communicative; but while at the tea-table this evening, where we were joined by the chaplain Mr. Andrew Bloxam, his brother, and Mr. Dampier the artist, he exhibited powers of conversation which must make him a charming companion to his intimate friends and family circle. He is a great favourite with the chiefs ; and in order most fully to secure every attention and service to himself and ship, Kaahumanu, her sister Hoapiri, and Wahine, accompany him to Hawaii. Mr. Goodrich of the Mission, who has paid a short visit at Oahu, improves this opportunity also, of returning to his station at Waiakea.

The Blonde is a forty-six gun ship, of fine model, and perfectly new, this being her first voyage. Lord Byron's accommodations consist of an after-cabin, fitted up as a reading and sitting room, in which tea is served; a for ward or large cabin, used as a breakfast and dining room ; and a sleeping and dressing cabin. The whole are substantially and handsomely finished and furnished, particularly the after-cabin.   In this there is a beautifully engraved likeness of his majesty George IV., from a full-length portrait by Sir Thomas Lawrence ; a half-length portrait of the present Lady Byron ; and one of the same size of Moore, the poet, who is an intimate friend of the Byron family.

Of Lady Byron, we have heard an admirable account. The expression of countenance in her portrait is uncommonly ingenuous and prepossessing, and, in addition to all that is amiable and benevolent in disposition, she is said, by those whom we have heard speak of her, to be eminently pious ; the plainness of her dress, and whole appearance, indicate a mind and heart little devoted to the vanities of high and fashionable life.

The library is in the after-cabin, and is of a character you would more expect to meet in a clergyman's study, than in a post-captain's cabin ; consisting principally of the British classical writers, with standard works on morals and religion.

Saturday evening, 11.   After being delayed all day yesterday between Maui and Hawaii, we this morning succeeded in doubling the north point of the latter island, and have been delighted with the romantic and verdant scenery of the windward side of Hawaii, including the precipices and waterfalls in the neighbourhood of the beautiful valleys of Wai-Pio, and Wai-Manu. One cascade, of which we had a full view for some time, could not have been less than six hundred feet in height, extending almost from the top of a mountain to its base. The quantity of water was small, but sufficiently great to be very beautiful, as in its descent it foamed from cliff to cliff, and from precipice to precipice. The windward, or eastern parts of all the mountains, are much more picturesque than the leeward, and abound in romantic and beautiful scenes, peculiarly refreshing from their verdure, to an eye long accustomed to the parched and dreary aspect of the opposite sides.

Lord Byron and myself are usually alone at the breakfast table, and his conversation then is less general, as to subjects, and often more interesting than at any other time. It was particularly so this morning, happening to turn on his late distinguished predecessor in the barony of the Byrons. He had often before spoken of him as a writer, and, in reference to his later publications, in terms of unqualified reprehension; but now his remarks regarded him as a man, and a member of his own family. They were of the same age, same education, and on terms of the closest intimacy, till after the poet's marriage.

The conversation also embraced Newstead Abbey, the ancient family mansion of the Byrons; in the appearance of which, although the death of its late celebrated possessor has given it a new master, no change whatever has taken place. All its ancient baronial character is retained, with as much reverence for the memory of the noble lord, as if he had consecrated it to the Muses, and interdicted every kind of alteration. The extraordinary genius, popularity, and whole character, of its late proprietor, has thrown an interest around it that few private mansions can boast; and it will, ever hereafter, be an object of curiosity to the scholar and traveller, if to no others.

Lord Byron has an estate in the vicinity of Newstead, and was kind enough to say, if I should ever visit England, he would be happy to see me in Nottinghamshire; with the promise of accompanying me to the abbey. The additional *if*, puts the event, humanly speaking, among the improbabilities of my life; but should such a thing take place, I am sure the gratification I might receive from treading the halls and cloisters of Newstead, would not arise from any feelings of veneration or respect for its former master. I admire the powers and brilliancy of his genius, less than I abhor their later monstrous perversion and prostitution.

Our nearness to the land and mountains gave us a beautiful sunset scene and evening, so much so as to call into exercise the poetic talent of our friend Mr. Bloxam, and secure the following effusion, which I found enclosed in a polite note on my writing-desk, on our return from the after-cabin.

Coasting along the ISLAND OF HAWAII—*Saturday Evening, June* 11, 1825.

> Eve, gentle Eve, the mourner's friend art thou
> Calming his lonely heart, his alter'd brow;
> Bidding again his former pleasures live
> With added charms, which thou alone canst give.
> Seen through thy misty veil, the years gone by
> Are dearest far to pensive memory.

When thy soft blending hues, along the West,
Calmly reposing in their tranquil rest,
Strew Hesper's cradle with their rosy light,
And shed bright tinges o'er the brow of night,—
Then let me hail thee ! for thy dewy star
Opens the gates of blessedness afar ;
And shining bright, and brighter from above,
Tells of a land where all is peace and love.

Fairest is Eve, where mild Ausonia's sky
Owns her bright hues ;—and where the Zephyr's sigh
Breathes the sweet tones of melody or song,
Or bears the fragrance of the groves along.

Lovely is eve, where Britain's western cloud
Throws round the sun her purple glowing shroud,
While even childhood, ere it sinks to rest,
Turns its blue eye enraptured to the West.

But *brightest*, most sublime, is Evening's reign
Where Hawaii links her seven-fold chain, *
And where the leader of her giant band†
Flings his broad shadows proudly o'er the land,
And soaring seeks among the snow-charged cloud,
His time-worn forehead's haughty height to shroud.
He sees the twilight shed her softening dyes
On Maui's mountains that contiguous rise ;
While his hoar brow is bright with hues of day ,
And glowing radiant 'neath the sun's last ray,
With timid hand, may evening scarcely dare
O'er his dark breast to draw her mantle fair.
But who at this soft hour is gaining now
The heights that frown o'er yonder vale below,
Who—winding down the craggy pathway there
In shadowy distance—seems some form of air !

* Seven Islands.   † Mounakea.

'Tis he—the *Pastor* of the numerous flock,
Who wait his coming under yonder rock;
Where (far from mild *Religion's* soothing ray)
Pale superstition late held direful sway :
But now—mysterious words—He speaks of Heaven,
Of Mercy—Hope—and Love—of sins forgiven :
He speaks of HIM, omnipotent to save,
Who died—who *lives* triumphant o'er the grave—
E'en now the savage, with unlifted eyes,
Drinks the sweet words, " Christ is our sacrifice."
No more (for past omissions to atone,)
He bows to forms of wood or gods of stone ;
But bends the knee, and humbly hopes to trace
Some glorious tidings of redeeming grace :
While gently stealing o'er the twilight dim,
Falls the soft cadence of the *Evening Hymn.*

Now all is peace.   Each sound has died away ;
The savage seeks his couch—till break of day
Again shall summon him, his vows to pay.

O blest seclusion !   Solicitude how blest !
Yes—soon on Mounakea's shaggy breast,
(Unless I idly dream) a Fane shall rise
To HIM, the great TRIUNE, who rules the earth and skies.

The whole is creditable to the writer, as an impromptu;
and the latter part is a pleasing and lively picture of our
ordinary evening worship with the natives.

Mission House, Hido, Monday, June 13.   Yesterday
morning, at the break of day, we were farther from the
harbour of Waiakea than we had the evening before
expected to be ; and Lord Byron gave orders to stand
off the land till the usual worship of the Sabbath was
performed.   The whole crew, in clean dresses, occupied

seats fronting the quarter-deck, where chairs were arranged for the officers. In addition to the morning service of prayers, at different parts of which the band played pieces of sacred music, Mr. Bloxam gave us a very excellent sermon on repentance. The whole was marked by much order and solemnity, and attended to by many with great devoutness, especially by the captain and our friend the surgeon.

As we approached the land after church, we were greatly delighted with the verdure, luxuriance, and beauty of the landscape opening to us, in the neighbourhood of the bay of Hido. The shore had lost in a great measure the abrupt and precipitous character of the coast along which we had been sailing on Saturday, and was only edged by a low cliff, richly mantled with shrubbery and creeping plants, and ornamented with several beautiful cascades. These in connection with the breakers which ran high upon the rocks, often dashing their spray many feet in the air, gave the cliff an uncommonly picturesque appearance. The land rose gradually from the cliff, to the distance of ten or fifteen miles, to a heavy wood encircling the base of Mounakea. Though in a state of nature, this large district had the appearance of cultivation, being an open country covered with grass, and beautifully studded and sprinkled with clumps, and groves, and single trees, in the manner of park scenery, with a cottage here and there peeping from beneath their rich foliage. The mountains were entirely covered with clouds, or the prospect would have been rendered more delightful from their sublimity. Such was the scene on our right, as we sailed close along the breakers to the narrow channel forming the entrance to the harbour, the gentlemen of the Blonde exclaiming " This is more like English scenery than any thing we have yet seen !" and we equally ready to say, " This looks something like America, it has some of *the features of a civilized land !*"

The channel is formed by the cliff on the right, and a sunken coral reef on the left, the point of which comes within two or three hundred rods of the shore, making it necessary for ships to pass so close to the breakers, as to appear in a dangerous situation. Seamen, how-ever, consider it perfectly safe. The reef runs in a curved direction, from the point at the channel, about half a mile to the east, where it joins a romantic little islet covered with cocoa-nut trees ; from that fact called " Cocoa-nut Island." A small channel runs between this and the main land, which is low, and sweeps round to the western cliffs in a beautifully curved sandy beach of about two miles, making the form of the bay that of a flattened horse-shoe. The beach is covered with varied vegetation, and ornamented by clumps and single trees of lofty cocoa-nut, among which the habitations of the natives are seen, not in a village, but scattered every where among the plantations, like farm-houses in a thickly inhabited country. The Mission Houses were pointed out to us, pleasantly situated near the water, about the middle of the curvature forming the head of the bay. At a very short distance from the beach, the bread-fruit trees were seen in heavy groves, in every direction, intersected with the pandanus and tutui, or candle-tree, the hibiscus and the acacia, &c. The tops of these rising gradually one above another, as the country gently ascended towards the mountains in the interior, presented for twenty or thirty miles in the southeast, a delightful forest scene, totally different in extent from any thing I had before witnessed on the Islands.

The Blonde anchored in the centre of the bay, and shortly after dinner the barge was lowered, to carry us to our friends on shore. After rowing half a mile, we entered a beautiful fresh-water creek, which winds its way close to the Missionary enclosure, and in a few minutes were welcomed to the cottage of Mr. Ruggles, where Mrs. Goodrich had resided during her husband's absence. They were greatly rejoiced at our unexpected visit to them in their remote and solitary abode, though their sympathy was deeply excited by the cause, and by the evidence of deep-seated disease, visible in the countenance and person of a beloved friend.

The gentlemen who accompanied us were so much pleased with the freshness and verdure of the shore, the simplicity and rural beauty of the gardens which surrounded the humble dwellings of our companions, that they permitted the barge to return to the ship without them, and spent the afternoon and took tea with us.

Besides a visit from the chaplain and surgeon to-day, we have had the pleasure of a call from Lord Byron, and the first lieutenant, Mr. Ball, an amiable and kind man, and a particular favourite of the captain.—They remained to tea with us, and expressed themselves highly delighted with Hido.

Tuesday, 14. The sunrise view of Mounakea yesterday was so charming, that I made an exertion to have

H—— witness the same this morning, before he should
be enwrapt in his daily robe of clouds. The morning
was delightful, and the whole atmosphere perfectly unobscured. The extensive region of upland country
intervening between us and the base of the mountain,
was gleaming in the brightness of the early sun, with all
the freshness and verdure of an American landscape in
June; while the mountain, in its whole extent of breadth
and height, glowed in the richest purple, except where
a broad line of ice and snow, still resting on its sides and
summit, added a cresting of silver. This scenery on our
left, the bay with its cliffs and islands, and beautifully
defined beach, and the Blonde at anchor immediately
before us, and the ocean in the distance, made a picture
highly calculated, in connection with the purity and
brightness of a summer's morning, to revive the spirits
and strengthen the nerves of one who, for more than
three months, had scarcely seen any thing but the dreary
walls of her sick chamber. After breakfast, supported
by my arm, she, with the same feeble and tottering step,
walked through the garden which separates the two
cottages, and was charmed with a variety of flowers,
shrubbery, herbs, and vegetables, which Mr. G. and Mr.
R. have collected and nursed, till they are beginning to
flourish exuberantly. Among the flowers, I saw many,
the seeds of which I brought to the Islands ; that which
is most prized by the natives, is the *purple globe ama-
ranthus.* They form beautiful wreaths from it, and you
scarcely pass a plantation without seeing a bed of it
cultivated for that purpose.

This afternoon I joined Lord Byron and party in a

visit to a large fish-pond, of which the creek or river is
the outlet. It is a pretty sheet of water in its natural
state, excepting strong stone dams, to prevent the escape
of the fish. These are *tabu* to all but high chiefs; and
no one of rank having lived here lately, the whole pond
is literally alive with the finest of mullet; the surface of
the water is almost in a constant ripple from their
motions; and hundreds can be taken at any time by a
single cast of a small net. Expressing our astonishment at the sight, *Sir Joseph Banks*,* who, from understanding and speaking some English, has been appointed
by her majesty interpreter, caterer, gentleman in waiting, &c. to Lord Byron, very seriously says, "O dis noting,
sir—noting—I see him before now;—he so full fish, I
see one man, he fall backwards in him, he no sink at all!"

After satisfying our curiosity here, we rowed down the
creek and across the bay, to another stream on the
western side of the harbour, called Wairuku—*river of
destruction*—where the ships get their water. The entrance of this river is highly romantic and beautiful, the
banks being precipitous and rocky, and covered with a
variety of vegetation. About a hundred yards above the
beach, it opens into a still deep basin, encircled by high
cliffs. Into this basin the whole stream is projected by
two cascades, the upper about twenty feet, and the lower
about eight feet, both rushing over their respective ledges
of rock in unbroken sheets. A rude bridge crosses the
stream just above the falls; and it is a favourite amusement of the natives to plunge from it, or from the ad
joining rocks, into the rapids, and pass head foremost

* A native so called.

2 g 2

over both falls, into the lower basin. Some of them were engaged in this sport when we arrived, for the gratification of Lieutenants Keith, Talbot, and Gambier, whom we found there. The accession of our party collected a greater crowd, and the cliffs and rocks were quickly covered with men, women, and children, many of whom not only passed over the falls in the manner described, but jumped also from a height of thirty, forty, and fifty feet, into the basin, which, though small, is of very great depth.

The inhabitants of Hido are in a state of much greater simplicity than those in many other parts of the Islands, owing to the infrequency of the visits of ships, and a less degree of the corrupting influence of foreign example in vice. More of the primitive character of the Islanders, its artless diffidence and timidity, is perceptible, than in the natives of Maui, Oahu, &c. And though these traits are far from being unmingled with licentiousness, and many of the abominations of heathenism, still they are more pleasing than the impu_ dence and unblushing vulgarity observable in those who have had long intercourse with the abandoned seamen and vagabonds, who frequent the less remote parts.

We passed near the chapel on our return. It stands almost midway between the Mission House and the watering place, close to the beach, and although small, is well built, and neatly thatched. The thatching of the houses in general, here, is altogether more neat and beautiful than at the leeward islands. It is made from the leaves of the pandanus, and so put on as to conceal

all the rudeness of the timber and sticks on the inside ;
while on the outside, a deep edging of fern, along the
peak and ends of the roof, and down the corners of the
house; having something of the effect of the cornice
and pilaster, give a finished and ornamental appearance, not seen in the common grass huts. The ease
with which stout timber can be procured here, enables
them also to build their dwellings much larger than at
Lahaina and Oahu, where the wood most accessible is
small and crooked.

Saturday, July 2, 1825. A party was formed a few
days since to visit the great volcano of Kirauea, and
set off early on Monday, the 27th ult. I was happy
enough to be one of the number ; and while the incidents of the excursion are fresh in my mind, I hasten
to give you an account of them.—Every preparation
having been previously made, we left the harbour
shortly after sunrise. The uncommon beauty of the
morning proved a true omen of the delightful weather
with which we were favoured during the whole of our
absence. The rich colouring of Mounakea in the early
sun, never called forth higher or more general admiration. The brightness of the sky, the purity of the air,
the freshness, sweetness, and cheerfulness of all nature,
excited a buoyancy of spirit favourable to the accomplishment of the walk of forty miles, which lay between
us and the object of our journey.

Lord Byron had invited Mr. Ruggles, who was also
of the party, and myself, to an early cup of coffee with
him, that we might all proceed together from his lodgings ; but besides the inconvenience of crossing the

river, it would have considerably lengthened our walk.
We therefore chose to take some refreshments at home,
and at an appointed signal proceeded up one side of
the stream and great fish-pond, while the gentlemen of
the Blonde followed a path up the other.   We met on
a rising ground at the end of two miles, and found the
company from the opposite side to consist of Lord
Byron, Mr. Ball the first lieutenant, Mr. Malden the
surveyor, Mr. Bloxam the chaplain, Mr. A. Bloxam
the mineralogist, Mr. Davis the surgeon, Mr. Dampier the artist, Mr. White, a son of the earl of Bantry,
and Mr. Powel midshipman.   Lord Frederick Beauclerc was to have been of the number, but was detained by sickness.

Maro, a principal chief of Hido, had been appointed
by Kaahumanu *caterer general ;* and about one hundred natives under his authority attended with our luggage and provisions. Sir Joseph, or, as more familiarly
styled, " *Joe Banks,*" was also in attendance, in his
diversified capacity.   The regent had left nothing
undone to render the trip as comfortable as her authority could make it.   Neat temporary houses for refreshment and sleeping, had been erected by her command
at intervals of twelve or fifteen miles, and the people of
the only inhabited district through which we were to
pass, had, the week before, been apprized of the journey
of " *the British chief,*" with strict orders to have an
abundance of pigs, fowls, taro, potatoes, and fruit, in
readiness, for the supply of his company.   When assembled, we formed quite a numerous body, and from
the variety of character and dress, the diversity in the

burdens of the natives, bundles, tin-cases, portman-
teaus, calabashes, kettles, buckets, pans, &c. &c. with
two hammocks by way of equipage, swung on long
poles, borne each by four men, (one for Lord Byron, in
case the fatigue of walking should affect his leg,
recently injured by a kick from a horse at Oahu,
and the other for the chaplain,) made, while marching
in single file along the narrow winding path which
formed our only road, quite a grotesque and novel appearance.

For the first four miles the country was open and
uneven, and beautifully sprinkled with clumps, groves,
and single trees of the bread-fruit, pandanus, and candle tree. We then came to a wood, four miles in width,
the outskirts of which exhibited a rich and delightful
foliage. It was composed principally of the candle-tree,
whose whitish leaves and blossoms afforded a fine contrast to the dark green of the various parasitical plants
which hung in luxuriant festoons and pendants from
their very tops to the ground, forming thick and deeply
shaded bowers round their trunks. The interior was
far less interesting, presenting nothing but an impenetrable thicket, on both sides of the path. This was
excessively rough and fatiguing, consisting, entirely of
loose and pointed pieces of lava, which, from their irregularity and sharpness, not only cut and tore our shoes,
but constantly endangered our feet and ankles. The
high brake, ginger, &c. which border and overhang the
path, were filled with the rain of the night, and added
greatly, from their wetness, to the unpleasantness of
the walk. An hour and a half, however, saw us safely

through, and refreshing ourselves in the charming groves
with which the wood was here again bordered.

The whole of the way, from this place to within a
short distance of the volcano, was very much of one
character.   The path, formed of black lava, so smooth
in some places as to endanger falling, and still shewing
the configuration of the molten stream as it had rolled
down the gradual descent of the mountain, led midway
through a strip of open uncultivated country, from
three to five miles wide, skirted on both sides by a ragged and stinted wood, and covered with fern, grass,
and low shrubs, principally a species of the whortle-
berry.   The fruit of this, of the size of a small goose-
berry, and of a bright yellow colour, tinged on one
side with red, was very abundant, and, though of insipid
taste, refreshing from its juice.   There were no houses
near the path, but the thatch of a cottage was occasionally observed peeping from the edge of the wood,
and here and there the white smoke of a kindling fire
curled above the thick foliage of the trees.   Far on the
right and west, Mounaroa and Mounakea were distinctly
visible; and at an equal distance, on the left and east,
the ocean, with its horizon, from the height at which
we viewed it, mingling with the sky.

We dined thirteen miles from the bay, under a large
candle tree, on a bed of brake, collected and spread by
a party of people who had been waiting by the wayside
to see the " *arii nui mai Perekania mai*," great chief
from Britain."   About two miles farther, we came to
the houses erected for our lodgings the first night.
Thinking it, however, too early to lie by for the day,

after witnessing a dance performed by a company from the neighbouring settlements, we hastened on, intending to sleep at the next houses, ten miles distant; but night overtaking us before we reached them, just as darkness set in, we turned aside a few rods to the ruins of two huts, the sticks only of which were remaining. The natives, however, soon covered them with fern, the leaves of the tutui, &c., a quantity of which they also spread on the ground, before spreading the mats which were to be our beds.

Our arrival and encampment produced quite a picturesque and lively scene; for the Islanders, who are not fond of such forced marches as we had made during the day, were more anxious for repose than ourselves, and proceeded with great alacrity to make preparations for the night. The darkness as it gathered round us, rendered more gloomy by a heavily clouded sky, made the novelty of our situation still more striking. Behind the huts, in the distance, an uplifted torch of the blazing tutui nut, here and there indistinctly revealed the figures and costume of many, spreading their couches under the bushes in the open air. A large lamp suspended from the centre of our rude lodge, entirely open in front, presented us in *bolder relief*, seated *à la Turc* round Lord Byron, who poured " to each the cup that cheers but not inebriates ;" the more curious of our dusky companions, both male and female, were in the mean time pressing in numbers round our circle, as if anxious to " catch the manners living as they rose." A large fire of brush-wood, at some distance in front, exhibited the objects of the fore-

ground, in still stronger *lights and shadows.* Groups
of both sexes, and all ages, were seated or standing
round the fire, wrapped up from the chilliness of the
evening air, in their large kiheis or mantles of white,
black, green, yellow, and red; some smoking, some
throwing in, and others snatching from the embers, a
fish or potatoe, or other article of food; some giving a
loud halloo, in answer to the call of a straggler just
arriving; others wholly taken up with the proceedings
of the sailors cooking our supper; and all chattering
with the volubility of so many magpies.

By day-light the next morning, we were on the road
again, and shortly after met Lieutenant Talbot, Mr.
Wilson the purser, and Mr. M'Rea the botanist, with
their guides and attendants, on their return; they
having preceded us three days in the same excursion.
As they intended to reach the frigate in time for
dinner, they stopped only long enough to say the volcano
was in fine action, and highly worth visiting. At nine
o'clock we passed the last houses put up for our
accommodation on the way; and at eleven o'clock had
arrived within three miles of the object of our curiosity.
For the last hour the scenery had become more
interesting, our path was skirted, occasionally, with
groves and clusters of trees, and fringed with a greater
variety of vegetation. Here also the smoke from the
volcano was first discovered, settling in light fleecy
clouds to the south-west. Our resting place, at this
time, was a delightful spot, commanding a full view of
the wide extent of country over which we had tra-
velled, and beyond, and around it, the ocean, which,

from the vast and almost undistinguished extent of its horizon, seemed literally an "illimitable sea." The smooth greensward, under the shade of a majestic acacia, almost encircled by thickets of a younger growth, afforded a refreshing couch on which to take our luncheon. Here we saw the first bed of strawberry vines, but without finding any fruit. We tarried but a few moments, and then hurried on to the grand object before us.

The nearer we approached, the more heavy the columns of smoke appeared, and roused to intenseness our curiosity to behold their origin. Under the influence of this excitement, we hastened forward with rapid steps, regardless of the heat of a noonday sun, and the fatigue of a walk of thirty-six miles, already accomplished. A few minutes before twelve o'clock, we came suddenly on the brink of a precipice, covered with shrubbery and trees, one hundred and fifty or two hundred feet high. Descending this by a path almost perpendicular, we crossed a plain half a mile in width, enclosed, except in the direction we were going, by the cliff behind us, and found ourselves a second time on the top of a precipice four hundred feet high, also covered with bushes and trees. This, like the former, swept off to the right and left, enclosing in a semi-circular form, a level space about a quarter of a mile broad ; immediately beyond which lay the tremendous abyss of our search, emitting volumes of vapour and smoke; and labouring and groaning, as if in inexpressible agony from the raging of the conflicting elements within its bosom. We

2 H

stood but a moment to take this first distant glance, then hastily descended the almost perpendicular height, and crossed the plain to the very brink of the crater.

There are scenes to which description, and even painting, can do no justice; and in conveying any adequate impression of which, they must ever fail. Of such, an elegant traveller rightly says, "the height, the depth, the length, the breadth, the combined aspect, may all be correctly given, but the mind of the reader will remain untouched by the emotions of admiration and sublimity which the eye-witness experiences." That which here burst on our sight was emphatically of this kind; and to behold it without singular and deep emotion, would demand a familiarity with the more terrible phenomena of nature, which few have the opportunity of acquiring.—Standing at an elevation of one thousand five hundred feet, we looked into a black and horrid gulf, not less than eight miles in circumference, so directly beneath us, that, in appearance, we might, by a single leap, have plunged into its lowest depth. The hideous immensity itself, independent of the many frightful images which it embraced, almost caused an involuntary closing of the eyes against it. But when to the sight is added the appalling effect of the various unnatural and fearful noises, the muttering and sighing, the groaning and blowing, the every agonized struggling, of the mighty action within, as a whole, it is too horrible! And for the first moment I felt like one of my friends, who, on reaching the brink, recoiled, and covered his face, exclaiming, " *Call it weakness, or what you please, but I cannot look again.*" It was sufficient employment for the afternoon, simply to sit and gaze on the scene; and though some of our party strolled about, and one or two descended a short distance into the crater, the most of our number deferred all investigation till the next morning.

From what I have already said, you will perceive that this volcano differs, in one respect, from most others of which we have accounts: the crater, instead of being the truncated top of a mountain, distinguishable in every direction at a distance, is an immense chasm in an upland country, near the base of the mountain Mounaroa—approached, not by ascending a cone, but by descending two vast terraces; and not visible from any point at a greater distance than half a mile, a circumstance which, no doubt, from the suddenness of the arrival, adds much to the effect of a first look from the brink.

It is probable that it was originally a cone, but assumed its present aspect, it may be centuries ago, from the falling in of the whole summit. Of this the precipices we descended, which entirely encircle the crater, in circumferences of fifteen and twenty miles, give strong evidence, they have unquestionably been formed by the sinking of the mountain, whose foundations had been undermined by the devouring flames beneath. In the same manner, one half of the present depth of the crater has, at no very remote period, been formed. About midway from the top, a ledge of lava, in some places only a few feet, but in others many rods wide, extends entirely round, at least as far as an examination has been made, forming a kind of gallery, to which you can descend in two or three places, and walk as far as the smoke, settling at the south end, will permit. This offset bears incontestable marks of having once been the level of the fiery flood now boiling in the bottom of the crater. A subduction of lava, by some subterraneous channel, has since taken place, and sunk the abyss many hundred feet, to its present depth.

The gulf below contains, probably, not less than sixty—fifty-six have been counted—smaller conical craters, many of which are in constant action. The tops and sides of two or three of these are covered with sulphur, of mingled shades of yellow and green. With this exception, the ledge, and every thing below it, are of a dismal black. The upper cliffs on the northern and western sides, are perfectly perpendicular, and of a red colour, every where exhibiting the seared marks of former powerful ignition. Those on the eastern side are less precipitous, and consist of entire banks of sulphur, of a delicate and beautiful yellow. The south end is wholly obscured by the smoke, which fills that part of the crater, and spreads widely over the surrounding horizon.

As the darkness of the night gathered round us, new and powerful effect was given to the scene. Fire after fire, which the glare of mid-day had entirely concealed, began to glimmer on the eye, with the first shades of evening; and, as the darkness increased, appeared in such rapid succession, as forcibly to

remind me of the hasty lighting of the lamps of a
city, on the sudden approach of a gloomy night.
Two or three of the small craters nearest to us were
in full action, every moment casting out stones, ashes,
and lava, with heavy detonations, while the irritated
flames accompanying them, glared widely over the
surrounding obscurity, against the sides of the ledge
and upper cliffs, richly illuminating the volumes of
smoke at the south end, and occasionally casting a
bright reflection on the bosom of a passing cloud.
The great seat of action, however, seemed to be at the
southern and western end, where an exhibition of ever
varying fireworks was presented, surpassing in beauty
and sublimity all that the ingenuity of art ever devised
Rivers of fire were seen rolling in splendid coruscation
among the labouring craters, and on one side a whole
lake, whose surface constantly flashed and sparkled
with the agitation of contending currents.

Expressions of admiration and astonishment burst
momentarily from our lips, and though greatly
fatigued, it was near midnight before we gave ourselves to a sleep, often interrupted during the night,
to gaze on the sight with renewed wonder and surprise.
As I laid myself down on my mat, fancying that the
very ground which was my pillow shook beneath my
head—the silent musings of my mind were,—"Great
and marvellous are thy works, Lord God Almighty!
greatly art thou to be feared, thou King of saints!"

On Wednesday, the 29th, after an early breakfast,
our party, excepting Lieutenant Malden, who was ill,
Mr Dampier, who remained to take a sketch, and

2 H 2

Mr. Ruggles, who chose to stroll above, prepared for
a descent into the crater.   One of the few places
where this is practicable, was within a rod of the hut
in which we lodged.   For the first four hundred feet,
the path was steep, and, from the looseness of the
stones and rocks on both sides, required caution in
every movement.   A slight touch was sufficient to
detach these, and send them bounding downwards
hundreds of feet, to the imminent danger of any one
near them.   The remaining distance of about the
same number of feet, was gradual and safe, the path
having turned into the bed of an old channel of lava,
which ran off in an inclined plane till it met the ledge
before described, more than a quarter of a mile west
of the place where we began the descent.   By the
time we arrived here, the natives acting as guides with
the Messrs. Bloxam and Mr. Powell, had preceded
the rest of our number too far to be overtaken, and
we became two parties for the rest of the morning;
the last, into which I fell, consisting of Lord Byron,
Mr. Ball, Mr. Davis, Mr. White, with Lord Byron's
servant and my native boy, to carry a canteen of water,
and the specimens we might collect.

Previous to our descent we had provided ourselves
with long canes and poles, by which we might test the
soundness of any spot before stepping on it, and
immediately on reaching the ledge we found the wisdom of the precaution.   This offset is formed wholly
of scoria and lava, mostly burned to a cinder, and
every where intersected by deep crevices and chasms,
from many of which light vapour and smoke were

emitted, and from others a scalding steam. The general surface is a black, glossy incrustation; retaining perfectly the innumerably diversified tortuous configurations of the lava, as it originally cooled, and so brittle as to crack and break under us like ice; while the hollow reverberations of our footsteps beneath, sufficiently assured us of the unsubstantial character of the whole mass. In some places, by thrusting our sticks down with force, large pieces would break through, disclosing deep fissures and holes, apparently without bottom. These however were generally too small to appear dangerous. The width of this ledge is constantly diminished in a greater or less degree, by the falling of large masses from its edges into the crater: and it is not improbable that in some future convulsion, the whole structure may yet be plunged into the abyss below.

Leaving the sulphur banks on the eastern side behind us, we directed our course along the northern part to the western cliffs. As we advanced, these became more and more perpendicular, till they presented nothing but the bare and upright face of an immense wall, from eight to ten hundred feet high, on whose surface huge stones and rocks hung, apparently so loosely as to threaten falling, at the agitation of a breath. In many places a white curling vapour issued from the sides and summit of the precipice; and in two or three places streams of clay-coloured lava, like small waterfalls, extending almost from the top to the bottom, had cooled, evidently at a very recent period. At almost every step, something new attracted our attention, and by stopping sometimes to look up, not without a feeling of apprehension at the enormous masses above our heads, at others to gain, by a cautious approach to the brink of the gulf, a nearer glance at the equally frightful depth below; at one time turning aside to ascertain the heat of a column of steam, and at another to secure some unique or beautiful speci men, we occupied more than two hours in proceeding the same number of miles.

At that distance from our entrance on the ledge, we came to a spot on the western side, where it widened many hundred feet, and terminated next the crater, not, as in most other places, perpendicularly, but in an immense heap of broken slabs and blocks of lava, loosely piled together as they had fallen in some convulsion of the mountain, and jutting off to the bottom in a frightful mass of ruin. Here, we had been informed, the descent into the depth of the crater could be most easily made; but being without a guide, we were entirely at a loss what course to take, till we unexpectedly descried the gentlemen who had preceded us, reascending. They dissuaded us most strenuously from proceeding farther; but their lively representations of the difficulty and dangers of the way, only strengthened the resolution of Lord Byron to go down; and knowing that the crater had been crossed at this end, we hastened on, notwithstanding the refusal of the guide to return with us. The descent was as perilous as it had been represented; but by proceeding with great caution, testing well the safety of every step before committing our weight to it, and often stopping to select the course which seemed least hazardous, in the space of about twenty minutes, by a zigzag way, we reached the bottom, without any accident of greater amount than a few scratches on the hands from the sharpness and roughness of the lava, by which we had occasionally been obliged to support ourselves. When about half way down, we were encouraged to persevere in our undertaking, by meeting a native who had descended on the opposite side, and passed over. It was only, however, from the renewed assurance it gave of the practicability of the attempt; for besides being greatly fatigued, he was much cut and bruised from a fall, said the bottom was " ino—ino roa—ka wahi O debelo !"—" excessively bad, the place of the devil !"—and he could be prevailed on to return with us only by the promise of a large reward.

It is difficult to say whether sensations of admiration or of terror predominated, on reaching the bottom of this tremendous spot. As I looked up at the gigantic wall which on every side rose to the very clouds, I felt oppressed to a most unpleasant degree, by a sense of confinement. Either from the influence of imagination, or from the actual effect of the intense power of a noonday sun beating directly on us, in addition to the heated and sulphureous atmosphere of the volcano itself, I for some moments experienced an agitation of spirits and difficulty of respiration, that made me cast a look of wishful anxiety towards our little hut, which, at an elevation of near fifteen hundred feet, seemed only like a bird's nest on the opposite cliff. These emotions, however, soon passed off, and we began, with great spirit and activity, the enterprise before us.

I can compare the general aspect of the bottom of the crater, to nothing that will give a livelier image of it to your mind, than to the appearance the Otsego Lake would present, if the ice with which it is covered in the winter, were suddenly broken up by a heavy storm, and as suddenly frozen again, while large slabs and blocks were still toppling, and dashing, and heaping against each other, with the motion of the waves. Just so rough and distorted was the black mass under our feet, only a hundred fold more terrific, independently of the innumerable cracks, fissures, deep chasms and holes, from which sulphureous vapour, steam, and smoke were exhaled, with a degree of heat that testified to the near vicinity of fire.

We had not proceeded far, before our path was intersected by a chasm at least thirty feet wide, and of a greater depth than we could ascertain, at the nearest distance we dare approach. The only alternative was to return, or to follow its course till it terminated, or became narrow enough to be crossed. We chose the latter, but soon met an equally formidable obstacle in a current of smoke, so highly impregnated with a suffocating gas, as not to allow of respiration. What a situation for a group of half a dozen men, totally unaware of the extent of peril to which they might be exposed! The lava on which we stood was in many places so hot, that we could not hold for a moment in our hands, the pieces we knocked off for specimens. On one side lay a gulf of unfathomable depth, on the other, an inaccessible pile of ruins, and immediately in front an oppressive and deadly vapour. While hesitating what to do, we

perceived the smoke to be swept round occasionally, by
an eddy of the air, in a direction opposite to that in which
it most of the time settled; and watching an opportunity
when our way was thus made clear, we held our breath,
and ran as rapidly as the dangerous character of the path
would permit, till we had gained a place beyond its
ordinary course. We here, unexpectedly, found ourselves also delivered from the other impediment to our
progress; for the chasm abruptly ran off in a direction
far from that we wished to pursue. Our escape from
the vapour, however, was that which we considered the
most important; and so great was our impression of the
danger to which he had been exposed from it, that when
we saw our way to the opposite side open, without any
special obstacle before us, we felt disposed formally to
return thanks to Almighty God for our deliverance.
But before this was proposed, all our number, except
Lord Byron, Mr. Davis, and myself, had gone forward
so far as to be out of call; and, for the time, the external
adoration of the Creator, from the midst of one of the
most terrible of his works, was reluctantly waved.

At an inconsiderable distance from us, was one of the
largest of the conical craters, whose laborious action
had so greatly impressed our minds during the night,
and we hastened to a nearer examination of it: so pro-
digious an engine I never expect again to behold. On
reaching its base, we judged it to be one hundred and
fifty feet high, a huge, irregularly shapen, inverted fun-
nel of lava, covered with clefts, orifices, and tunnels,
from which bodies of steam escaped with deafening explosion, while pale flames, ashes, stones, and lava, were

propelled with equal force and noise, from its ragged
and yawning mouth. The whole formed so singularly
terrific an object, that, in order to secure a hasty sketch
of it, I permitted the other gentlemen to go a few yards
nearer than I did, while I occupied myself with my
pencil. Lord Byron and his servant ascended the cone
several feet, but found the heat too great to remain
longer than to detach, with their sticks, a piece or two
of recent lava, burning-hot.

So highly was our admiration excited by the scene,
that we forgot the danger to which we might be exposed, should any change take place in the currents of
destructive gas, which exist, in a greater or less degree,
in every part of the crater ; till Mr. Davis, after two or
three ineffectual intimations of the propriety of an immediate departure, warned us in a most decided tone,
not only as a private friend, but as a professional gentleman, of the peril of our situation ; assuring us, that
three inspirations of the air by which we might be surrounded, would prove fatal to every one of us. We
felt the truth of the assertion, and notwithstanding the
desire we had of visiting a similar cone, covered with a
beautiful incrustation of sulphur, at the distance from
us of a few hundred yards only, we hastily took the
speediest course from so dangerous a spot. The ascent
to the ledge was not less difficult and frightful than
the descent had been, and, for the last few yards, was
almost perpendicular ; but we all succeeded in safely
gaining its top, not far from the path by which we had
in the morning descended the upper cliff.

We reached the hut about two o'clock, nearly ex-

hausted from fatigue, thirst, and hunger ; and had immediate reason to congratulate ourselves on a most
narrow escape from suffering an extreme danger, if not
from death. For, on turning round, we perceived the
whole chasm to be filled with thick sulphureous smoke;
and within half an hour, it was so completely choked
with it, that not an object below us was visible. Even
where we were, in the unconfined region above, the air
became so oppressive, as to make us think seriously of
a precipitate retreat. This continued to be the case
for the greater part of the afternoon. A dead calm
took place both within and without the crater, and
from the diminution of noise, and the various signs of
action, the volcano itself seemed to be resting from its
labours.

Mr. Ruggles, during his morning ramble, had gathered two large buckets of fine strawberries, which made
a delightful dessert at our dinner. The mountains of
Hawaii are the only parts of the islands on which this
delicious fruit is found. A large red raspberry is also
abundant on them ; but even when fully ripe, it has a
rough acid taste, similar to that of an unripe black-
berry. The flavour of the strawberry, however, is as
fine as that of the same fruit in America.

Towards evening, the smoke again rolled off to the
south, before a fresh breeze ; and every thing assumed
its ordinary aspect. At this time, Lieutenant Malden,
notwithstanding his indisposition, succeeded in getting
sufficient data to calculate the height of the upper
cliff : he made it nine hundred feet ; agreeing with the
measurement of Mr. Goodrich and Mr. Chamberlain some

months before. If this be correct, it is judged that the height of the ledge cannot be less than six hundred feet; making the whole depth of the crater, that which I have stated in the preceding pages, fifteen hundred feet. On similar grounds, the circumference of the crater at its bottom has been estimated at a distance of from five to seven miles; and at its top, from eight to ten miles.

Greatly to our regret, we found it would be necessary to set off on our return early the next morning, all the provisions of the natives being entirely expended. We could have passed a week here with undiminished interest, and wished to remain at least one day longer, to visit the sulphur banks, which abound with beautiful crystallizations, and to make some researches on the summit. We would have been glad, also, to have added to the variety of specimens already collected, especially of the volcanic sponge, and capillary volcanic glass, not found on the side of the crater where we encamped. But it was impossible; and we made preparations for an early departure. Just as these were completed, in the edge of the evening, another party from the Blonde, consisting of about a dozen midshipmen, arrived, with whom we shared our lodgings for the night.

The splendid illuminations of the preceding evening were again lighted up with the closing of the day; and after enjoying their beauty for two or three hours with renewed delight, we early sought a repose, which the fatigue of the morning had rendered most desirable. The chattering of the Islanders around our cabins, and the occasional sound of voices in protracted conversation among our own number, had, however, scarcely ceased long enough to admit of sound sleep, when the volcano again began roaring and labouring with redoubled activity. The confusion of noises was prodigiously great. In addition to all we had before heard, there was an angry muttering from the very bowels of the abyss, accompanied, at intervals, by what appeared the desperate effort of some gigantic power struggling for deliverance. These sounds were not fixed or confined to one place, but rolled from one end of the crater to the other; sometimes seeming to be immediately under us, when a sensible tremor of the ground on which we lay, took place; and then again rushing to the farthest end with incalculable velocity. The whole air was filled with the tumult; and those most soundly asleep were quickly roused by it to thorough wakefulness. Lord Byron sprang up in his cot, exclaiming, "We shall certainly have an eruption; such power must burst through every thing!" He had barely ceased speaking, when a dense column of heavy black smoke was seen rising from the crater, directly in front of us, the subterranean struggle ceased, and immediately after, flames burst from a large cone, near which we had been in the morning, and which then appeared to have been long inactive. Red-hot stones, cinders, and ashes, were also propelled to a great height with immense violence; and shortly after, the molten lava came boiling up, and flowed down the sides of the cone, and over the surrounding scoria, in two beautiful curved streams, glittering with indescribable brilliance.

At the same time a whole lake of fire opened in a more distant part. This could not have been less than two miles in circumference; and its action was more horribly sublime than any thing I ever imagined to exist, even in the ideal visions of unearthly things. Its surface had all the agitation of an ocean; billow after billow tossed its monstrous bosom in the air, and occasionally those from different directions burst with such violence, as in the concussion to dash the fiery spray forty and fifty feet high. It was at once the most splendidly beautiful and dreadfully fearful of spectacles; and irresistibly turned the thoughts to that lake of fire, from whence the smoke of torment ascendeth for ever and ever. No work of Him who laid the foundations of the earth, and who by his almighty power still supports them, ever brought to my mind the more awful revelations of his word, with such overwhelming impression. Truly, *"with God is terrible majesty"*—" Let all the nations say unto God—*how terrible art thou in thy works!"*

Under the name of *Pele*, this volcano, was one of the most distinguished and most feared of the former gods of Hawaii. Its terrific features are well suited to the character and abode of an unpropitious demon; and few works in nature would be more likely to impose thoughts of terror on the ignorant and superstitious, and, from their destructive ravages, lead to sacrifices of propitiation and peace. It is now rapidly losing its power over the minds of the people; not one of the large number in our company, seemed to be at all apprehensive of it as a supernatural being.

After an almost sleepless night, we early turned our

faces homeward, not without many "a lingering look behind," even at the very entrance of our path. It was precisely six o'clock when the last of our party left the brink. Never was there a more delightful morning. The atmosphere was perfectly clear, and the air, with the thermometer at 56° Fahrenheit, pure and bracing. A splendid assemblage of strong and beautifully contrasted colours glowed around us. The bed of the crater still covered with the broad shadow of the eastern banks, was of jetty blackness. The reflection of the early sun added a deeper redness to the western cliffs, those opposite were of a bright yellow, while the body of smoke rising between them, hung in a light drapery of pearly whiteness, against the deep azure of the southern sky. Mounaroa and Mounakea, in full view in the west, were richly clothed in purple; and the long line of intervening forest, the level over which we were passing, and the precipice by which it is encircled, thickly covered with trees and shrubbery, exhibited an equally bright and lively green.

On gaining the top of the first precipice, the distant view of the crater was so strikingly beautiful, that I stopped long enough to secure a hasty sketch, though most of the gentlemen had preceded me. A copy I hope to send with this account of our excursion. We walked rapidly during the morning, and by twelve o'clock reached the houses built for our accommodation, about half way between the harbour and the volcano. We determined to spend the night here, and, after a refreshing nap, washed and dressed ourselves for dinner, which we took at four o'clock, on a bed of leaves, spread on the shaded side of one of the houses. We set off before daylight the next morning, and about one o'clock arrived at the bay. H—— was more ill than when I left her; and for the last twelve hours, the family had become so much alarmed, as to think seriously of sending an express for me.

CHAPTER XV.

Mission House, Waiakea, July 4, 1825. Lord Byron informed me on Saturday, when dining with him, that the Blonde would leave this harbour, now called Byron Bay in honour of his lordship, on Wednesday of this week, for Kearakekua, on the opposite side of the island. We are seriously apprehensive that H—— will not be able to go in the frigate. She is exceedingly ill, and every hope seems again to be threatened. Mr. Davis called me aside on the Sabbath, and told me he thought nothing but a speedy removal to a more bracing climate could save her, and urged an immediate departure from the Islands as soon as she might gain strength to undertake a voyage. Mr. Bloxam, who has been deeply interested in her situation, after a short visit to-day, during which he was particularly affected by her appearance, sent home an album belonging to her, with the following lines, written on returning to his lodgings. I am sorry to say to those who love her, but from whom she is removed too far to receive their sympathy and their special prayers, that they only express the general sentiment, as to her present state.

" Hark—they whisper—angels say,
Sister spirit, come away."
" Hark ! from realms of rest above
Steals the hymn of peace and love :
As the enfranchis'd spirit flies
To her home in yonder skies,
Strains which Eden never knew,
Guide her untrod pathway thro' !

" Sister—ransom'd spirit—come !
Exile ! seek thy native home !
Come—the Spirit bids thee—here,
Never falls the parting tear ;
Spread thy wings for speedy flight,
To the realms of love and light !"

On board the Blonde, Wednesday, 6, 11 *o'clock, P. M.*

H—— was carried from her bed to the barge, which
brought us off at four o'clock his afternoon, and is
now quietly reposing in the after-cabin, far from the
noise of the ship. When we came on board, we fully
expected to proceed to the leeward of the island for
eight or ten days ; but when Lord Byron saw how very
ill H—— is, partly that she might meet her children
as soon as possible, and partly on account of a letter
he has received respecting a piratical squadron, he, an
hour since, determined to bear away directly for Oahu.
This is joyful tidings to us, for we had much reason to
fear that H—— would not have survived to see Honoruru by the other route. We are overwhelmed by the
kindness and affectionate attention of Lord Byron. He
has insisted upon relinquishing his own private accommodations to us, that we may be as free as possible from
all the inconvenience of shipboard. Mr. Davis, wh

manifests deep solicitude for H———, on hearing of the determination to proceed immediately to Oahu, said to her. "In his Lordship, madam, you have really met a brother, he is one of the kindest of men." He has our warm gratitude and affection.

Mission House, Oahu, Saturday Night, July, 9. We passed Diamond Hill this morning at sunrise, and at eight o'clock came to anchor. Soon after breakfast, the barge came alongside, to carry us on shore. H——— was removed to the deck, and lowered to the boat in an arm-chair, where a mattress and cot were ready to receive her. On reaching the shore, the crew of the barge carried her in her cot to Mr. Bingham's cottage, where she was safely placed in her own room, less exhausted than we had feared she would be. It was thought advisable that she should take an apartment at the Mission House, on account of the greater quietude of the upper rooms, and accordingly, this afternoon at four o'clock was removed. Meeting the children in good health, &c. has produced an excitement of spirits which makes her appear rather revived this evening.

Tuesday, July 12. A report from the Spanish main has hastened the departure of the Blonde. Yesterday some of the gentlemen, who did not expect to be on shore again, paid us a farewell visit. Among others, Lieutenants Ball and Talbot, and Mr. Wilson the purser, all of whom resquested permission to say farewell to H———. This morning I met Lord Byron, Mr. Davis, and Mr. Bloxam at breakfast, at Mr. Bingham's, after which they came over to express to Mrs. S———, for the last time, the interest they felt in her situation, and leave their best wishes for their recovery. Immemediately afterwards, they went to the Point, where the captain's gig was in waiting. Gratitude for their very polite and unwearied attentions, led me to accompany them to the beach, where, with affection and sincere regret, I gave them the parting hand in this world : and in the course of an hour, the frigate weighed anchor under a salute from the fort, and early in the afternoon faded from our sight for ever.

POSTSCRIPT.

For nearly three months after the departure of the Blonde, I was confined, almost exclusively, to the sick chamber of Mrs. Stewart ; and kept brief notes only of passing events. Incidents of a most interesting character, in reference to the success of the Mission and the state of the people, were daily taking place, incidents which testified to a change in the intellectual and moral condition of the nation, almost beyond credibility. The number of schools was multiplying as rapidly as books and teachers could be furnished ; and already contained fifteen thousand pupils, ten thousand of whom were supposed to be capable of reading intelligibly in their own language : while the population of the whole group were calling for the means of instruction. Drunkenness had become a public crime : and the manufacture of intoxicating drinks was prohibited by law. In the region of every Missionary establishment, the songs, and dances, and games, and dissipation, once so universal, had entirely ceased. Theft was becoming unpopular and disgraceful ; and proclamations against every vice had been made by order of the government through all the Islands. The Sabbath was extensively regarded as the day of God, and two-thirds of the whole population in the vicinity of the Missionary chapels, regularly attended the preaching of the Gospel ; forming congregations, at all the principal stations, of three thousand, four thousand, and even five thousand hearers. But to fill out the Journal with the proof of these data, would be to extend the volume, already enlarged beyond the promised size, to an undesirable length ; and I can but briefly add, from a record of a later date, the closing scenes of our residence in the Pacific.

The apprehension excited, during the visit of the Blonde, of the necessity of a removal from the Islands, for the preservation of Mrs. Stewart's life, was deepened soon afterwards, by the professional opinion of Dr. Blatchely of the Mission : and in the course of a few weeks, became the settled conviction of all who had a knowledge of her situation. As early as the first of September, we considered the certainty of our return, to rest entirely on the fact of her surviving, in a state to undertake a voyage, till an opportunity of leaving the Islands should offer.

That we should meet with a suitable opportunity, at a period sufficiently early, was very improbable. Three requisites were essential, which we could not expect to find united in the same ship in so remote a part of the world—a *physician* attached to the vessel; *accommodations* sufficiently large for a family; and a ship *homeward bound.* Indeed, our whole expectation of making a voyage, after the departure of the Blonde, rested on a visit from Commodore Hull, in the frigate United States, which letters from the Secretary of the Navy had led us to anticipate. But Commodore Hull might not arrive for months—might not come at all—and if he did, even in time for our purpose, it might not be in his power to accommodate us with a passage.

Such was our attitude, when the ship Fawn, Captain Dale, of London, touched at Oahu for refreshments in the early part of October. Mr. Short, a surgeon attached to her, soon visited Mrs. Stewart; and added his opinion to that of others already given, that her rescue depended solely on an early removal from the Islands. From him we learned, that the Fawn was bound directly to London; ascertained that her accommodations were large, and superior to those of most ships navigating the Pacific; and immediately afterwards had proffered to us by Captain Dale, in a most kind and delicate manner, a passage to England, with every comfort his ship could secure; but only on condition of its being accepted gratuitously, as an expression of his friendship and good-will. Mr. Short, at the same time, made a similar tender of his professional services to Mrs. Stewart and family. I could only acknowledge myself deeply affected by the unmerited kindness and generosity of those, who till then were entire strangers; and refer them to the decision of my associates for an answer.

A meeting of the members of the Mission then at Oahu was called, and the subject submitted to them in two propositions: 1st—" Whether it was my duty, under the existing circumstances of my family, to return, at least for a time, to the United States?" and, 2d,—" If so, whether the kind offer of Captain Dale, of a gratuitous passage to London, should be accepted?" both of which were fully and unanimously decided in the affirmative: and we began to prepare for embarkation at the end of eight days.

After the first emotions of a decision so important, my thoughts and affections were hurried to Maui; a spot interesting above all others to my heart, and which I could not think of leaving, without the farewell visit of at least an hour. This, through the very great kindness of a principal mercantile house at Oahu, I was enabled to do by express, in a small vessel, under the command, for the occasion, of Mr. Elwell, of Boston; a gentleman connected with the establishment, to whom I have often been indebted for similar marks of friendship. We arrived at Lahaina at midnight, and, as we had been delayed three days, by head winds, on a passage usually made by such vessels in one, and no time was to be lost; in despite of the great darkness of the night, and the danger of the surf, I landed immediately.

The Mission House had been removed from the place on which it originally stood, but familiarity with every spot, enabled me easily to grope my way through the luxuriant plantations by which it is now surrounded. But how great was my astonishment, at the peculiar circumstances in which I found our inestimable friends,

2 K

Mr. and Mrs. Richards.   Instead of being permitted, unobserved, to break their slumbers by the salutations of friendship and affection, how was I surprised to meet, at my first approach to the house, the presented bayonet, and to hear the stern challenge of the watchful sentry, " *Who goes there* ?" and when assured that it was a friend, how inexplicable to my mind the fact of receiving the cordial embraces of my brother, not in the peaceful cottage of the Missionary, but in the midst of a *garrison*, apparently in momentary expectation of the attack of a foe ; and to find the very couch, on which was reclining one, who to us has been most emphatically *a sister*, surrounded by the muskets and the spears of those, known to the world only by the name of savages !

My first thoughts were, that a revolt of the island against the general government had taken place, in which our friends had been seized, and were guarded as captives; or that some formidable party of unfriendly natives had risen with the determination of destroying them, and from whom they were protected by the higher chiefs ; but, as soon as an explanation could be given, I learned that their peril was not from the heathen, but from the degenerate sons of a civilized and Christian country !   The seamen of a large British ship at anchor at Lahaina, exasperated at the restraints laid on their licentiousness, through the influence of the Mission, had carried their menaces and open acts of violence, against Mr. and Mrs. Richards, to such an extent as to cause the chiefs to arm a body of men, and defend them at the hazard of life : and at that very hour, three armed boats' crews, amounting to near forty men, were on shore, with the sworn purpose of firing their houses, and taking their lives, before morning !

Only two days before, after a succession of fearful threats and gross insults, the same party, countenanced and upheld by their captain and officers, and armed with knives and pistols, had landed under the black flag of death, and surrounding the Missionary enclosure, then unprotected, offered life to our friends, only on condition of their retracting their instructions to the people founded on the Seventh Commandment. The firmness with which they were met by Mr. Richards, only made them doubly infuriate ; and, as they seemed ready to fall upon him, to execute their horrid threats, Mrs. Richards, with the spirit of a martyr, rushed between them and her husband, exclaiming, " My only protection is in my husband and my God ; I had hoped, that the helplessness of a female, surrounded only by heathen, would have touched the compassion of men from a Christian land—but, if such cannot be the case, know that I stand prepared to share the fate of my husband ! When I left my country, I took my life in my hand, not knowing when I might be called to lay it down ; if this is the time, know that I am prepared—sooner than disgrace the character I sustain, or dishonour the religion of my Master, by countenancing in the people we have come to enlighten, a course of conduct at variance with the word of God." For a moment the heroism of a refined and lovely woman appeared to shake the firmness of their purpose, and they retired from the ground : but it was only to return with

a more relentless determination, and the interference
of the natives took place in time, barely to rescue
the lives of their teachers at the hazard of their own.
So resolute were they, however, in the defence, when
once commenced, that three thousand men were
armed, and in readiness to seize the ship, and to
make prisoners of her crew, should another outrage of
the kind be attempted.

The statement of these circumstances, with the
unfolding of the character and object of my visit,
made our interview most deeply affecting; and the
remainder of the night was spent in thought and conversation, of unmingled sorrow at the termination which
was about to take place, of that union and intercourse,
which, for near three years, had been the source of
some of our highest and sweetest enjoyment.

A first resolution, on the mention of our embarkation
in four days, was, to return with me to Oahu, for a last
interview with H——; but, after beginning to prepare
for the visit, it occurred to them, that, under existing
circumstances, it might appear like deserting their
post; or, at least, might afford an occasion to their
enemies to say, that they had been driven from their
station; and with sadness, but with firmness, they
determined, from a sense of duty, to forego the melancholy satisfaction they had contemplated.

At sunrise, Mr. Richards and myself visited the
spacious, well-built and finished chapel, lately erected
by the chiefs: and in the pulpit, from which we had
fondly hoped jointly to proclaim the glad tidings of
salvation, in tears and in prayer we looked to God,

the arbitrator of our destinies, for his blessing on our future divided labours in his cause. And, in the course of an hour, after having bade a hasty adieu to the chiefs and such of the people as were best known to me, we sorrowfully interchanged embraces, which we had great reason to fear would prove our last in this world.

I can never forget the last words of Mrs. Richards, especially as connected with the scenes through which she had just passed, and which then might be renewed at any moment—" It is true, I weep, and shall weep again and again. A heavier affliction could scarce befall me, than the removal of your family from the Islands, leaving us alone on Maui, in the midst of twenty thousand heathen; but I weep not at my own loss only, I weep also at yours, I have always been contented in my situation, but I never knew *the happiness of the Missionary life* till within the six months past. It seems but yesterday, that we went forth weeping with the precious seed of eternal life, and now we are returning from our work daily, bringing our sheaves with us, and shouting the harvest home!"

Never did the field of labour I had hoped to occupy for life, appear so truly desirable : and I found my heart clinging closely to every object included in it, from my associates, and the thousands eagerly desirous of my instruction, to the very trees and shrubbery I had planted and nurtured in our garden. The struggles of strong affection filled me with sadness and gloom, and during the passage to Oahu, I had almost fully determined, to permit the Fawn to depart

2 K 2

without us, and venture a delay till the United States
should arrive.   How great then was my surprise and
satisfaction to hear before landing, that there had
been an arrival from South America, and that a
packet from Commodore Hull was waiting my return.
That gentleman could not know my peculiar situation.
Still I was persuaded, that his communication would,
in the providence of God, make my path plain, and
remove every doubt then resting on it.   And such was
fully the case; for on breaking the seal of a long and
kind letter from him, though utterly unaware of the
importance of the information to me, he gave the
most unqualified assurance that it would be impossible
for his vessel to make the proposed voyage to the
Sandwich Islands. This was all that was necessary
to render our duty clear as noon-day, and we prepared
cheerfully to follow the path we believed pointed out
of God.

Still, warm affection for our companions, some of
whom, besides Mr. and Mrs. Richards (especially
Mrs. Bingham) were in circumstances of affliction
greatly to aggravate the sorrow of a separation—love
to their work, and to our work, and the highly
encouraging state of the people, thousands of them
delighting in our instructions, and tens of thousands
perishing, from a want of more labourers, in a field
ripe for the sickle—all caused us to bid farewell to
the Sandwich Islands with feelings of the most painful depression.   Rude as was the throng which
covered the beach as our boats shoved off, unlike as
was the whole scene, except in the murmur of sym-

pathy and the salutations and tears of affection, to the enlightened and pious multitude, and the beautiful and classic ground on which our eyes rested, as we waved a last adieu to the American shores—it was scarce less affecting, and caused an agitation of heart far more oppressive, than any we experienced, ON THE 19TH OF NOVEMBER, 1822.

THE END.

ADDENDA.

During a visit to Philadelphia some months since, I presented to Professor Green of that city, a few specimens in conchology, which I had brought with me from the Sandwich Islands for that purpose. After an examination of them, he was kind enough to transmit to me, for insertion in my Journal, a description of two. A point of delicacy, arising from the friendship with which he honours me, is involved in the publication, as will be perceived from the article. But, I do not feel at liberty to withhold from the lovers of science, the result of his investigation; and trust I shall be excused for acknowledging, in this manner, the unmerited politeness of the distinguished naturalist.

Description of two new Species of ACHATINA, *from the Sandwich Islands.* By J. GREEN, A. M. Prof. of Chem. in Jeff. Med. College.

ACHATINA *Stewartii.*

A testa sinistrorsa—ovato—oblonga—lutescente, minutissime striata—colore varia, nunc unicolore, nunc divertissime fasciata—columella rosea—labro tenui— intus albido.

STEWART'S ACHATINA.—*Shell* heterostophe—conical—oblong—about one inch in length and half an inch in diameter—*whorls* six or seven, rounded and marked with numerous oblique and delicate striæ—*apex* rather obtuse, and not eroded—a deeply impressed line along the upper part of the whorls, parallel with the suture, *periostracha* smooth and very glossy, *colour* and *markings* exceedingly various, the ground colour is usually greenish or some shade of yellow, sometimes a single blackish coloured band accompanies the suture, sometimes this band is double and of different shades, and on many specimens there are two bands, one at the suture and one in the middle of the whorls. In some varieties the base of the body whorl is dark brown, the rest of the shell being of a dark fawn, and not unfrequently the whole shell is without any markings whatever; in which case the colour is yellow, the *aperture*, when inverted, is ear-shaped, the truncation of the *columella* is rounded and thickened in a remarkable manner at its edge; along the inner margin of the *outer lip* there is a strong callous ridge, as in most of the species of this genus, which gradually attenuates towards the edge of the lip, which is thin and sharp *inside*, white and pinkish round the *columella*.

This splendid little ACHATINA was brought from Oahu, one of the Sandwich Islands, by the Rev. C. S. Stewart. He informs me that it is found in considerable numbers in the deep valleys of Oahu, at all seasons, adhering to the under surface of the large leaves of a plant called, in the language of the natives, Ti, and from the roots of which they brewed an intoxicating liquor, which was in general use before the arrival of the Missionaries. Though the leaves of the ti are the favourite

resort of this ACHATINA, it is by no means confined
to that plant. The Islanders sometimes eat the animal
which inhabits this shell, as they frequently do fish,
without cooking; but a favourite mode of preparing it,
is to tie up, in the large leaves of the ti, considerable
numbers of them at once, bake them thus with heated
stones, and then pick out the animal with a small
pointed instrument. The beautiful and shining colours
of this ACHATINA, and the manner of their arrangement, forcibly remind us of the HELIX *nemoralis* or
hortensis, so common in the woods and hedges throughout France and England.

There are two very distinct varieties of A. *Stewartii*,
one dextral, or with whorls revolving from right to left.
In the numerous specimens which I have received, there
is no individual of single uniform colour, they are all
greenish, with a single brown band at the sutures. The
columella in this, as in the first variety, has the remarkable thick plait or callosity resembling the TOR-
NATELLA *fasciata*. The other variety is more globose,
and much depressed, being three-fourths of an inch in
length, and half an inch in diameter; this shell is almost always dextral, and of a light yellowish colour,
and the callous ridge along the inner margin is peculiarly striking. The contour of this variety resembles
that of the VOLUTA *fasciata*, Linn.; the lip of that
species, however, is reflected.

ACHATINA *Oahuensis.*

*A testa oblonga—tenuissime striata—colore ferugineo
rufescente—columella rosea—apertura alba et rosea
—labro tenui.*

OAHU ACHATINA—*Shell* dextral — oblong—about
three-fourths of an inch in length, and one fourth of an
inch in diameter—*whorls* seven or eight, slightly rounded—*sutures* deeply impressed and crenulated—*periostracha* finely striated, and of a light dirty reddish
brown colour—*body whorl* with an obsolete carina—
apex chesnut colour—*collumella* plaited, as in A. *Stewartii*—*outer lip* thin—*inside* pinkish, darker near the
edge.

This ACHATINA is a native of the Sandwich Islands.
It does not appear to be so common as the A. *Stewartii,*
which it resembles a little ; but it differs from that
species in being much more elevated in proportion to its
diameter, in the number of its whorls, in the absence
of the impressed line near the suture, and in many other
characters.

INDEX

People

Places

Subjects